WITH THE INNISKILLING DRAGOONS

DURING THE BOER WAR, 1899-1902

Photo: Ellis & Walery.

H.R.H. THE DUKE OF CONNAUGHT, K.G., &c.
Colonel-in-Chief, Inniskilling Dragoons.

WITH THE

INNISKILLING DRAGOONS

THE RECORD OF A CAVALRY REGIMENT
DURING THE BOER WAR, 1899–1902

BY

LIEUT.-COLONEL J. WATKINS YARDLEY

B.A. TRIN. COLL. CAMB.

LATE INNISKILLING DRAGOONS

WITH ILLUSTRATIONS AND A MAP

LONGMANS, GREEN, AND CO.

39 PATERNOSTER ROW, LONDON

NEW YORK AND BOMBAY

1904

TO MY READERS

THESE rough notes were not penned with a view to publication, but at the request of my brother officers and several friends I offer them in the hope that they may give a good idea of some of the work done by our Cavalry in the late war. They are plain facts narrated in a simple manner, which may be read as a letter-diary.

Serving as a regimental officer, I give, as a sample, the daily records of one regiment. The good work of our severely criticised Cavalry has not yet been publicly appreciated; and it must be remembered that the gallant Imperial Yeomen, and many of our true Colonial corps, to whom we owe so much, were trained and led by the Regular Cavalry officers.

Owing to being wounded I was, to my regret, unable to serve with my old regiment during the whole period of the war; but, thanks to the excellent diaries of Lieut.-Colonel Thursby Dauncey and the Staff diary of Brigadier-General M. F. Rimington, C.B., compiled by Brevet-Major G. K. Ansell, with notes from Colonel Allenby, C.B., and from other officers in the regiment, I have been able to complete these records.   Without such aid I could not have accomplished it.

My thanks are further due for the excellent photographs kindly placed at my disposal by Brevet-Major G. K. Ansell and Captain E. C. Holland.

J. WATKINS YARDLEY.

CONTENTS

ILLUSTRATIONS

WITH THE INNISKILLING DRAGOONS

DURING

THE BOER WAR

CHAPTER I

TO THE FRONT—UNDER GENERAL FRENCH

WAR! The regiment ordered to the front. Oh! the enthusiasm, the hopes and aspirations, the hustle-bustle of preparations, and the farewells!

Mobilisation was rapidly followed by marching orders and embarkation. So hurried was the de-
_{Mobilisa-} parture that the service kits from Pimlico
_{tion.} had not reached the Curragh before the first squadron of the regiment entrained there for embarkation at Queenstown. Luckily, after being nearly lost, they arrived in the nick of time to be bundled on board.

It was originally intended that on mobilisation the Inniskilling Dragoons should be brigaded with the Royals and Scots Greys in order to form again the old fighting Union Brigade—the cavalry of England, Scotland, and Ireland. This, to our disappointment, fell through, owing to regiments, and even squadrons, being sent off to the front directly they landed, so urgent was the need for troops. Thus

B

brigades were necessarily formed as the troops came to hand. The Inniskillings and Scots Greys were, however, brigaded together during the earlier stages of the war, but the Royals were separated owing to their starting on the campaign from the Natal theatre of war. This was the first regiment of the brigade to land at Cape Town, but the immediate need of troops in Natal caused their re-embarkation for Durban, and so separation from the brigade. Later they worked with the Inniskillings when forming part of Colonel Pulteney's column.

The 6th Inniskilling Dragoons, comprising 23 officers, 558 non-commissioned officers and men, with Strength.   496 horses, embarked at Queenstown in the s.s. *Jamaican*, s.s. *Siberian*, and s.s. *Persia* on Embarka- October 23, 24, and 28, 1899, respectively. (Detail as below.)

On the *Siberian* were the Headquarters and A Squadron.

Headquarters :

Lieut.-Colonel H. C. Page Henderson (Commanding Regiment).

Lieut. G. K. Ansell (Adjutant).

Lieut. T. G. Jackson, 7th D.Gs., attached as Transport Officer.

Lieut. J. R. Siddall (Quartermaster).

Major H. T. Wyatt (R.A.M.C.).

Veterinary-Captain J. Cooper (A.V.D.).

A Squadron :

Captain A. R. Mosley (Commanding Squadron).

Lieut. C. F. Dixon Johnson.

Lieut. H. C. Higgin.

INNISKILLING DRAGOONS GOING ON BOARD THE "SIBERIAN" AT QUEENSTOWN.

A MAKE-SHIFT TARGET.

Lieut. H.S.H. Prince Alexander ot Teck, 7th
Hussars, attached.
Second Lieut. G. H. Earle.
Second Lieut. E. C. S. Jervis.

Total, 12 officers, 246 non-commissioned officers
and men, 167 horses, and 23 chargers; of the horses
6 were lost on the voyage.

On the *Jamaican* was B Squadron :

Major Thursby Dauncey (Commanding Squadron).
Lieut. Ewing Paterson.
Lieut. J. Lawlor.
Lieut. R. B. Johnson.
Second Lieut. G. Meek.

Total, 5 officers, 156 non-commissioned officers
and men, 142 horses, and 10 chargers; of the horses
7 were lost on the voyage.

On the *Persia* was C Squadron :

Major E. H. Allenby (Commanding Squadron).
Captain E. A. Herbert.
Lieut. Viscount Fincastle, V.C., 16th Lancers,
attached.
Second Lieut. C. E. Amphlett.
Second Lieut. T. G. Gibson.

Total, 6 officers, 156 non-commissioned officers
and men, 142 horses, and 12 chargers; of the horses
31 were lost on the voyage.

Captain Stevenson Hamilton joined C Squadron
later, from exploration in Central Africa. Coming
out at Quilimane on the East Coast, he learnt of the

war and that the regiment was already at the front, so he obtained a passage in the *Herzog*, a foreign ship laden with freight and passengers of many nationalities, bound for Delagoa Bay. The ship was seized off Delagoa Bay by our men-of-war as containing contraband of war and passengers going to fight for the Boer cause. Several of the latter were foreign titled officers, but all ostensibly proclaimed that they were going to work under the Red Cross! After representations to the Home Government, this ship was allowed to go back with its freight and passengers to Delagoa Bay. Captain Hamilton then obtained passage in one of our own ships and reached Port Elizabeth ; there he was detained by the military authorities, who, owing to his ragged appearance after two years' wanderings in the wilds of Central Africa, mistook him for a Boer spy and doubted his identity.

Captain J. W. Yardley (retired) rejoined the regiment from a shooting expedition in India, and commanded A Squadron from April 13, 1900, until October 16, when he was wounded.

The s.s. *Jamaican* and s.s. *Siberian* made good passages, arriving at Cape Town on November 18 and 20. The s.s. *Persia* (Anchor Line), commanded by Captain Osborne, encountered very rough weather during the first week of the voyage, the horses suffering severely, and many dying from exhaustion. Early on the morning of November 8 she broke her ' thrust block,' and was totally disabled. She was then about twenty miles from St. Vincent and some six miles east of San Antonio. The wind was S.E. and fresh, with a heavy swell setting towards the shore. Several men from C Squadron volunteered to row to St. Vincent under

Wreck of
Persia.

MAXIM GUN IN ACTION OVER THE STERN.

MAITLAND CAMP, LOOKING TOWARDS TABLE MOUNTAIN.
The mountain is clothed with its usual cloud, termed "the table cloth."

command of the second officer of the ship. Although soldiers, they performed a fine feat of seamanship in gaining St. Vincent (twenty miles), and reporting to H.M.S. *Diadem*, Captain Niblett. He at once secured a tug, fortunately with steam up, and immediately despatched it to the rescue.

Meanwhile the *Persia* was drifting on to the rocks; the boats were launched in readiness for emergency, preparations made to cast the horses overboard, and an anchor hung out on 60 fathoms of cable on the chance of its catching on to something. At about 2 P.M., when the ship had drifted to within three-quarters of a mile of the rocks, the anchor held. Would it hold long enough? Yes; for, directly after, all eyes were gladdened by the sight of the tug arriving, followed by H.M.S. *Diadem*. It was found impossible to get the boats on board again, and ten out of the eleven were lost. With great difficulty, but, happily, without accident to life or limb, hawsers were attached and the *Persia* was towed to St. Vincent. The injury to the ship could not be repaired, so the squadron had to wait the arrival of the Union Castle s.s. *Goth* (Captain Travers), which had been cabled for to England. The troops were then transhipped and proceeded to Cape Town, disembarking there on December 11. This stormy weather and shipwreck caused delay and great loss of horses to the C Squadron.

The regiment, having disembarked at Cape Town, encamped at Maitland—a hot, exposed, and, later, Maitland a blinding dusty camp, of which few troops Camp. cherish pleasant recollections. A few horses died here from sand colic, and were almost the only horses honoured with a burial throughout the war.

Apart from the discomfort, all were eager to get to the front, and the continual arrival and departure of corps of every description—Regulars, Irregulars, and Colonials—caused chaos to reign, which was especially trying for camp commandants, adjutants, and quartermasters.

The work of the Inniskillings during the war may be divided into three periods : *First*, when working, The Innis- more or less, by squadrons, up to the occupa- killings. tion of Bloemfontein. *Second*, when they formed part of the First Cavalry Brigade, under General French. *Third*, during the later stages of the war, when serving in different columns.

From first to last the regiment was worked hard in the fighting line, without a single rest, and I doubt if any regiment experienced and accomplished so much without serious disaster of any kind. From beginning to end, commanded and led in turns by Colonels Page Henderson, Allenby, Rimington, and Dauncey, its dash and gallantry were conspicuous.

The first period comprises the work round Colesberg, the relief of Kimberley, Paardeberg, and the occupation of Bloemfontein.

On November 27 B Squadron, under Major Dauncey, made a start. They entrained to Victoria Nov. 27, Road station on the De Aar line, remaining 1899. there for eleven days, patrolling the country and visiting the town of Victoria West, seven miles distant, which was very disaffected.

They then proceeded to Arundel and joined the Dec. 10. regimental headquarters and A Squadron, which arrived the same day from Maitland Camp, Cape Town.

Next day Major Dauncey, with Lieut. Paterson

and six men, set off before dawn to endeavour to get round the enemy's position at Taaiboschlaagte, in

Dec. 11. Recon-naissance Patrol.

order to obtain information. They got as far as Vaalkop, when they encountered fifty of the enemy, who separated into three parties and attempted to surround them. A stern chase ensued; twice the small patrol found itself wired in under heavy fire; but, thanks to skilful leadership and to wire-cutters, of which every man carried a pair on his saddle, and which proved invaluable throughout the war, they eventually made a successful reconnaissance and got back to Arundel, a distance of six miles, without a scratch.

The following morning Vaalkop was shelled and occupied by two guns R.H.A. and a squadron of cavalry, which was relieved daily. This occupation lasted till the 16th, when the Boers attacked and re-occupied it, the squadron 10th Hussars, Mounted Infantry, and guns which held it at the time, being obliged, in face of such superior force, to retire on Arundel.

The enemy then attempted to work round our right flank. The troops, which consisted of R Battery

Dec. 13.

R.H.A., 6th Dragoon Guards (Carabiniers), two squadrons 6th Dragoons (Inniskillings), two squadrons 10th Hussars, one company Mounted Infantry, and Colonial Troops—all under command of Colonel Porter, 6th Dragoon Guards—repulsed them after a hard day's fighting. Amongst the

Captain Mosley wounded.

casualties was numbered Captain Mosley, 6th Inniskilling Dragoons, who was shot through the bone below the knee, which invalided him home; but later in the war he rejoined the regiment. Many horses, also, were shot. The enemy's 'Long

Tom,' whose first shot fell amongst B Squadron Inniskillings without doing any harm, was silenced by our guns after two rounds; we found afterwards that our shells had broken the carriage, killing several of its gunners. Our own gunners had a trying time; being out in the open all day, they were continually under long-range Mauser fire, but luckily escaped with only a few men wounded.

On the 14th, Major-General Brabazon, A.D.C., assumed command from Colonel Porter of the force at Arundel. His instructions were to prevent the enemy moving from their present position, by holding Arundel as a pivot, and acting energetically against their detachments. Next day he visited Vaalkop and from there sent the two guns to shell from the railway line a Boer convoy on the Colesberg road. The enemy replied, without loss to us.

At daybreak shelling was heard from the direction of Vaalkop. The Boers were attacking it, and the small force previously mentioned as holding it was compelled to withdraw. General Brabazon at once took out four guns of R Battery R.H.A., two squadrons Inniskillings, and two squadrons Colonial Troops. B Squadron Inniskillings, reconnoitring in advance, interrupted the enemy while breakfasting off the captured tinned meats and biscuits at the small farm at the foot of Vaalkop; the remainder of the force under General Brabazon came through a 'poort' into the Vaalkop plain *en masse*, forming a beautiful target for the enemy's guns. Their shells, however, fell harmless, and the Boers once more fled from Vaalkop, but before doing so they fired about twenty shells, one of which pitched almost under an ambulance wagon, and another close

Dec. 16.

Photo: Lambert Weston & Son.

LIEUT.-GEN. SIR J. D. P. FRENCH, K.C.B., K.C.M.G.

to Prince Teck. Later in the afternoon a patrol, under Captain Jackson, 7th Dragoon Guards, attached to the Inniskillings, reconnoitred towards Rensburg; they came under a heavy fire, and Captain Jackson was mortally wounded. Sergeant Broadwood and Private McKinnon gallantly stuck to him, amidst a hail of bullets, and successfully carried him in.

Death of Captain Jackson.

On December 17 Lieut.-General French, fresh from his successes in Natal, assumed command, to the delight of all ranks. He appointed Major-General Brabazon second in command, and formed a division, viz. : 1st Brigade, under Colonel Porter, 6th Dragoon Guards, consisting of the Carabiniers, New South Wales Lancers (one squadron), one company Mounted Infantry, and New Zealand Mounted Rifles (one squadron) ; 2nd Brigade, under Lieut.-Colonel Fisher, 10th Hussars, consisting of the Inniskilling Dragoons, 10th Hussars, and one company Mounted Infantry.

Dec. 17. Arrival of General French.

Forma- tion of Cavalry Division.

Next day C Squadron Inniskillings, under Major Allenby, which had been delayed, owing to the wreck of their ship, the *Persia*, arrived, completing the regiment.

Dec. 18.

The usual daily routine was to start off at 2 A.M. to relieve outposts towards Rensburg, which were over four miles distant. The kopje always occupied by a squadron of the 2nd Brigade was named ' Epsom Kopje,' owing to the wonderful ' Epsom finish ' made by two Boers (1,800 yards distant) after one shot from Major Dauncey's carbine, which pitched just in front of them, and caused them to race away, flogging their ponies with their rifles. This shows the range

of the carbine, which was afterwards repeatedly
proved.

Sports for the Force were held in the afternoon
of Christmas Day, the officers' pony race being
Christmas won by Captain Kenna, V.C., the Provost-
Day, 1899. Marshal. The men's Christmas dinner consisted of tinned sausages, raw onions, plum-pudding,
with lemon squash to drink, and a 'tot' of rum to
put all right. A much-needed troop of Royal
Engineers also arrived this day.

The Suffolk Regiment later increased our force,
and the following day Major Rimington and his
Guides, 'The Tigers,' joined from Modder
Dec. 26. River. These famous Guides were raised,
on the outbreak of the war, entirely by Major
Rimington, Inniskilling Dragoons. He enlisted only
men who knew the country and spoke Dutch; unless
found absolutely efficient they were at once dis-
charged. The sobriquet 'Tigers' was given them
from the cat-tails worn round their hats and for their
daring. They are famous for the splendid work they
did under their dashing leader throughout the war.

Daily shelling took place; but on the 29th,
during a terrific hailstorm, the Carabinier horses
stampeded. They galloped four miles from
Dec. 29. camp; thence into and through the Boer
position of Taaibosch without a shot being fired at
them, thereby showing that the Boers had vacated
their position. A patrol of the Inniskillings, under
Lieut. Harris, which had been out all night, returned
at the same time, confirming the fact, as they had
been all through the position. Major Dauncey, with
our outpost squadron on Epsom Kopje, immediately
heliographed the information to Headquarters.

"A" SQUADRON PICQUET ON EPSOM KOPJE.

PACK MAXIM ON AN ARGENTINE.

Rimington's Guides and the New Zealanders then reconnoitred round the Rensburg hills, reporting them unoccupied. The stampeded horses, meanwhile, returned round the other flank, bringing with them several Boer ponies.

As a result, General French, at daylight next morning, sent forward the 1st Brigade, under Colonel

Dec. 30.
Occupation of
Rensburg.

Porter, to occupy the Rensburg Ridge and reconnoitre to the front. This was successfully accomplished and they established themselves on one of the ridges which was termed ' Porter's Hill.' The following day the 2nd Brigade, under Lieut.-Colonel Fisher, less A Squadron Inniskillings left to guard Arundel, marched to Rensburg, pitched camp there, and, at 5 P.M., commenced a night march on Colesberg. The column, consisting

French attacks the Colesberg position.

of the Inniskilling Dragoons, 10th Hussars, O and R Batteries R.H.A., and the Berkshires, halted at 9 P.M. at Maeder's Farm. General French was present commanding. The men were lying by their horses' heads till 2 A.M., when the column received the order to advance; progress was slow owing to the difficulty with the guns in the dark, but it arrived just underneath Coleskop before dawn; the Berkshires, under Major McCracken, were in front. Suddenly fire was opened on the column from a picquet with a Maxim on the right front. The Berkshires gallantly rushed this kopje and the firing ceased, but at first streak of dawn a heavy shell (shrapnel) and pom-pom fire was opened from the hills in front (west), and also from the hills south of Colesberg. One man of B Squadron Inniskilling Dragoons was killed by a shrapnel bullet, and several horses were shot.

The Inniskilling Dragoons and R (Major Burton's) Battery R.H.A. at once galloped to the Berkshires' kopje, and found them in possession of it, firing merrily from its summit.   The Berkshires lost Lieut. West, and one man killed and ten wounded, that morning.   R Battery at once proceeded to endeavour to silence the pom-pom on the hill south of Coles-berg, being simply raked by pom-pom shells in doing so, and losing two men wounded and many horses killed.   The steady, plucky way they stood this most nerve-shaking fire, and the accurate shooting of the battery, were splendid.   They silenced it in about a quarter of an hour, the remainder of the force occupying positions on the hills to the north. This Berkshire kopje, or ' Much Cracking Hill '
Mc-   (McCracken's Hill), as it was afterwards
Cracken's styled, was about 1,000 yards from Coleskop,
Hill.
           the rear of Coleskop being used as a kind of base of operations.

During the afternoon R Battery was relieved by O Battery.   During the operation they were simply enveloped with dust from pom-pom and rifle fire, but only had a few men wounded and horses killed. Crossing this open space was dangerous work ; order-lies galloping to and fro were watched with interest and some amusement as the bullets spluttered around them.

Meantime the cavalry pushed forward and suc-cessfully accomplished their task of seizing important positions threatening Colesberg.   The 1st Brigade, under Colonel Porter, co-operating from Rensburg to the south, gave valuable assistance ; the Carabiniers, New South Wales Lancers, New Zealanders, and Rimington's Guides, guarding the flank, being all

GRAVE OF AN INNISKILLING UNDER COLESKOP—
PRIVATE LAWRENCE.

VIEW FROM THE TOP OF COLESKOP.

heavily engaged in repulsing an attempt of the enemy to outflank.

This New Year's Day of hard fighting, after the long night march, was very trying for the troops; the horses could not be watered until night-time; the men also were mad with thirst and got no water fit to drink until midnight.

Next morning an orderly from the Inniskilling Squadron (B), which remained to hold McCracken's Hill, as he galloped past Coleskop, found a wounded artilleryman groaning and shouting in a water-spruit, where he had been lying all night, shot in the head! Volunteers went out and brought him in, being heavily fired on, notwithstanding that they carried a stretcher and waved a Red Cross flag. An Inniskilling sentry on this hill was mistaken by some eight Boers at daylight for a wounded man; they shouted, ' Are you sick ? ' On which he bolted from rock to rock back to his picquet, followed by bullets; the picquet replied, and a duel, at only 80 yards' distance, was kept up between the two small parties all day.

At 5 P.M. the squadron was ordered to retire and escort R Battery from behind Coleskop to Maeder's Farm Camp. The men were retired in single file at 300 yards' distance, each man receiving a storm of bullets, but not a horse or man was hit!

The Suffolk Regiment arrived at Colesberg this day. B Squadron Inniskilling Dragoons, under Major Dauncey, occupied Windmill Well, one mile west of Coleskop, the extreme left of the position; C squadron, under Captain Herbert, occupied a kopje at the end of the hills N.W. of Coles-

Jan. 3, 1900.

berg (Herbert's Kopje) ; A Squadron, under Major Allenby, was still at Arundel.

Desultory fighting continued. Captain Viscount Fincastle and Lieut. Harris, from C Squadron, succeeded in cutting the telegraph line north of Colesberg.

The following morning, as day was dawning, Lieut. Gibson, from the C Squadron on Herbert's

Lieut. Gibson wounded.

Kopje, whilst riding to one of the detached posts, came suddenly under a hot fire at close range. He was wounded in four places, but managed to reach his post, and there lay in charge of it, protected by a rock. The Boers had been creeping into positions during the night, and now poured a heavy fire into the squadron.

Later on, in obedience to orders, Captain Herbert sallied out with thirteen men towards Barnard's Nek Ridge. About 200 Boers suddenly issued from under a kopje to his left and tried to cut him off. Captain

Captain Herbert's charge of the Inniskillings.

Herbert, without hesitation, most gallantly charged them, routed them and gained his kopje, but with five of his thirteen men killed and five wounded : his own horse was shot under him, and Trumpeter Price brought him in on his horse. He then held the kopje until a company of the Suffolks came to his assistance, and by so doing saved the situation, which had been most critical. At the same time, Captain de Lisle, with his Mounted Infantry, assisted by shell fire from near Coleskop, charged the Boer kopjes and drove them off with heavy loss. It was a fine performance executed with great dash. The kopjes were afterwards named ' De Lisle's Kopjes.' The enemy had occupied them in the night, and were attempting in

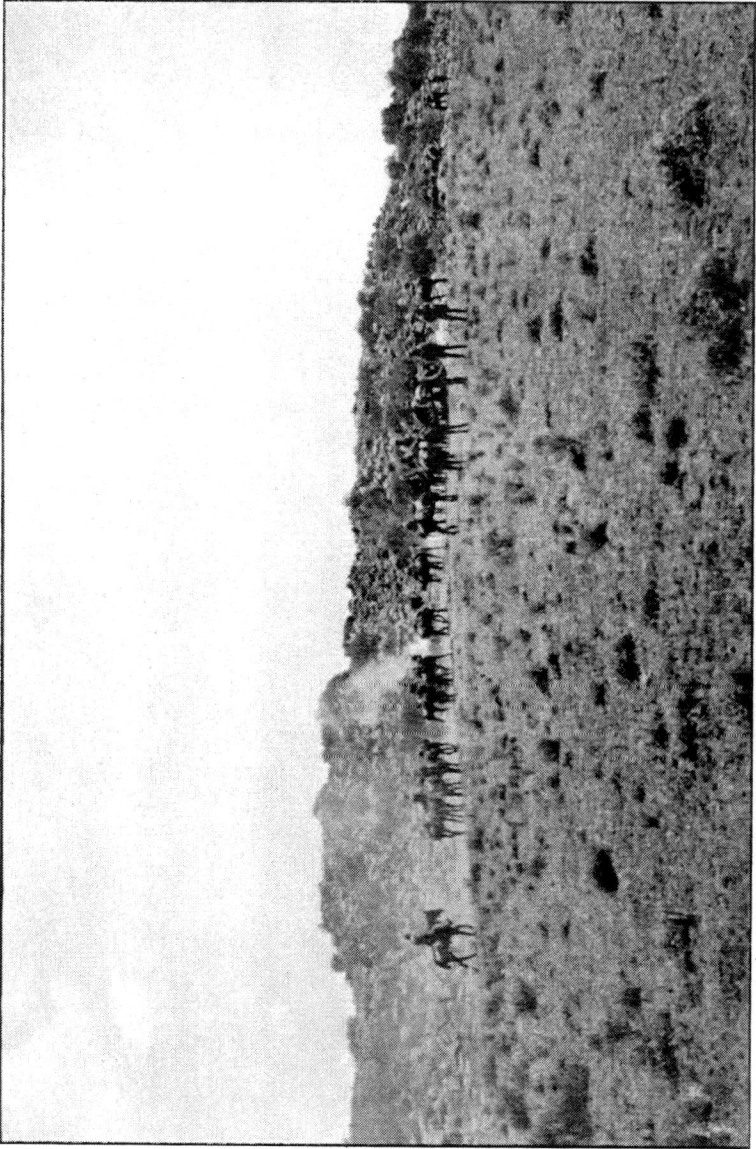

AN OUTLYING PICQUET ON DE LISLE'S KOPJE.

large force to turn our left flank. Meantime B
Squadron Inniskillings joined the 10th Hus-
Charge of
the 10th   sars in a charge across the open towards
Hussars.   Colesberg, Colonel Fisher finally dismount-
ing his men and taking the end of the ridge on foot.
Death of   The 10th Hussars lost Major Harvey, killed,
Major   Major Alexander, wounded, and several men
Harvey.   killed and wounded ; many of our horses also
were killed.

By noon the enemy's attempt to turn our flank
had been quite defeated by General French, and they
were repulsed with heavy loss, about 100 being killed
and wounded. It is unfortunate that the cavalry
charge across the open was not carried right through,
in which case Colesberg might have been captured.

During Captain Herbert's charge, Sergeant
McNaughten, Inniskilling Dragoons, had his clothes
Escape of   riddled with bullets without sustaining any
Sergeant   wound, and was later shown to General
McNaugh-
ten.   French as a ' curiosity ' ! He drove his lance
through one Boer and snatched the Boer's rifle from
his hand, bringing it away ; it was a Royal Irish
Fusilier Lee-Metford rifle.

Major Allenby, with A Squadron from Arundel,
moved to Rensburg.

Next day a despatch was received that the
General Officer Commanding intended attacking a
Attack on   large kopje known as the Red Hill, close
Red Hill : north of Colesberg, early the following morn-
Disaster
to the   ing, the duty assigned to the two squadrons
Suffolks.   Inniskilling Dragoons being to hold De
Lisle's Kopjes, which protected the left flank. Whilst
they were taking up position an ambulance passed
conveying Sir John Milbanke, 10th Hussars, who had

been wounded while gallantly rescuing a sergeant of his regiment, a feat for which he was afterwards awarded the V.C.

About 3 A.M. heavy firing was heard in the direction of Red Hill ; later it was reported that the Jan. 6. Suffolks had attacked it with half a battalion, the result not being known. C Squadron Inniskilling Dragoons, under Captain Herbert, was sent at dawn to reconnoitre around the left flank of the hill. This reconnaissance was an extremely hazardous undertaking. In very open order they approached close to the hill, where a Red Cross flag was seen, surrounded by a number of men. Captain Viscount Fincastle and Lieut. Harris approached within 200 yards to discover what was going on, when suddenly fire was opened on the squadron from all sides ; but, thanks to the open formation, they effected a retirement without casualty.

The night attack of the Suffolks had failed ! One wounded officer and about 200 men escaped ; the remainder, including their commander, Colonel Watson, and ten officers, being killed, wounded, or taken prisoners. It was a sad affair. It would appear that the Boers were expecting and prepared for the attack, having occupied overnight the hill which Colonel Watson believed tenantless. The hill was a mass of loose, sharp stones, which made a great noise when walked over, and was covered with very strong, well-built sangars echeloned upon each other to half-way down the hill. These sangars were quite invisible to telescopes from Coleskop. Later in the morning Lord Fincastle made a most valuable reconnaissance of the ridge of hills to the north-west of Red Hill ; he found a portion of them, ending in

Hobkirk's Farm to the west, unoccupied, but occupied to the north of Red Hill.

From January 6 till February 10 B Squadron Inniskilling Dragoons took up permanent possession of Windmill Post, fortified it with trenches, and held it until the later date, when the force was driven back on Arundel, after General French had weakened the troops by withdrawing for his march to Kimberley. Later it was strengthened by 110 Victorian Mounted Rifles and 57 Australians, and much severe fighting was done by it at the Windmill, and especially when trying to retain Hobkirk's Ridge.

A commando of 300 Boers, coming into Colesberg from the north, was shelled by the 4th Battery Field Artillery, under Major Butcher, at 6,000 yards range, an extreme range obtained by tilting their guns; this same battery, later, caused the death of General de Villebois-Mareuil.

Jan. 7.

Half the Essex Regiment arrived at the Waterkloof and the composite regiment of Household Cavalry arrived at Rensburg. A squadron of the latter was severely engaged next day reconnoitring, losing Captain Ricardo and four men, taken prisoners.

O Battery R.H.A., escorted by A Squadron Inniskillings, had a fierce duel with the Boer artillery to the East, having two men and seventeen horses killed. Lieut. Aldridge, R.H.A., had his horse's head blown off by a shell, but luckily escaped unhurt himself. A patrol of Mounted Infantry sent to Seacow river at night captured three Boer prisoners. One had Lieut. Collis' (Carabiniers) saddle, this officer's horse having been previously shot near Arundel on December 12.

Jan. 9.

C

Lord Roberts now arrived at Cape Town and

assumed command of all our forces in South Africa.

Major Butcher, 4th Battery R.H.A., performed a great feat in getting one of his 15-pounders on to the

top of Coleskop. With a rope on each side of the gun and about forty men to each rope, a series of tugs were given to order, and thus, in a wonderful way, the gun was dragged to the top of the hill—a performance that appeared impossible. Later on he got up a second gun. The Boers were surprised next morning by his shelling Red Hill and their laagers S.E. of Colesberg. He cleared them all out, and for a long time they could not understand where the shells came from.

The weather of late had been very wet, causing great discomfort to the troops.

A column, consisting of A Squadron Inniskillings, one squadron 10th Hussars, two guns R.H.A., and

Jan. 13.
Recon-
naissance
of Coles-
berg
Road
Bridge by
Major
Allenby.
four companies Mounted Infantry, all under command of Major Allenby, Inniskilling Dragoons, starting at 10 P.M., moved round by the left flank to reconnoitre Colesberg Road Bridge, and, if possible, to destroy it. Next day, about noon, they got within 3,000 yards of the bridge and found the enemy in overwhelming force. The enemy attempted to cut off the column, but Major Allenby made good use of his artillery, and, having skilfully effected a most useful reconnaissance, retired without a casualty, taking five prisoners with him. General French sent out troops to cover the retirement of the column, which arrived back safely on the morning of the 15th;

GETTING 15-POUNDER ON TO COLESKOP.

THE INNISKILLING POLO TEAM AT ARUNDEL CAMP.
Lieut. ANSELL. Major RIMINGTON. Lieut. HAIG. Lieut. HIGGIN.

its object of misleading the Boers had also been accomplished.

The Boers this day made a bold attack at Slingersfontein, the brunt of the attack being borne by the Yorkshires and New Zealand Mounted Rifles. Gallantly they repulsed it, inflicting heavy loss on the enemy, their own casualties being small, but including Captain Orr, of the Yorkshires, and several men wounded. On this occasion the situation was saved at the critical moment by Captain Maddocks. Fixing bayonets, he headed the New Zealanders and charged into the Boers, who fled before the impetuosity of this counter-attack, leaving about thirty dead and many wounded behind.

Attack of Boers at Slingers- fontein.

Situation saved by Captain Maddocks,

Two howitzers, newly arrived, bombarded the Boer position with lyddite. At night some ostriches stampeded a good many of the horses at the Windmill in the pitch dark ; all except four were recovered next day, but it was found necessary to shoot three that were badly lacerated by having galloped into barbed wire.

Jan. 20.

A force consisting of A and C Squadrons Inniskilling Dragoons, 10th Hussars, R Battery R.H.A., and two companies Mounted Infantry, all under Major-General Brabazon, moved to Du Plessis Farm, bivouacking there preparatory to operations on the morrow. Sir Ashmead Bartlett accompanied this force. The Mounted Infantry held Bastard's Nek, and at daylight the force moved, by a wide détour, to the right flank of the enemy's position at Rietfontein Poort, with the intention of making a demonstration so as to enable the infantry, which was moved along the Bastard's Nek

Jan. 24. Opera-' tions by General Brabazon.

ridge, to seize the 'poort'; at the same time another demonstration was made against Red Hill by B Squadron Inniskilling Dragoons. The operation was unsuccessful, the enemy's position being too strongly guarded. The Wilts lost several men, but their commanding officer, Colonel Carter, behaving with great gallantry, got his wounded away. There were no casualties amongst the mounted troops; the Inniskillings, when under very heavy fire, being greatly protected by a violent storm of rain and hail which occurred most opportunely.

At this time regimental transport, with the exception of ammunition and water-carts, was done away with, being handed over to the Army Service Corps.

Jan. 27.

Transport.

THE 15-POUNDER ON TOP OF COLESKOP

CHAPTER II

AT the end of the month General French left for Cape Town to meet Lord Roberts and arrange for the famous relief of Kimberley. He handed over the command of the forces before Colesberg to Major-General Clements. These now consisted of the 18th Royal Irish, Worcesters, Berks, Wilts, and Essex Regiments, J Battery R.H.A., four 15-pounders, 4th R.F.A., two howitzers, Victorian Mounted Rifles, South and West Australian Mounted Infantry, &c., but early in February they were much weakened by the departure of all the Regular Cavalry, except B and C Squadrons Inniskilling Dragoons, for Orange River *en route* to Kimberley. A Squadron Inniskilling Dragoons, under Major Allenby, was attached to the Scots Greys and left with them for Modder River.

Jan. 29. Major-General Clements takes over command from General French.

The Boers at this time were in great strength at Colesberg, nearly 10,000 strong, with many guns, and were most aggressive. They were daily being increased, whereas our forces were being lessened for the Kimberley relief, so General Clements was left in a most trying position, but he proved himself equal to the task.

Boer strength.

The Inniskilling Squadron (B) under Major

Dauncey, at Windmill, was reinforced by 100
Victorian Mounted Infantry under Captain McLeish,

Feb. 4.   and occupied Hobkirk's Farm and Bastard's
Nek, two most risky posts 3 and 2½ miles
distant, respectively.

The Inniskilling Squadron (C) proceeded with
four guns J Battery R.H.A., 100 West Australians,

Feb. 6.   and a howitzer, brought up a few days later
disguised as a wagon, from Maeder's Farm to
hold Slingersfontein. This squadron, under Lieut.

Feb. 7.   Harris, made a reconnaissance east, six miles
Recon-   from Slingersfontein, towards Potfontein;
naissance. they found it strongly held, and had one man
killed, one wounded, and three captured.

Next day, owing to the illness of Captain Herbert,
Lieut. Neil Haig took over command of C Squadron,

Feb. 8.   and made a 'demonstration' on Potfontein,
having one man wounded. At daylight
Lieut. Haig, with C Squadron Inniskillings and 100
West Australians, tried to surprise a farm four miles

Feb. 9.   distant, which was held by the Boers. The
surprise failed; the advanced guard was
heavily fired on at 500 yards, from the hill behind
the farm; at the same time a heavy fire was opened
from the ridge on the right of the squadron, parallel
to which they had to retire, sniped all the way. The
West Australians eventually occupied a kopje about
100 yards from this ridge, and kept the enemy at bay
the whole day, suffering some loss; they behaved
most gallantly, and Private Kruger (?) was afterwards
recommended for the V.C. In the evening they
retired by detachments in very open order, under a
storm of bullets. The Boers then occupied this kopje
and sniped all night, wounding one Inniskilling.

THE FIRST BOER PRISONERS CAPTURED BY THE REGIMENT.

FIRST BOER HORSE CAPTURED BY THE REGIMENT.
This horse went right through the war.

At dawn the Boers shelled Slingersfontein Camp for the first time, putting twenty-seven shells into it before our artillery silenced their guns.

Feb. 10. Boer attacks.

Simultaneously the enemy in force attacked the Windmill posts of Hobkirk's Farm and Bastard's Nek, occupied by the Victoria Mounted Rifles, driving them in, with the loss of one killed and three wounded. Lieut. Raymond Johnson, with

Gallant repulse by Inniskillings.

his troop of Inniskilling Dragoons, who were inlying picket, and therefore ready saddled, at once galloped off to seize Hobkirk's Ridge before the enemy could reach it ; he was just in time, but was attacked from right front and left rear, being almost surrounded. He dismounted the men, who fought splendidly. One corporal was killed ; another corporal was shot through the sleeve at close range by a young Boer of about fourteen years, whom he had to shoot in self-defence. Another man from one side of a bush poked a Boer in the stomach with the barrel of his unloaded carbine, loaded quickly, and shot the Boer. Five men were cut off, but hid in a kloof, and rejoined later. Gallantly the little troop held on to the ridge until Major Dauncey, reinforced by the remainder of the Inniskillings and the South Australians, drove back the enemy, who remained all day sniping from Hobkirk's Farm. Later Colonel Carter, in command of the left wing of the main position, arrived with two guns and some of his battalion, the Wilts. He agreed with Major Dauncey that the position would be untenable when the enemy got his guns on the hill behind Hobkirk's Farm ; but, in order to prevent our left being turned, ordered him to hold on as long as possible.

Sniping continued all next day and all night.

The gunners of the 4th Battery R.F.A. were busy building an épaulement for one gun to reach Bastard's Nek; and it was lucky that they did so, for at dawn two long-range guns opened on Windmill Camp from Bastard's Nek. Thanks to cover from the épaulement and a high dam near, and despite the enemy's well-timed shrapnel fire, Major Butcher, with his one gun, silenced the enemy's in an hour or so, having only one man wounded.

Feb. 12.

A fierce attack was made at dawn with gun and rifle fire simultaneously upon Hobkirk's Ridge. Major Eddy, with twenty-five of his South Australians, most gallantly held the extreme edge of the ridge overlooking Hobkirk's Farm. The enemy stormed this in the most determined manner, sending up armed Kaffirs in the first line (so the Australians affirmed); at the same time the shell and pom-pom fire from the hills high above made it so hot that they had to retire. They were at such close quarters with the enemy when they did so that, although their horses were quite close, several of them were shot down whilst mounting. Major Eddy himself was shot through the head just as he rose and gave the order to retire. Out of his twenty-five men only twelve came back! The two troops of Inniskillings there under Lieut. Lawlor also fought bravely, having one corporal killed and one corporal wounded. The Wilts, too, lost some men, and had to retire eventually on Windmill Camp; many of them, who were quite exhausted and would have been captured, were taken up by our men behind them on their horses. Corporal Coleman, Inniskillings, endeavouring to assist a wounded man, was himself wounded. An Australian

Gallantry of South Australians under Major Eddy.

who was taken prisoner informed us that a Boer came up to the corporal while he was lying wounded and took his water-bottle from him. Corporal Coleman protested, and the Boer at once shot him through the head. Later we found his dead body. He was such a good, brave soldier.

Death of Corporal Coleman.

The enemy, having obtained possession of Hobkirk's Ridge, outflanked our guns, which had to retire under a fusillade of segment shells, which were pitched into and far beyond Windmill Camp without doing much harm. At dusk all retired to the ridges close to and west of Coleskop.

Meanwhile, on our other (right) flank at Slingersfontein, the Boers fiercely stormed a ridge held by the Worcesters. The attack was repulsed with heavy loss to the enemy; but the Worcesters suffered great loss in doing it, both their colonel and adjutant being killed. During the day the Inniskilling Squadron (C) here was engaged continuously in severe fighting, and finally covered the withdrawal of the Worcesters at dusk from their ridge.

Worcesters repulse attack.

In face of such overwhelming numbers General Clements ordered a midnight retirement of the whole force on Rensburg. Accordingly the guns were got down from the top of Coleskop. One, breaking away, rolled to the bottom of the hill, smashing its carriage; nevertheless, it was brought away somehow. The Essex were collected from Waterkloof, McCracken and his Berkshires from Berkshire Kopje, and on the other flank the troops from Slingersfontein. The Inniskilling Dragoons and Victorian Mounted Rifles protected the flanks and formed the advanced guard during the

Midnight retirement on Rensburg.

midnight retirement, all arriving safely at Rensburg before daylight.   The Boers, following up, contented themselves with sniping during the day.   At midnight General Clements continued the retirement on Arundel.

At 10 P.M. Major Dauncey, with B Squadron Inniskillings and the Victorian M.I., relieved the Wilts on the hills to the north-west of Rensburg, remaining there until 1.30 A.M., in order to cover the retirement of the column.   The Wilts retired when relieved, but neglected to warn two of their companies who were occupying a high hill close by. Colonel Carter had sent orderlies to inform them, but it was a difficult place to find amongst the hills, and the orderlies evidently did not find them, though Colonel Carter believed that they had done so.   So these two companies did not discover the retirement until dawn, when all the remainder were nine miles away at Arundel.   It was not till then, also, that they were missed.

Feb. 14.
Retire-
ment on
Arundel.
Loss of
two
companies
Wilts.

Although worn out with two nights and days of incessant fighting, and without any sleep, the Inniskilling Dragoons, with a Battery R.H.A., under Lieut.-Colonel Page Henderson, immediately raced back four and a half miles towards Rensburg to their former old position at Epsom Kopje, but, alas! only just in time to save twenty men of the Bedfordshire Regiment, who had also got left behind, and a few stragglers of these two Wilts companies.   The remainder had already been captured with heavy loss in killed and wounded.   These twenty men of the Bedfordshires were already at bay in the Epsom Kopje, firing volleys into the enemy, who were surrounding them, when our Horse Artillery guns came into action.

The Boers, having retired, continued shelling from their old position at Taaibosch, until noon, when, leaving outposts out, the Inniskillings returned to Arundel.

The same day Lieut. and Adjutant Ansell, Inniskillings, went out with one attendant only on a special reconnaissance through the enemies' lines to Capture of the north-west. He had previously per- Lieut. Ansell. formed similar daring feats with success, but on this occasion, owing to his horse being exhausted and to the dastardly treachery of a supposed loyalist farmer, who, seeing the patrol in the distance, galloped over to a Boer commando at Bastard's Nek and gave information, he was surrounded by a Boer force and taken prisoner. Lieut. Lawlor was now selected as Acting Adjutant in place of Lieut. Ansell, a duty he performed with great success.

On February 17, General Clements, having received information that a Boer convoy, on the road to Colesberg Wagon Bridge, was at Pleuman's Farm, to the north-west of Arundel, despatched a mounted force of the Inniskillings, two companies Mounted Infantry (the Oxfords and Australians), and Major Butcher's battery R.F.A., under Lieut.-Colonel Page Henderson, to try to cut it off. On arrival opposite Vaalkop, the convoy turned out to be the enemy's main advanced laager. It was at once reinforced from Rensburg, and our mounted force, which had no cover but that afforded by the irregularities of the ground, was subject to a cross fire of shells, pom-poms, and musketry. An attack with such a small mounted force was impossible. Major Butcher fought his battery splendidly, while shells were bursting all amongst it, and the troops were safely withdrawn to Arundel.

On February 20 the Boers made a determined attempt at daybreak to get round both our flanks at Arundel, and the fighting lasted till evening. The defence of our right was under Major McCracken, with Lieut. Haig in command of the mounted troops, consisting of C Squadron Inniskillings, and the Colonials, who completely checked the Boers there. It was reported that a detachment of Cape Town Volunteers (Prince Alfred's), who were at Naauwpoort, hearing the firing, occupied a hill covering the town, thus appearing on the left flank of the Boers, and undoubtedly helping materially to check them. They nearly succeeded, however, in gaining a position commanding the camp, when Lieut. Paterson, with B Squadron Inniskilling Dragoons, who was luckily returning from a reconnaissance at the time, perceived their intention. With great promptitude he raced for the position, seized it first, and drove back with heavy loss the astonished Boers who were advancing up the further side.

By this time General Clements had been reinforced, and, believing that the Boers were working round his left with the intention of seizing the railway at Hanover Road, and so getting between him and De Aar, he despatched a mounted force consisting of one battery R.H.A., C Squadron Inniskilling Dragoons, the Oxford and West Riding Mounted Infantry, and the Australians, all under Lieut.-Colonel Page Henderson, to Mooifontein, about nine miles to the west, with instructions to effect there a junction with Colonel Price

Boer attack repulsed.

Feb. 22.

and his Colonials, who were to move from Hanover Road. On arriving at Mooifontein at daybreak, this force surprised the Boer outposts already there, and a heavy fire with two pom-poms and Mausers was opened on it. Having taken up positions, an artillery duel was maintained until the afternoon, when Colonel Price's force was seen approaching from the south.

The combined forces then succeeded in driving off the Boers and taking several prisoners and arms, and bivouacked on their position, receiving the congratulations of General Clements.

It was on this day that Sergeant Hanwell, Inniskilling Dragoons, having his horse shot, and having lost his helmet, lay behind an ant-heap all day, unable to move on account of the Boer bullets. The latter he escaped, but the terrible heat of the sun gave him a stroke from which he eventually died.

Loss of Sergeant Hanwell.

The following morning an advance was made round the Boer flanks, to support an attack by General Clements to the north; but it was not successful. Next day the operations were renewed. A detachment of mounted infantry, under Major King-King, of the 2nd Queen's, dashed through a ' nek ' in the Boer position at daybreak; Lieut.-Colonel Page Henderson, with the Inniskillings and the rest of the mounted troops, followed, leaving half the force behind in order to cover and support the movement. Lieut. Jervis, reconnoitring with his troop of Inniskillings, advanced with Corporal Hamilton only, to discover the enemy's dispositions. They were joined by two of Rimington's Guides and two Australians. About eighty Boers attempted to cut off their retreat, nearly

Feb. 23.

Feb. 24.

surrounding them. Under heavy fire they had to cut their way back through a wire fence. All were hit, but Lieut. Jervis, slightly wounded, and two others, also wounded, regained the troop. Corporal Hamilton was shot through the bladder, captured by the Boers, stripped and left. Afterwards he managed to crawl back to his squadron, three miles off. The West Ridings drove the Boers from two kopjes and took them, losing their captain, killed, and one subaltern, shot in the head. Meantime, the Boers in force had occupied all the hills to the left rear, so lack of water and reinforcements rendered further progress impossible. The casualties included one officer killed, three wounded, one prisoner, and several men killed and wounded. That night torrents of rain rendered the country a bog. This, and the fatigue of the horses, prevented a pursuit of the enemy, who retreated.

Lieut. Jervis and Corporal Hamilton wounded.

Feb. 26. Lord Kitchener visited the camp at Arundel.

Feb. 27. Recapture of Rensburg by Inniskillings. On the 27th, B Squadron Inniskilling Dragoons, under Lieut. Paterson, reconnoitred Rensburg. Finding it weakly held, they seized the position commanding it, drove off the Boer rear-guard, and took the town—a very smart performance.

Feb. 28. Capture of Colesberg. The following day General Clements moved the troops to Rensburg and occupied Colesberg without opposition. The enemy were now withdrawing their forces north, the surrender of Cronje the previous day, no doubt, hastening them. Thus, after all these weary weeks of fighting backwards and forwards, our troops once more occupied Rensburg and, at last, entered Colesberg.

INNISKILLING OFFICERS' MESS SHELTER.

Lieut. RAYMOND JOHNSON.   Lieut. HAIG.   Major WYATT, A.M.D.   Capt. HERBERT.

The permanent advanced guard from Colesberg Junction (March 1), until arrival at Norval's Pont (March 7) and the crossing of the Orange River (15th), was under the command of Major Butcher, R.F.A., and consisted of two sections 4th Battery R.F.A., one squadron (B) Inniskillings, under Major Dauncey, 100 Victoria Mounted Rifles (Captain McLeish), 200 West Australians (Major More), and 100 mounted infantry (Oxford L.I. ?). The remainder of General Clements' force was at Rensburg; the Royal Engineers being busy with the repair of Colesberg Junction bridge, which had been blown up.

March 1.

A patrol of thirty Inniskillings and twenty Victoria M.R. (Lieut. Thorne), all under the command of Lieut. Paterson (Inniskillings), started at 7 A.M. to reconnoitre towards Norval's Pont. After proceeding twelve miles they fell in with the Boer rear-guard and a smart encounter ensued. Lieut. Paterson attacked boldly, inflicting considerable loss on the enemy, many of whom were seen to fall. The ponies of a Cape cart endeavouring to escape were shot, but the Boers coming on in great force effected the rescue of the occupants. It transpired later that one of these was an important officer of the Boer Artillery who was coming to select positions for their guns to retard our forces. On our occupation of Bloemfontein this same cart was found there riddled with bullet-holes, and had been exhibited by the Boers as a curiosity. Lieut. Paterson's own horse was shot as he was mounting, and several others were killed and wounded, but, having made a useful reconnaissance, he brought back his patrol without casualty, the

March 3.
Successful reconnaissance.

dismounted men riding in on donkeys they had captured.

Next morning General Clements started on a forward advance from Colesberg Junction in the direction of Norval's Pont. With the Inniskillings' advanced guard, the forces moved to a very strong pass, Achtertang. The river (the Oorlogspruit) rushes through the pass, flowing north into the Orange River, the road winding close along the right bank through the gorge. The advanced guard seized the pass, the main body encamping in the rear. Lieut. Raymond Johnson, with six men, Inniskillings, reconnoitred to the north-west, finding several small parties of the enemy in that direction. One of his men, scouting around the further side of a long kopje, was suddenly held up by a couple of Dutchmen who jumped out from behind a rock.

'Hallo! What's up?' shouted one of them.

'Oh, nothing ; just having a look round,' said the Inniskilling.

'So are we,' said the first spokesman, 'but you'd better be sharp off unless you want to see Pretoria.' And they let him go without disarming him. They told him, in slang English, that a good many of them were 'fed up' with the war ; also that there was a large force of Boers behind them coming up from the Colesberg wagon bridge.

The Inniskillings, reconnoitring north-east, found the Rietfontein bridge blown up, so General Clements moved his forces there, took up a position, and set the Engineers to repair it. Moving on next day the Inniskillings in advance seized Norval's Pont. No opposition was met until

March 4. Forward advance.

Mar. 5–7. Capture of Norval's Pont.

NORVALS PONT BRIDGE, DESTROYED BY THE BOERS.

WATER CART COMING INTO CAMP.

they arrived at the small village of tin houses, when sharp sniping took place. Having occupied the hills and obtained a sketch of the broken bridge the force encamped, guarding the pass through which the road debouches, about one mile from the village.

The next few days were spent in preparing to cross the Orange River. Two 5-inch guns arrived and were placed in position ; the Bedfordshire Regiment also arrived. The opposite side of the river was bombarded, and the Stockenstroom Drift was guarded.

At daylight on March 15, the Engineers threw a pontoon bridge across the Orange River, but, owing to some of the boats filling and sinking, it was evening before B Squadron Inniskillings, who were the first to cross, reached the other side. They at once pushed on six miles north and occupied Donkerpoort.

March 15.

A very sad affair occurred during the morning by which Lieut. Dent, Inniskilling Dragoons, lost his life. The Orange River was very full and flooded, with dangerous whirlpools. Lieut. Dent got into one of these and was carried away by the current and drowned. Lieut. Haig, Lieut. Harris, and Sergeant Williams, Inniskillings, made heroic efforts to save him, but without avail, all narrowly escaping the same fate themselves. For this gallant conduct each was awarded the Royal Humane Society's medal.

Lieut. Dent drowned.

The force having successfully crossed the Orange River, the 4th Battery R.F.A., under Major Butcher, left for Kimberley, and General Clements started to march to Bloemfontein, *viâ* Philippolis, Jagersfontein, and

March 20. Clements' march to Bloemfontein.

D

Fauresmith, in three columns: himself with the centre column of infantry; Major Slee, 2nd Battery R.F.A., commanding the left column; Major Dauncey, Inniskilling Dragoons, the right column. Major Slee's column consisted of two guns R.F.A., C Squadron Inniskilling Dragoons, under Lieut. Haig, and the 6th Victoria Mounted Rifles under Captain McLeish. Major Dauncey's column consisted of four guns R.F.A., under Captain Crockett; B Squadron Inniskilling Dragoons, under Lieut. Paterson; 100 M.I., Oxford Light Infantry, under Captain Colvile; 100 West Riding Mounted Infantry; 80 West Australians under Major More; 60 South Australians under Captain Howland, and a Colt gun.

The columns marched to Bloemfontein without opposition, the inhabitants coming in and surrendering their arms. The march occupied sixteen days, the forces arriving at Bloemfontein on April 5. During the march much buried ammunition was discovered: for instance, on March 26, in two different mine shafts, a Maxim (Martini-Henry) and an Armstrong gun were found; in Mr. Rorick's paddock at Koppiesfontein sixty shells, 60 lb. of powder, and eight boxes of small-arm ammunition were buried; next day, at Rondefontein, three wagonloads of shells and small-arm ammunition were unearthed and sent into Jagersfontein. Much pacification of the country was also accomplished.

On April 7 B and C Squadrons Inniskilling Dragoons joined A Squadron and the 1st Cavalry Brigade at Springfield Camp, about six miles south-east of Bloemfontein. The squadrons were now at last united and the regiment complete

April 7.

INNISKILLING DRAGOONS CROSSING THE
ORANGE RIVER FOR THE FIRST TIME.

STORE OF BISCUITS AT MACHADODORP,
USED AS A HELIOGRAPH STATION.

A 4'7" GUN GOING INTO ACTION.

GENERAL CLEMENTS' COLUMN MAKING PONTOON
BRIDGE OVER THE ORANGE RIVER.

A SAND DEVIL AT ARUNDEL.

A COLD MORNING.

under the command of Lieut.-Colonel Page Henderson; but on the 13th he was appointed to command the Cavalry Depôt at Bloemfontein, and Major Allenby, who had been away with A Squadron on the Kimberley relief march, assumed command of the regiment.

I must now return and briefly relate the doings of this squadron.

CHAPTER III

THE RELIEF OF KIMBERLEY

AT the beginning of February, when the cavalry were quietly withdrawn from before Colesberg for Feb. 2. the relief of Kimberley, A Squadron Inniskilling Dragoons, under command of Major Allenby, marched from Rensburg to Arundel, proceeding next day to Naauwpoort, where it entrained for Modder River Camp. After a tedious nineteen hours' railway journey, it arrived there on the 4th, and camped on the southern (left) bank of the river alongside the Household Cavalry. It was a sandy spot, where violent storms of wind and dust occurred almost daily, and was situated inside Lord Methuen's entrenched camp, opposite the Magersfontein position, which his big guns were continually bombarding.

During the next three days the Scots Greys, 10th Hussars, 9th, 12th, and 16th Lancers, with other Formation of Kimberley Relief Column. mounted troops, had assembled. Although the troops were not yet all present, a cavalry division of three brigades was now organised under General French—viz. : *First Brigade*, under Colonel Porter, consisting of the Carabiniers, Scots Greys (one squadron), Inniskillings (one squadron), 14th Hussars, and New South Wales Lancers.

Second Brigade, under Colonel Broadwood: Household Cavalry, 10th Hussars, and 12th Lancers. *Third Brigade*, Colonel Gordon: 9th and 16th Lancers; Royal Horse Artillery, Colonel Eustace, G, O, Q, R, T, and U Batteries. Also two brigades of Mounted Infantry under Colonel Hannay and Colonel Ridley. These brigades did not join till February 13, when the army was on its march. Colonel Porter, with the Carabiniers, arrived the same day; in the meantime Lieut.-Colonel Alexander, of the Scots Greys, took over command of the 1st Cavalry Brigade.

The Inniskilling Dragoons' A Squadron was attached to the Scots Greys, and was treated by them as if it belonged to their regiment, being shown constant kindness and consideration. Colonel Broadwood and Colonel Gordon (who had only just arrived from India) took over command of their brigades at Ramdam.

The secret plan, now, was for this force to assemble at Ramdam on February 11, and make a rapid dash on Kimberley.[1] Ramdam was a large farm and dam about twenty-five miles south-east, just inside the Orange Free State. Two infantry divisions, under Generals Tucker and Kelly-Kenny, were to follow up in support of the movement. To deceive the Boers as to our real intentions, General Macdonald, with his infantry, and General Babington, with cavalry, made a feint attack on the right of the Magersfontein position, *i.e.* on our left, thereby causing Cronje to move his forces to that flank.

Plan.

[1] The total strength of the relieving force was 209 officers, 3,783 men, 3,932 horses.

Major Rimington, Inniskilling Dragoons, who knew the country so well, was entrusted, with his Guides, with the all-important task of guiding the army.

Lord Roberts personally addressed the cavalry, telling them that he entrusted to them the relief of Kimberley ; that it was a grand opportunity for them ; that he relied on its being done with dash and at all costs—thereby causing the greatest enthusiasm.

At 3 A.M. on Sunday, February 16, the troops started by moonlight for Ramdam, where the real
Start.   assembly took place.   The few Boers about,
being surprised, fled, and Major Rimington, in advance with his Guides, occupied it without opposition.   At 10 A.M. the cavalry reached Ramdam and were joined by General Tucker's division of infantry. Roberts's and Kitchener's Horse also joined, and, with the exception of the Mounted Infantry Division and the Carabiniers, General French's force had assembled.

At 2 A.M. next day the Cavalry Division moved off in brigades on the Waterfall and De Kiel's drifts of the Riet River, about twelve miles distant, in order to force a passage at one or the other. With daylight came opposition, the Boers opening fire with two guns and placing some shells in the midst of General French and his Staff. Our own artillery at once replied. Meantime, A Squadron Inniskilling Dragoons, who were advanced guard to the 1st Brigade, advancing on Waterfall Drift, had become engaged and were
Narrow   directed to guard the flank, supported by
escape of
Captain   Rimington's Guides, who had been reconnoi-
Rankin.   tring ahead. One of their patrols, under
Captain Rankin, climbing a high kopje, on the left,

found themselves face to face with the Boers already in possession, and marvellously escaped with only their clothes riddled with bullets.

The 3rd Brigade (Gordon's) now made a feint of crossing the Waterfall Drift, drawing the Boer

De Kiel's Drift rushed.

forces to oppose, whereupon General French moved to the east and, with Roberts's Horse and the First Brigade, rushed De Kiel's Drift. It was a race between Roberts's Horse and a force of the Boers, but the former, urged on by Major Hunter Weston, R.E., of General French's Staff, gained the north bank and, after some severe fighting, in which

Death of Captain Majendie.

Captain Majendie of the Rifle Brigade, attached to Roberts's Horse, was killed, the drift was secured, and a battery R.H.A. passed over to make it good. General Tucker's Infantry Division and the transport arrived later.

At nightfall the Inniskilling Dragoons, A Squadron, which, under Major Allenby, had been guarding the left flank, crossed De Kiel's Drift and rejoined the 1st Brigade on the north bank, having lost three men wounded and two horses killed. Here the cavalry parted from their transport wagons, many of which were not seen again till Paardeberg.

Early next morning Lord Roberts arrived and witnessed General French's departure with the Cavalry Division. The Modder River, which was in the possession of the enemy, lay about twenty-four miles off, and there was no intermediate water. Our objective, the river, had to be gained that day. To add to the trial, the day was intensely hot and the march lay over a sandy, parched country. It was a perilous adventure.

Directly the advance began fire opened on the left

flank and continued all day, but the division pressed
on, driving back opposition. About midday Major
Allenby's squadron of Inniskillings, which was guarding the right flank, was severely engaged, losing
Lieut. D. Johnson and two men wounded and five
horses killed. The heat was intense ; men and horses
were parched with thirst, many of the latter dropping
down dead or exhausted. The gun-horses could
scarcely drag the guns, and gradually they lagged
behind.

At last the green bushes in the distance marked
the line of the river and the longed-for water. The
division was making for Klip Drift. The enemy, in
force on the opposite bank, were gathering to oppose,
so General French headed for Klip Kraal Drift on the
extreme right. The enemy at once followed suit,
whereupon General French, suddenly changing his
direction again, dashed the 2nd and 1st Brigades on
Klip Drift and the 3rd Brigade to threaten Rondavel
Drift on the extreme left. This manœuvre was
crowned with success. The Boers being much scattered,
the 12th Lancers and Mounted Infantry rushed
through the Drift with but slight loss from the
enemy's fire, drove them off, and captured their laagers
beyond. The laagers were full of provisions and
forage, which were most needed, also ammunition,
sheep, wagons, and oxen.

The day had been a great success. The admirable
tactics of General French, the rapid advance of the
cavalry, necessarily leaving their guns behind them,
had completely surprised, out-manœuvred, and scattered the Boers, so that, with trifling loss, we secured
the Modder River, and, in addition, some rations
and forage for the horses from their captured laagers.

It was not, however, sufficient; the Inniskillings, coming in late, from guarding the right rear of the division, only secured a little flour, which was made into paste for the horses.

As a set-back, the loss in horses had been terrible. The long, hot, waterless march had killed many, and hundreds were too exhausted to be fit to move on. At nightfall the 1st and 2nd Brigades bivouacked in a hot dust-storm on the right bank of the river, the Mounted Infantry on the left bank, and the 3rd Brigade at Rondavel Drift.

A forward movement next day was impossible, as it was essential to wait until the infantry closed up, and also for the Supply Column. The outposts were heavily engaged all day, and the Boers shelled the bivouac with their long-range guns, without inflicting much damage. Late in the afternoon the Supply Column, escorted by Colonel Porter with the Carabiniers, arrived, and during the night General Kelly-Kenny's Infantry Division marched in.

Feb. 14.

On the morning of the 15th all was ready for the do-or-die charge of the cavalry on Kimberley, now only twenty miles distant. All were eager, but longing for fresher horses. The division moved off up the right bank of the river, the 3rd Brigade (Colonel Gordon) in advance; then the 1st Brigade (Colonel Porter), 2nd Brigade (Colonel Broadwood), and the Mounted Infantry (Colonel Alderson). Our guns were heavily engaged on the left as the column proceeded, and soon the Boer position was revealed. Their centre was on a long 'nek' rising from the open plain, with high ridges on each flank, on which the enemy were in great force with their guns.

The leading regiment, 16th Lancers, had already

got within rifle shot of the main position. The Boers opened fire with their guns, pitching shells into the midst of squadrons with, luckily, little harm, and were getting a cross fire on the division, when our batteries took up position in the open, making splendid practice on the ridges and keeping down the enemy's fire. Then, at the right moment, came the command to charge.

Gordon's Brigade of the 16th Lancers, with the 9th Lancers opening out on their right, went straight at the Boer centre, the men riding at open intervals. General French himself followed with the 2nd Brigade, forming the second line and charging in succession of regiments, whilst Porter's Brigade and the Mounted Infantry followed on, forming a third line. Major Allenby's squadron of Inniskillings and Major Middleton's squadron of Scots Greys were first employed dismounted to the right flank, to keep down the enemy's fire, and then followed on.

The charge was met by a terrific fire, but, owing to the open order, pace, and clouds of dust, there were few casualties, and the Boers, appalled at the terrific approach, broke and fled. Many were ridden down and left dead on the field ; many escaped through the intervals ; but the majority mounted quickly and made their escape good round the flank.

It looked as if the carnage must be awful, and, had there been any hesitation, or had the Boers stood their ground, it certainly would have been. As it was, the position was taken with comparatively small losses, and the Boers were in flight everywhere. Who shall say that the days of cavalry are over ?

Amongst the casualties, the Royal Horse Artillery lost one officer killed and several men wounded ; the

16th Lancers lost Lieut. Hesketh and two men killed whilst gallantly leading their charge; several horses, too, were killed and wounded.

The division having reformed and watered at a farm beyond Roodekalkfontein, the advance on Kimberley was continued. There was but little subsequent resistance; but the march was long and thirsty, and the horses were badly done up; for instance, A Squadron Inniskilling Dragoons could only muster forty-two horses on its arrival at Kimberley. There the New South Wales Lancers, under Major Lee, were attached to it under Major Allenby, making the squadron up to 120 horses, and thereafter they remained with the regiment, rendering yeoman service until their return to New South Wales.

At last, late in the afternoon, the columns reached Kimberley, and the relief was accomplished, General French joining hands with Colonel Kekewich, its defender, and riding into the town amidst the cheers of the garrison and the populace. The sudden arrival of our cavalry was a welcome relief to them, for they mistook them for reinforcements to the enemy, so made no effort to assist us entering the town, or to cut off the enemy's retreat towards the Vaal and prevent them taking off their big gun.

CHAPTER IV

THE PURSUIT OF CRONJE

THE 1st and 3rd Brigades bivouacked after dark at Blankenberg's Vlei, outside the town, the 2nd Brigade at Alexanderfontein. There was, however, little rest, for at 4.30 A.M. next day General French, accompanied by Colonel Kekewich and some of the garrison, moved out with the 1st and 3rd Cavalry Brigades (Porter's and Gordon's) and the Mounted Infantry, the object being, if possible, to cut off some of the enemy and secure the big gun with which they had been bombarding the town. Owing to the worn-out condition of the horses, it was an unsatisfactory day : intense heat, no food, no water, continuous severe fighting, severe losses, and the object not achieved.

The Boers were in a strong position at Dronfield and also on a ridge by Macfarlane's Farm, leading to it. After some gallant attacks the Macfarlane Ridge was taken and occupied, but the Dronfield position was too strong. The Boers could be seen retreating with their convoy, but it was impossible to pursue ; our horses were dying by scores from thirst and exhaustion. The brunt of the fighting fell on the Cavalry Brigades, of which two officers were killed and five wounded, and about thirty men killed. The

Feb. 16.

Scots Greys lost Lieut. Bunbury, killed, and two officers wounded ; the 9th Lancers, Lieut. Brassey killed, Captain Gordon and Lieut. Durand wounded. The Inniskilling squadron, strange to say, had no casualties.

In the attack on the Macfarlane position Major Allenby was directed to outflank it, and led his men round to within 500 yards of the position, where, with little cover, they were engaged for over an hour in a heavy fire with the Boers until the Boers retired.

It was 9.30 P.M. before the horses and men of the Inniskillings, who were rear-guard, covering the Scots Greys while they were bringing in their wounded, crawled back to Kimberley, utterly done up.

The enemy retreated from Dronfield during the night, leaving a gun and their laager there in our hands.

At midnight one of Rimington's ubiquitous Guides came in, after a daring and successful ride, with a despatch from Lord Kitchener, informing General French of Cronje's retreat and giving urgent orders to head him off.

Collecting every horse that could move, the 2nd Cavalry Brigade (Broadwood's), consisting of Household Cavalry, 10th Hussars, 12th Feb. 17. Lancers, Rimington's Guides, and two batteries R.H.A. (the only available troops), left at 3 A.M., followed, a few hours later, by General French with a squadron of the Carabiniers.

Colonel Porter was left with the 1st and 3rd Brigades to recoup his horses as far as possible and protect Kimberley, in conjunction with Colonel Kekewich, until Lord Methuen arrived with his infantry. Food was very scarce, but Mr. Cecil

Rhodes came to the rescue and helped to the best of his ability, sending forage for the horses, soup, fire-wood, cooking-pots, &c., for the men.

Meantime, during the early hours of the 17th, General French, with an unerring instinct, led the 2nd Brigade straight for Koodoosrand, some thirty-five miles from Kimberley. It was reached about 10 A.M. : considering the state of the horses, a most remarkable performance and a splendid achievement. A few minutes more and it would have been too late, for the vanguard of Cronje's army was approaching the drift, which, once in their possession, would have left them an open road to Bloemfontein and escape. Even now, it was a close thing. Our guns at once opened on the surprised and astonished army, bring-ing them to a sudden halt ; and then ensued a race between the 10th Hussars and a Boer force to seize the position commanding the drift. The Hussars won and, as it turned out, sealed Cronje's fate. General French at once attacked with his small force ; the 12th Lancers seized the drift and crossed, but were driven back. Meantime, the guns were hurried up and drove back the Boers into the banks of the river at Paardeberg. Later in the day, a force of the enemy under De Wet, hastening from the south to the relief of Cronje, made a bold counter-attack on General French's flank, but were repulsed by the 12th Lancers.

Had Cronje only realised the smallness of General French's force holding him, he might have over-whelmed it. It was an anxious day and night, for no sign of the pursuing infantry could be seen. The brigade bivouacked on the position they were hold-ing, in grim determination to be sacrificed to a man before Cronje's army should escape them. All the forage and rations possible were obtained from the surrounding farms.

Rescue forces were already attacking from the south, and others were racing from Bloemfontein and the north. It was a question whether General French would first be overwhelmed by the Boers, or Cronje by our forces.

At length, next morning, heliographic communication was established with Lord Kitchener,

Feb. 19. and the welcome sight of our army approaching was seen. Certainly, but for General French and the 2nd Cavalry Brigade, Cronje and his army would, long ere this, have been in safety. As it was, they had spent the night entrenching themselves in the honeycombed banks of the river. Lord Kitchener at once directed an infantry attack, which was repulsed with a loss of over 1,000 killed and wounded.

The 3rd (Gordon's) Brigade, which had left Kimberley the previous day, now joined General French, but not without severe fighting, in which they repulsed the enemy. Lord Roberts also arrived and directed the complete surrounding and bombarding of Paardeberg, which continued mercilessly during the next few days, until the surrender on the 27th. During this period the Cavalry Brigade, under General French, much hampered by the terrible condition of the horses, were severely engaged every day with the Boer forces attempting the relief of Cronje.

On February 21 the 1st (Porter's) Brigade, Scots

Feb. 21. Greys, Inniskillings, and Carabiniers, left Kimberley for Paardeberg, arriving next day at Koodoosrand Drift on the Modder, where it rejoined the division.   Here it met its transport, which had not been seen since leaving De Kiel's Drift on February 12 ; it was now passed up by General Kelly-Kenny and truly welcomed.   Henceforward, until Cronje's surrender, all were continuously engaged on reconnaissance and outpost duty, with little food for man or beast, and no shelter from the heavy and frequent thunderstorms.

Feb. 22.

On the evening of the 26th all were on picquet, forming a cordon to prevent the possible attempt of Cronje to break out, and the early hours of the 27th witnessed the magnificent attack of the Canadians and Cronje's unconditional surrender. Needless to say, despite all our hardships and losses, unstinted admiration was expressed for the brave and plucky stand these 4,000 Boers had made in the face of overwhelming numbers.

Feb. 27.

Owing to the disastrous capture of our supply wagons following the main army in their march up-country, the horses were daily becoming weaker from lack of food, and an immediate forward move was impossible ; but on March 3 the Cavalry Division made a reconnaissance to the north, locating the enemy in position near Poplar Grove, higher up the right bank of the Modder. Major Allenby's squadron of Inniskillings and the New South Wales Lancers stayed out to watch and keep in touch with them.

March 3.

The 1st Brigade now crossed over to the left (south) bank of the Modder, a manœuvre carried out with great difficulty, owing to the flooded state of the river.   This was in view of Lord Roberts's dispositions to attack the Poplar

March 6.

Grove position on the morrow, and his despatch of the cavalry earlier round the left flank to cut off any Boer retreat. The division accordingly started at 3 A.M., having over thirty miles to go. As soon as it was light the enemy, having perceived our intention, at once commenced to evacuate their position, opened on the cavalry with their guns, and laid themselves out to obstruct our plans. Small parties of the Boers courageously placed themselves in the cavalry's line of advance, fighting magnificently; thus they delayed it until their force and guns had made good their retreat. Again the cavalry were hampered by the condition of their horses; the day had been intensely hot, there was little water, and the march was long, so that pursuit, when the Boer guns and transport should have been at our mercy, was impossible. The fighting had fallen entirely upon the cavalry, who lost about fifty killed and wounded. The Inniskillings were on the left advance of the 1st Brigade, which was the left brigade of the division, and only lost a few horses, most of the fighting being opposite the 2nd and 3rd Brigades.

The infantry, especially General Kelly-Kenny's 6th Division, had done some magnificent marching, and the strong Boer position was occupied, one gun only being captured.

Presidents Kruger and Steyn were spectators of this fight, and escaped capture by our cavalry by only a few minutes.

Next day General French, with the 1st Cavalry Brigade, Alderson's Mounted Infantry, and the 6th (General Kelly-Kenny's) Division, moved some eight miles up the river towards Abram's Kraal, where they revelled in a welcome day's halt.

March 7.

March 8.

E

In the morning Lord Roberts continued the march on Bloemfontein in three columns, the three Cavalry Brigades advancing in three lines: on the left the 1st (Porter's) Cavalry Brigade, with Alderson's Mounted Infantry and 6th (General Kelly-Kenny's) Division on its left rear; in the centre the 2nd (Broadwood's) Cavalry Brigade, with Le Gallais's and Martyr's Mounted Infantry and General Tucker's Division; on the right the 3rd (Gordon's) Cavalry Brigade, with Ridley's Mounted Infantry. Lord Roberts was in the centre with the Guards' Brigade and 9th Division.

March 10.

The 1st Cavalry Brigade, on the left, was the first to locate and engage the enemy in position at Driefontein; the 2nd Brigade, which came up on their right in conjunction with them, worked round the Boer left. The 6th (General Kelly-Kenny's) Division now attacked the main position, and took it with great gallantry, but not until after desperate fighting, which ended with a splendid charge of the Essex with fixed bayonets. Our losses were heavy—fifty killed and 300 wounded; but the Boer losses were much heavier, 200 dead being picked up on the battlefield. The 1st Cavalry Brigade lost ten men and eleven horses killed. U Battery R.H.A., which did splendid work under a hail of shell and rifle fire, escaped with seven casualties. The Inniskillings early in the day were detached on the Boer left flank, and later worked with the Scots Greys to their left rear; but the horses again were too exhausted to pursue. The Boer leaders in this desperate battle were De la Rey, Celliers, and De Wet. The Johannesburg Police made the most fierce stand, and suffered terrific loss.

Our troops bivouacked on the battlefield, moving

on next day without opposition to Venter's Vlei.
Early the following morning the cavalry pushed on.
March 11.   Major Allenby, with his squadron of Inniskilling Dragoons and New South Wales
Lancers, led the advanced guard of the 1st Brigade,
and, after a long day's march, at 4.30 P.M. seized some
March 12.   detached kopjes five miles south of Bloemfontein, and immediately opened a heavy fire
upon the enemy on the plateau (Brandkop) which
commanded the town. Although late in the day,
General French, working the division round to the
right, directed the 1st Brigade to seize the plateau.
Major Scobell's squadron of Scots Greys, supported
by U Battery R.H.A., at once dashed for it. Several
wire fences were encountered, and while cutting
through them many horses were shot, but, strange
to say, not a man wounded. Arrived at the foot of
the kopje, Major Scobell dismounted and led the
men up ; reaching the plateau, they beheld, about
100 yards off, many hundred Boers mounting and
galloping away. Volleys poured into the Boers in
the gathering darkness rendered their flight and
confusion complete.

This squadron, reinforced by Major Rimington
and his Guides, held the position all night. Meantime Alderson's Mounted Infantry had occupied
another kopje, from which the Boers also fled, but
they kept shelling the division long after darkness.
At midnight Major Hunter Weston, R.E., on General
French's Staff, set off with a daring little band of
Engineers—Lieut. Charles, R.E., and seven men, with
two guides, Mr. Hogg and Private Penny, French's
Scouts—and an escort of eight Mounted Infantry,
to pierce the enemy's lines and destroy the railway

E 2

north of Bloemfontein. The first Boer scout met was
soundly rated in Dutch for being out of his district
and sent frightened away.   Cleverly avoiding the
Boer picquets, they successfully reached the line near
Karee Siding, cut the telegraph wires, and blew up a
culvert by placing 10 lb. of gun-cotton on booms
and web.   Then, after various adventures and charging
a Boer outpost, they cut their way back in the early
dawn, with the loss of only two horses.   They came
suddenly on this outpost, which blocked their way
at a donga, but boldly rushed in and cut their way
through.   Lieut. Charles's horse fell back on him
in the donga, but, although much bruised, his men
got him away.   It was a magnificent night's work,
and of the utmost value, for it prevented twenty-eight
locomotives that already had steam up, and a huge
quantity of rolling stock from leaving Bloemfontein.
Further, it stopped communication with Pretoria and
prevented the arrival of reinforcements.   A special
train, with General Joubert, had been timed to arrive
at Bloemfontein at 8.20 A.M.

At dawn General French bombarded all the
positions round the town, drove off the Boers, and
March 13. occupied the positions with the division, com-
Capture of
Bloem- pletely surrounding the place.   At 10 A.M. a
fontein. deputation came out from the city and surrendered it.   At midday Lord Roberts entered at the
head of Gordon's 3rd Cavalry Brigade, the remainder
of the cavalry and Mounted Infantry throwing a line
of outposts round the town four miles out.

The Cavalry Division was now very weak, owing
to the terrible loss in horseflesh caused by casualties
in action and the late fearful work, in trying weather,
with scanty water and food.   But for the cavalry

there could be no rest.   The Waterworks, twenty
miles east of the city, had to be occupied, and General
French himself conducted a column, consisting of the
Household Cavalry, 10th Hussars, Q and U Batteries
R.H.A., Mounted Infantry, and Rimington's Guides,
further afield to Thaba 'Nchu, in order to pacify the
neighbourhood.   General French, being required at
headquarters, left the column there under the command of Brigadier-General Broadwood.

There was a false, optimistic feeling about, that all
opposition was over—a feeling that was soon to be
rudely dispelled.   At Thaba 'Nchu the submissive
Boers (?) were holding a race meeting with the
troops ; a few days later they were shooting them
down.

About March 15, Major Allenby, with an escort
of 100 Inniskillings, New South Wales Lancers, and
Carabiniers, safely escorted a convoy to
March 15. Thaba 'Nchu, *viâ* Sanna's Post, and back.

On the 29th the 1st (Porter's) and 3rd
(Gordon's) Cavalry Brigades and 12th Lancers, under
General French, took part in the action of
March 29. Karee Siding.   Before they had completed
their turning movement the general attack was
delivered.   The object of clearing away the enemy
in that neighbourhood was accomplished, but with
severe loss to the infantry—100 being killed and
wounded ; the cavalry lost only five.   The infantry
occupied the positions, and the cavalry returned, late
at night, to their camps near Bloemfontein.

March 31. Next morning, at 10.30, a messenger
arrived from General Broadwood at Sanna's
Post, asking for reinforcements.   Immediately the
1st and 3rd Brigades saddled up and started for

Bosmanskop, *en route* to Sanna's Post, some twenty
miles distant.   On the way came the sad news of
General Broadwood's disaster and the capture of the
guns.

The following day the 1st Brigade reconnoitred
Sanna's Post and brought away General Broadwood's

April 1.   wounded, although hotly engaged by the
Boers.   But for the kindly support by a regiment of General Smith-Dorrien's Brigade of General
Colvile's Division, which was retiring on Bosmanskop, this could hardly have been effected.

The 1st Brigade returned to Springfield Camp,
six miles east of Bloemfontein, but was out again

April 3.   next day, engaged in a slight skirmish to the
south-east.   In order to show the attenuated
condition to which the severe work had reduced it, I
may mention that the whole brigade this day mustered
only 120 horses, the Inniskilling Squadron (A) being
reduced to about twelve men and five officers.

A few days later (April 7) the remainder of the
regiment, B and C Squadrons, under Major Dauncey,
arrived at Springfield Camp from their march with
General Clements, and the regiment was once more
united.

BRIGADIER-GENERAL T. C. PORTER, C.B.
1st Cavalry Brigade.

BRIGADIER-GENERAL J. R. P. GORDON, C.B.
1st Cavalry Brigade.

COLONEL E. H. H. ALLENBY, C.B.

THE REV. FATHER F. KNAPP.
Acting Chaplain, 1st Cavalry Brigade.

GENERAL M. F. RIMINGTON, C.B.

LIEUT.-COL. H. C. PAGE-HENDERSON.

COLONEL H. E. THURSBY DAUNCEY.

CHAPTER V

BACK TO MY REGIMENT—THE ADVANCE FROM
BLOEMFONTEIN

Early in April, after wanderings in other theatres
of the war and previous futile attempts to get
back to my old regiment, I received the Commander-
in-Chief's order to join it. Thus, on April 12,
I found myself riding into its lines at Springfield
Camp near Bloemfontein, where I received a right
hearty welcome, with cheers from the men. I was
at once appointed to take over the command of
A Squadron, and it was sad to see the state and
reduction of the horses, the result of the terrible
work, hardships, and sufferings already narrated.

Many of the men also were suffering from enteric
fever and dysentery, caused by lying in their wet
bivouac, for many were now sleeping in the open, in
mud, with their saddles only for pillows.

Owing to the great losses in horses and transport
animals, and the need of large supplies for the army,
Lord Roberts found it imperative to wait at Bloemfontein the remainder of the month in order to
establish a new base, and make good the ground
won, before attempting his great move forward.

Long reconnaissance and outpost work, however,
allowed little rest for the cavalry. On the 22nd the

regiment, Inniskillings, marched by night on sudden orders to Fischer's Farm (fourteen miles), in order to take up a long outpost line there. Fischer's Farm itself, a pretty spot, was being used as a depôt for sick horses under charge of Captains Tomblings (8th Hussars) and Cooper Smith (I.Y.). Mr. Fischer himself had retired to Europe as one of the Boer delegates. The dead and dying horses scattered about were a painful sight ; many were too weak even to graze, and some ten were shot daily. It was impossible to bury more than the entrails, so that hundreds of carcases were lying about putrefying, the atmosphere for miles round being redolent and most nauseating. After holding an extensive outpost line for three days the regiment was relieved by General Hutton's Mounted Infantry. The General informed us that he had 6,000 mounted infantry, but only 3,000 horses.

April 22.
Fischer's Farm.

Returning to Springfield Camp, C Squadron, under Lieut. Haig, left to escort a convoy to Thaba 'Nchu. An epidemic of enteric fever was at this time rife. Three thousand were lying stricken with it in the hospitals at Bloemfontein, in addition to numbers in the camp hospitals. The daily funeral processions were pitiful. Poor Major Horley, of the Scots Greys, after only a week's illness, was amongst the number borne this day to their graves.

April 28.
Epidemic of enteric fever.

Death of Major Horley.

Two more squadrons, A and B, proceeded to Bushman's Kop, to hold the position there, and next day the remainder of the Inniskillings, one squadron Scots Greys, one squadron Carabiniers, all under Major Allenby, went to Waterfall Drift to hold it until General Colvile's Highland

April 29 and 30.

Brigade had safely crossed. It was a long day, with thirty miles marching, but we only heard the sounds of fighting.

May 1.   Preparations were being urgently hurried on for Lord Roberts's general advance.

The New South Wales Lancers, under Major Lee, who had hitherto been attached to A Squadron, N.S.W. Lancers. were formed into a distinct squadron of the 6th Inniskilling Dragoons. They were proud to be considered a part of the regiment ; all officers will testify to their usefulness, the fine scouting, and efficient work they rendered. Under splendid officers, their coolness, self-reliance, and dash brought them out of difficulties where other troops might have suffered severely. Some of this corps came out direct from England, where they had been to attend the Queen's Jubilee, after which they had been going Australian Horse. through a regular course with our cavalry at Aldershot. The Australian Horse was similarly attached to the Scots Greys.

The 1st Cavalry Brigade (Greys, Carabiniers, Inniskillings, and T Battery R.H.A., under Colonel Porter) were remounted May 3, 4, and 5, at Springfield, near Bloemfontein. The remounts were soft and unfit for hard marching ; many were received only the afternoon before starting, so there was no time to re-shoe or properly fit saddles.

This fault of starting off horses absolutely unfit for hard work was continued throughout the war. It Saddles. was one of the chief factors in our lack of mobility. When the weight carried on the horses was reduced, and when the horses were started fit for hard work, then, and not till then, were our columns as mobile as those of the Boers. During the later stages of the war weight on the saddles was reduced to a minimum. But the demand for remounts always exceeded the supply. We were always working the horses at too high a pressure ; it was not until the general halt of all columns during the final peace negotiations that the supply was equal to, and exceeded, the demand. From then on, till the supply was stopped, there were too many horses. But during the war we were never able to halt all round for ten days, to let the supply catch up with the requirements.

The Brigade marched to Rondeheuvel ; on the 7th, through Brandfort, beyond Constantia ; on the 8th across the Vet River, where the bridge had been destroyed by the enemy, to Smaldeel. Five remounts in my squadron were unfit to go on, and three died on the march.

May 6-8.

On May 9 we crossed the Zand River at Du Preez Drift, and bivouacked on the north bank. Lord Kitchener visited General French. Colonel Alderson, with his Mounted Infantry, joined the Cavalry Division, reporting the railway bridge over the Zand River destroyed, and the Boers in force with guns on the north bank.

We advanced at 5.30 A.M. to Diamond Mine, finding all clear. About four miles north of this we encountered our first opposition, the enemy, from Vredes Verdrag, a kopje a few miles to the east of Kopje Aileen, shelling the brigade in mass. The New South Wales Lancer squadron was ordered to keep touch with the Mounted Infantry to our right rear, and a troop of A Squadron Inniskillings to occupy a farm to our left front. Open order was at once taken by the regimental commanders, shells

May 9.

SMALDEEL RAILWAY BRIDGE, DESTROYED BY THE BOERS.

AN OLD TRANSVAAL BOER.

being beautifully placed in our midst ; but again the harmlessness of the Boer shell-fire was evident, as little damage was done, although it looked most effective : shells crashed into the ground within a few feet of us, horses and riders being hidden in the cloud of dirt and dust thrown up, but it was a matter of surprise nearly always to see both advancing unscathed. Our Brigadier directed that open order was not to be taken, and we rapidly closed again into mass, forming a splendid target for the Boer marksmen.   They were, however, getting alarmed for their guns, and rapidly limbered them up to retire to a safer spot ; so we luckily escaped any disaster from shells falling into our closed mass. Colonel Porter, in command, continued the advance in mass to the foot of the kopje, ordering one squadron of the Inniskillings to occupy it.

Fighting, Zand River.

The brigade being at close range, Captain Elworthy's squadron of Carabiniers and C Squadron Inniskillings, under Lieut. Haig, rushed the kopje and occupied the ridge.   There was no time to reconnoitre it in any way, and it seemed quite possible that the squadron would be into the enemy's guns before they could cross the ridge.   The guns were, however, rapidly galloped away.   The squadrons gained the top, dismounted, threw themselves down, and returned the severe fire to which they were subjected. A squadron of Greys was sent to support, but all came under the terrible fusillade.   The ridge was dominated by the enemy's fire ; the horses were shot from the flank ; no officer was specially in command, and severe losses were sustained. Lieut. Haig was taken prisoner, his horse being shot, and the Inniskilling squadron, while endeavouring to hold the ridge, was practically annihilated—many men being killed and several taken prisoners through their horses having been shot. Lieut. Harris had his horse shot in two places while carrying a man away, but bore his man to safety just as the horse fell dead. Amongst the casualties,the gallant Captain Elworthy, of the Carabiniers, was killed, Lieut. Collis and Lieut. Moncreiff, of the same regiment, being severely wounded.

The brigade, in mass, were moved under a heavy fire to the left flank, and repelled an attack from that quarter by dismounted fire. Lieut. Lawlor, Adjutant Inniskilling Dragoons, had his horse shot in two places ; several men (Inniskillings) were wounded, and many horses killed and wounded. Some of the enemy, who had hoisted a white flag, did good execution out of a pit in a mealie field. Lieut. Walton, R.A.M.C., showed conspicuous bravery, attending to the wounded under heavy fire. Our battery of Artillery were of little use, as at first they were not employed, while later they were short of ammunition and, still later in the day, were outranged.

We joined the 4th Cavalry Brigade, which was moving to the left flank and threatening the enemy's rear, under direction of General French. General French had himself led the 4th Brigade round and ordered a charge on the Boers in the open country. The tired and heavily-weighted horses, however, were unable to catch the Boers, so the enemy got away, leaving seven dead and three prisoners behind. This caused the enemy, who consisted chiefly of the Johannesburg Police and were fighting a rear-guard action, to retire, and the

Charge of 4th Brigade.

GUNS CROSSING THE VAALSCH RIVER.

Mounted Infantry took the ridge with little opposition.

As regards the 1st Cavalry Brigade, it was an unfortunate day; there were fifty casualties, but otherwise it was a long successful advance. General French pushed on about another ten miles till after dark, and the division bivouacked at Graspan.

We advanced again as day was dawning, General French's orders being that the enemy were in full retreat and the cavalry must pursue. A

May 11.

genial smile spread over everyone's countenance at the word ' pursue,' for, alas ! who had a horse that could raise more than a trot ? No wonder that we were losing our horses wholesale, from want of food and water, with 18 to 20 stone on their backs, saddled from morning to night and perhaps all night, and then on again next day ! Nevertheless we pushed on as rapidly as possible, leading our horses a great part of the march and with difficulty dragging them along, and, without opposition, we reached the Valsch River Drift early in the afternoon, arriving just in time to seize it as a large force (about 3,000) of the enemy was approaching to oppose. Our guns commanding the drift were brought into action, and troops which were rapidly passed over drove the enemy back. It was indeed a fine piece of smart work to gain this important drift without a casualty. We then bivouacked, on a lovely evening, on both sides of the drift by the farm of Boshof, a truly beautiful spot—the 4th Brigade on the north side, the 1st Brigade on the south.

I was selected to escort Major Hunter Weston, under cover of darkness, to destroy the railway to the north, and, if possible, to prevent the enemy from getting their big guns away from Kroonstad. The following account, which I saw later in the *Times*, is, as far as I was concerned, and as Major Hunter Weston after described to me, a truthful account of this enterprise :

When the Cavalry Division under General French arrived at the farm of Boshof, on the night of May 11, Major Hunter Weston, commanding the Royal Engineers with the division, volunteered to attempt a raid on the railway communication north of Kroonstad, similar to the excursion which he carried out so successfully on the night previous to the occupation of Bloemfontein. General French gave his sanction. Volunteers were called for, and again it had to be a matter of selection. Taking Mr. Burnham, the American scout, and Lieut. Charles, R.E., Major Weston chose the following eight sappers :—Corporals C. Hyde and F. Kirby ; Sappers J. Austin, C. Collins, T. Costin, J. Crisp, B. Fearnley, and T. Pearce. As it was anticipated that it might be necessary to employ force to pass the demolition party through the outer picquet line, Captain Yardley, Inniskilling Dragoons, and Lieut. Harrison, Scots Greys, accompanied the expedition with a squadron of 50 men and 60 horses picked from the 1st Cavalry Brigade.

[margin note: Major Hunter Weston's Expedition.]

Crossing the Bospoortspruit, the little column of desperate men moved north, parallel with the Valsch River. Major Weston led the column, steering by the stars, and Burnham brought his extraordinary faculties of sight and ear into use to prevent the party from running into any outlying patrol or picquet. About a mile north of the Modderspruit Burnham discovered a patrol of three men moving across the front. As it was impossible for the column to avoid detection, Major Weston determined to capture the group. The cavalry divided and charged in upon both flanks. It was a wonderful scene : the thud of the galloping horses in the deep silence of night, the sabres flashing bare in the strong moonlight, the intense excitement of the moment. The mounted men proved to be Kaffirs, and formed a patrol which had been sent out by a Boer picquet lying about a mile to the east. At this point Major Weston considered that the outlying cordon was pierced. So he left Captain Yardley with the cavalry, in observation of a strong Boer picquet on the right, with orders to return to camp as soon as the raiding party was clear. Then the little group, now eleven strong, with two led horses, moved north-east to a point in the Fairfield property. Here, at the juncture of a wire fence, a mounted picquet of the enemy was descried. Burnham made out others all along the fence. This is the custom of the Boers when throwing out night out-posts. Vedettes are stationed all along wire fences, with their heads against the posts. As soon as a wire is touched or cut, some one of the vedettes is im-mediately aware of the fact. Major Weston tried to avoid the patrol, but when the party returned to the fence they found that it had moved parallel with them and had collected the vedettes along the line. Burnham dismounted and reconnoitred the group. He found that it was, as had been thought, in obser-vation of the party, and that four dismounted men had been detached to lie in ambush under a small nek which lay in the line of advance. To shake off this following the party dived into the deep and wooded Dornspruit, and when they reached the dam found that they were clear. They then crossed the Dam-fontein Hills, from which position they could see the Boer camp-fires, extending in an almost unbroken line from Kroonstad to Honing Spruit. The retreating force seemed to be encamped all along the railway line. So, slipping past two mounted patrols, the party turned in to hit it off. Burnham again went forward and found a spruit in which it would have been possible to have hidden the horses. But, just as the party arrived at the edge of the depression, a Boer camp-fire flared up in their faces from within the cutting.

Time was now getting short. There was only half an hour of moonlight and an hour of darkness left before dawn. Retiring west from the spruit and passing round a farm full of Boers—even moving through their hobbled horses—the gallant little band made another attempt to reach the railway. As had been hoped, the railway fence was here. But just as the party struck it the head of a large commando of mounted Boers turned up over a fold in the veldt. Thanks to Burnham, the Boers were seen before they made the English out. Major Weston at once moved his party twenty paces into the veldt, and in a whisper ordered the men to lie flat upon their horses' necks. As the commando passed the leading file challenged. For a moment it seemed that it would be necessary to give the preconcerted signal that the little party might break up and as individuals make a bid for safety. But as no response was given the Boers apparently mistook the group for a bunch of loose horses and passed on. It was a moment of extreme suspense, a moment when you hear each beat of your heart. But the crowd of burghers pressed on and, laughing and joking, passed into the shadow. The horses were then led further away from the line. Again the party stumbled upon another wire fence running parallel to the line. As Lieut. Charles was cutting this, three Boers suddenly sprang up out of the grass. Hunter Weston and Burnham each immediately 'covered' a man, and Lieut. Charles with great promptitude seized the carbine of the third. They proved to be three scouts of the Afrikander Horse. They were left with Lieut. Charles and the sappers beyond the wire fence. Major Weston and Burnham then went forward alone and on foot to attempt the demolition. Almost at once they met a picquet in search of the prisoners. Avoiding these by lying flat on the ground, they waited until they heard the men move on before again going forward. The Boers disappeared, accusing the patrol of deserting its post.   Boers were all round, but the two desperate men crawled on to the road.   Here they lay in the grass and waited while another long commando passed.   Then came some wagons, and under the dust and noise both crossed the road in safety. Moving thus in the intervals between wagons and troops, they were able to crawl to the top of the embankment and worm themselves flat against the ballast of the permanent way.   The charges were fixed and the fuses lighted under Burnham's broad-brimmed hat while the enemy were passing within ten yards of the spot.   They waited until Burnham's practised ear told him that there was an interval in the wagon-train, and then they hazarded the journey back towards the horses.

Then came the explosion.   It was followed by a babel of noise from waking men, scared cattle, and a rush ' to horse.'   Under cover of this tumult Major Weston and Burnham reached the horses, and, mounting the prisoners on the led horses, the whole party moved off north-west.

They were soon clear of the surrounding Boers, and they trotted steadily on for three miles till they were out of all possible contact with the disturbed convoy round the railway.   At sunrise they were clear.   But the increasing light suddenly disclosed a picquet of twenty Boers directly across their path. Fortunately they were dismounted and engaged in catching their horses.   One man only remained by the fire.   The party galloped down upon this man. He surrendered at once ; the stock of his rifle was immediately broken, also those of six others lying by him.   There was no time to wait, and the party pressed on to get clear of the rest of the Boers before they could collect their scattered horses and rifles. At first the burghers seemed dumfounded.   But they then collected and opened fire, slightly wounding Sapper Collins in the hand.

Seeing that it would be necessary to check this Boer picquet now left with twelve rifles, Major Weston ordered everyone to gallop on, and himself remained behind to cover the retreat with rifle fire. Providence aided him, for his first shot emptied a saddle. The whole pursuit was checked, and the Major was able to rejoin his party unmolested. An hour later the gallant little *cortège* with its three prisoners was clear of danger. They returned quietly to camp, having accomplished an expedition which, in its sequence of miraculous escapes, reads more like a fairy tale than a stern episode in war, and which presents one of the most stirring, gallant, and self-sacrificing side-histories of this war.

It was a successful enterprise, but a full moon, which did not set till the early hours, delayed the explosion and caused the loss of great results. My plan with Major Hunter Weston was, if engaged, to occupy the enemy with fighting whilst he slipped through with his small party. When I had taken him safely through the main outposts, Major Hunter Weston rightly considered our numbers too great, so we parted with mutual regret. It was a difficult task to get the escort safely back, and the temptation to surround picquets and Boer farms *en route* was great ; but to avoid giving alarm was our task. Two things helped me : one was the fact that, when near any life, I advanced reconnoitring by myself, and, by crawling and placing the ear to the ground, strove to discover the cause. The other was that I made use of one of the Kaffir prisoners, who, under the muzzle of my revolver, proved an efficient guide.

Finally, we safely reached our bivouac in the early

hours of the morning, eluding even our own sentries. Our rest was a short one, for we marched again at dawn. One of our squadrons was detailed to reconnoitre at daylight for the enemy in the direction of our previous night's expedition. They espied Major Hunter Weston's small party attempting to return and pursued them, thinking that they were Boers. Major Hunter Weston similarly mistook them for Boers and tried to avoid them, so much delay arose before each discovered the error. My squadron was first detailed for this duty, and it would have been strange if, after escorting them out, I had been hunting them when returning. But in this vast country, where the air is so clear, figures can be seen at great distances, and you are within range of rifle fire ere it can be decided whether it is that of friend or foe.

We marched at daylight, with all precautions, and without opposition. Our guns took up a position on

May 12. the hill commanding Kroonstad, advanced
Capture troops occupying the town. About 11 A.M.
of Kroon-
stad. the Landdrost, with a white flag, rode out on
a fine chestnut horse and surrendered the town to General French. Later, on the arrival of the main army, the formality of handing over the keys to Lord Roberts was gone through. The previous capture and occupation of the town by General French was ignored by the Press, and when the Guards triumphantly marched through the town the cavalry were ten miles ahead, clearing the surrounding country. The boasted Kroonstad position had been turned by our cavalry and evacuated without defence. Our army could be seen advancing from the south, and the Cavalry Division at once pushed

F 2

on to Jordan Siding and drew on the farms for forage and rations. Of these we were very short, and our orders were that we must live on the country, so officers' patrols were quickly out making good hauls.

During the week the division had marched about 170 miles on direct route, and men were seldom out of the saddle. The loss of horses was great—*e.g.* in the regiment (Inniskillings) alone, 200. The direct route being 170 miles, the enormous distance our cavalry horse must have done reconnoitring can be imagined, and this, carrying about 20 stone, as each man had to carry three days' supply of forage and rations. I have previously mentioned the condition of horses at the start. From May 13 to 19 we remained halted, our scouts each day locating a few of the enemy some miles off.

I took A Squadron (Inniskilling Dragoons), forty-eight strong, with orders to reconnoitre the railway to

May 19.
Recon-
naissance
by squad-
ron 6th
Dragoons.
Honing Spruit, and report on its condition. Opposition I expected, as our patrols had daily been a short distance in this direction at the same hour, and always returned reporting that they had seen the enemy. As we started Major Hunter Weston joined me, being anxious to inspect the line where he had previously destroyed it on our night raid. Whilst doing this, my patrols reported the enemy in considerable force on the right flank, so I doubled the flankers, placed a rear party to prevent the possibility of being cut off, and changed my direction to the more open country on the left of the railway. Meantime, my advanced patrols had pushed on nearly to Honing Spruit. The fact that there was no sniping made me suspicious,

so I halted in the centre of the open plain and sent forward to reconnoitre. Then the enemy suddenly showed their hand : they had crawled into mealie fields and culverts by the railway between my main body and advanced patrols, and were only waiting in expectation to bag the lot of us.

Seeing that they were frustrated, they attempted to get the patrols, and opened a heavy fire behind them. I took up a strong rallying position. Lieut. Harris gallantly galloped into the thick, and, the patrols scattering, galloped back through the enemy under our cover. Sergeant Kirby was captured through his horse falling over wire and stunning him, but the horse galloped back. Private Watson was also captured, being dangerously wounded when he halted, thinking himself clear. On the right, Sergeant Bland and Private Dunn were captured ; the former was in command of a strong patrol which I had sent to guard our right flank. The sergeant walked into the middle of the enemy, and only perceived them on the cries of ' Hands up ! ' This gave the opening on the right, of which the enemy quickly availed themselves, and they got in behind the advanced patrols. Sad scouting ! Collecting my small force, and the enemy declining to advance, we returned to bivouac with one prisoner, and sent ambulances out which met Private Watson, seriously wounded, who was being sent back by Captain Theron on a trolly down the line.

The enemy, under Captain Theron, who had been reinforced the previous day by a commando under Colonel Blake, were in strength near Honing Spruit, and laid ambush with a view to cutting us off. Released prisoners informed me later that they were expecting us, as our patrols had come daily at the same hour in the same direction. This is the very worst system in any sort of fighting ; patrols should never be sent in a similar manner two days running, or picquets posted in the same place two nights running. Something different and unexpected should always be done. Our reconnaissance was accomplished with a good deal of fighting, and the railway found intact. Three dragoons were cut off and taken prisoners, and one wounded. We killed one Boer and brought back one prisoner. One scout was invited by women at a Boer farm to have a cup of coffee. Whilst drinking, a bullet just missed the cup ; dropping it, he galloped off, successfully running the gauntlet of fire from some Boers lying in a field by the house.

Remounts not fit for hard work arrived with Second-Lieut. Swanston and Second-Lieut. Gibbs, who had just come to join the regiment ; and the division, under General French, marched to Kroonbloom, near Rhenoster Kop. On the 21st they marched to Welgelegen, the Carabiniers seizing the drift at the junction of Rhenoster River and Honing Spruit ; on the 22nd all crossed the ridge beyond, which was not held.

May 20.

This evening, with fifty Inniskillings and fifty Scots Greys, under Major Scobell, I formed an escort to Major Hunter Weston to destroy the railway in the neighbourhood of Grootvlei or Wolverhoek Station, so as to prevent the enemy, if possible, from getting two 6-inch guns away. We took forty led horses, and rode twenty-five miles in three hours without drawing rein or meeting opposition ; our plan being, had we done so, to charge through it. We saw a Cape cart

May 22.

Major H. Weston's expedition.

in the distance, galloping away from a large farm-house, but too far to pursue. We found the line already destroyed by the enemy, several commandos being bivouacked near it. Avoiding them, we rode all night, raiding Olivier's farm for some bread. It was about midnight and very dark when we silently surrounded the house. There was a difficulty in find-ing any entrance, and our feeelings must have been akin to those of burglars. The barking of dogs was the only sign of life. Our time was precious, and Major Scobell tried with me to effect an entrance at doors and windows, expecting at any moment we might be fighting hand to hand. At last, after nearly breaking down a door, a Kaffir boy appeared, and, rushing in, we demanded the inhabitants. A female voice only was heard from an inner room, and pre-sently, half-dressed, Madam Olivier appeared. She seemed more alarmed for our own safety than any-thing ; assured us that she had not seen her husband for over a year ; that the Boers had been there in force in the afternoon, eaten everything, were close by, and would assuredly kill us ; and, oh ! we must be careful. On our demand she produced a few loaves of bread and some eggs—luxuries we did not often see, and for which we duly paid. Then we made a rapid search. The good lady denied the existence of any arms, and, in deference to her feel-ings and the probability of our troops being there next day, we did not burst open some cupboards of which, she said, her husband had taken away the keys.

According to later lessons, perhaps we were wrong ; but our object was only to get food for the men and accomplish our special mission, so we

hurriedly left and went on through the night. It was
very dark, and, beyond a general direction, we got
quite lost, a native we were trusting to as a guide
being quite out of his reckoning. Once we got into
a very bad piece of ground, with mealie fields and
wire all round us; the sound of animals moving in
the dry mealies made us suspicious that we were in
close proximity to a Boer force or picquet. Silently
we dismounted. I crawled off with Major Scobell
to reconnoitre. We first got into a small hovel,
where we dared to strike a match in order to consult
our compasses ; and, having done so, we decided our
bearing was right. Then he went off to satisfy himself about the moving horses, and returned still very
suspicious.

Meantime our native boy guide, a servant of
Lieut. Paterson, had found a kraal, and brought
another native from it, whom we impressed to our
aid. It was difficult to get our small force silently
started, as many, being dog-tired, were sound asleep,
with reins over their arms. How is it the British
soldier can sleep on such emergencies ? One man
I could not shake to life ; so, kicking him with
all my might, I placed a revolver at his head and
growled ' Hands up ! ' This successfully brought
him to life, and once more we got on our weary
march.

At 2.30 A.M. we struck Du Plessis's farm. Having
fixed outposts with Major Scobell, we repaired to the
farm, where the Du Plessis made themselves most
obliging, procuring anything we wanted. Du Plessis
was one of the good old Dutch who had fought
against us for seven months, being a field-cornet outside Ladysmith. He complained that his sons were

still away on commando, but was, I think, himself
sincere in his protestations of belief in our cause.
After our fifty-mile ride, those not on outpost were
glad to throw themselves down for one or two hours'
welcome slumber. At 6 A.M. General French

May 23.
arrived with the division, which we rejoined.
We then marched on to Essenbosch. My bay pack
pony foaled on the march to-day, but came on as if
nothing had happened. In the afternoon we halted,
and I looked in vain for something to shoot. The
night was bitterly cold, but we had a peaceful rest.
Two long reconnaissances were made to-day by
B Squadron Inniskillings, under Major Dauncey,
and the New South Wales Lancers Squadron, under
Major Lee, to the railway near Leeuwspruit and
Vredefort Stations respectively. Both returned, after
covering about forty-five miles and being in the saddle
sixteen hours, with reports that the enemy in strong
force, with guns, had all retired the previous day
north of the Vaal.

CHAPTER VI

ADVANCING ON JOHANNESBURG

THE division marched at 6 A.M. on Parys, the
Mounted Infantry leading. General French explained his plans to rush the Vaal River
drifts—a perilous enterprise. We were
astonished---in fact, amazed—to find them
unoccupied. The 4th Brigade occupied
Parys and crossed the Parys Drift unmolested.
The 1st Brigade marched along the southern bank,
through rough, hilly country, to a *bad* drift, about
six miles east, near Lindequee, and crossed into
the Transvaal. A few of the enemy were seen
retiring, and could have made our march and crossing
a hard task. The country was a regular 'Chitral' of
hills. We bivouacked on the north bank, drinking
her Majesty's health on our entry into the Transvaal
on her birthday, and congratulated ourselves on the
successful crossing of the drift at the end of a long
thirty-mile march. We quite expected severe fighting; in such awful country a few hundred of the
enemy could have effectually stopped us, and we
decided that the Boers must have some scheme on or
be quite demoralised. Considering yesterday and the
night, my horses stood the march well, and I only
lost two.

May 24.
*Crossing
the Vaal.*
*Entering
the Trans-
vaal.*

Next day the division marched along the north bank of the Vaal, through intricate country, to Zeekoefontein, two miles east of Lindequee.

May 25.

Small parties of the enemy opposed and sniped us. The regiment (Inniskillings) took one terrible position, where the loss would have been great but for the excellent dispositions made by Major Allenby, who was in command. It was again my fate to select an outpost line in the dark and post picquets — a hazardous proceeding on unknown ground, and productive of many hours' tumbling about on the veldt. The strain of night outpost duty is one of the severest duties, which falls so heavily on our cavalry, especially after a day of hard work; often, after fighting all day and when still at it at nightfall, comes the order : ' Hold the hill you are on, keeping touch with So-and-so on your flank, fresh ·troops not being available.' Then comes a night of anxious watching. This nervous strain is also made much greater owing to the ridiculous red tape and chain of responsibility in our Service, so well described by the story of the inspecting general, who complains to the regimental colonel that a horse is dirty. The colonel passes the complaint on to the second in command, he to the squadron officer, he to the subaltern of the troop, and so on to the sergeant-major, N.C.O. of squadron, and finally to the trooper who owns the dirty horse. The trooper then gives his horse a violent kick in the belly, ejaculating ' What the devil do you mean by being dirty, you brute ? ' Luckily this war has done much to change all this ; but, oh ! how much it hampered us !

On the 26th we reconnoitred Riet Spruit, Viljoen's

Drift, and Vereeniging. We found our troops in occupation of the latter, and got in touch with General Broadwood's brigade. Two squadrons of Carabiniers and Captain Stevenson Hamilton's squadron of Inniskillings, all under Colonel Sprott, reconnoitred to Vereeniging, and returned next morning, reporting it just occupied by our troops. Meanwhile we encountered the enemy to the north-east, numbers unknown, and retired at dark to Vakplaats, across the Riet Spruit, having killed five and wounded nine Boers and taken three prisoners ; our loss was one man wounded.

Reconnaissances.

The following day we marched to Houtkop, where we received orders to turn west and march to Rietfontein. The enemy were visible in large force, with transport, retiring north. Distances seem so short in this clear atmosphere that they seemed quite close, and we were longing to have a gallop for them, but the orders were to move west, and later the reason became apparent. Our Commander-in-Chief, unknown to us, was making a fine cast. In the afternoon our 1st Brigade were advancing along the valley, with the 4th Brigade on the left flank, but for some reason it converged in rear of the 1st, leaving our left flank quite unprotected. The enemy were in front and on both flanks ! At the head of the valley the road crossed the range of hills, the Gatsrand, which commanded Klip Spruit and the west flank of the Klipriversberg position. The main hill at the head of the valley was essential to us.

May 27.
Advancing on Johannesburg.

B Squadron Inniskillings, under Major Dauncey, supported by A Squadron, under Captain Yardley, were sent to take it. On our approach the enemy

opened fire with two pom-poms and a gun. Arrived
at the base of the hill, we formed one line, took what
cover we could, and returned the fire. We drove a
good many Boers out of a farmhouse, Vlakfontein,
which, later, the Scots Greys occupied. Owing to
the nature of the ground the enemy were able to get
away along a sheltered nullah, so were bold in remaining till late at the house. Then, mounting, we
advanced with a rush, B Squadron on the right,
A Squadron on the left. B Squadron gained the top,
but heavy fire from the ridge beyond drove them
back. With two troops of A Squadron I held on to
the left edge, sending the other two to try to get
round the flank. At this juncture Colonel Clowes,
8th Hussars, with his Adjutant, Lieut. Jones, galloped up, followed by about twenty men only of the
8th Hussars, with urgent orders from General French
that we must take the hill.

Major Allenby, who had joined the firing line,
drew his sword, heading B Squadron; I drew my
revolver, and with a cheer we all galloped for the top
ridges, dismounted, and lined them. Two corporals
of B Squadron were at this time dangerously wounded.
To show oneself was to be shot. But the enemy also
could not advance, and darkness came on and enveloped us as we lay, grim and cold, holding on to
the ground we had gained. Owing to the fact that
good cover was taken, only a few men were hit.
Meantime the Scots Greys, with slight opposition,
occupied the farm at the foot of the hill and the hill
commanding the road on the right front, Lieut.
Connolly doing good practice with his Maxim, disabling and preventing the enemy from retiring their
transport. After dark Colonel Lowe, with the 7th

Dragoon Guards, relieved us, and arrangements were made to get guns up. During the night, however, the enemy retreated, and the Gatsrand, the key to the advance on the west of Johannesburg, was in General French's possession, opening the road for General Ian Hamilton's forces.

Our losses were remarkably slight. General French's bold attack late in the day, and the feeble resistance of the surprised enemy, gave us this important position, Elandsfontein. Our Brigadiers did not make much use of our artillery, and once Major Allenby and myself were nearly killed by one of our own shells. Every credit must be given the Inniskillings for taking this essential position, and, when matters were critical, the arrival of Colonel Clowes, cheering, with only about twenty of the 8th Hussars, put fresh life into us, as we certainly thought they were backed up by their brigade, as was probably intended.

At daylight, after a cold night, we occupied the high ridge, from which there was a fine view of the Klipriversberg position, with the mines of Johannesburg in the distance. The enemy were visible about three miles off, and trains could be seen running to Johannesburg.

May 28.

General French moved the cavalry down across the Klip River by the store at Van Wyk's Rust where the bridge was intact, as soon as they were relieved by the Mounted Infantry. The Inniskillings (again the gallant Inniskillings) were advanced to clear the situation. The New South Wales Lancers, with B (Major Dauncey's) Squadron on the left and A (Captain Yardley's) Squadron on the right, supported by Major

Recon-
naissance
in force
before
Johannes-
burg.

Allenby with the rest of the regiment, a pom-pom and, later, two guns, led the advance. Our orders were to advance to a road running across our front, about four miles ahead, and prevent small parties of the enemy from moving along it. It was really a road running just under their position, but General French wanted to make a reconnaissance in force. We soon found out what we were in for. The enemy showed in strong force on the Johannesburg position, and at once opened a heavy fire from Creusots, a 40-pounder, and several pom-poms. We were for hours under terrific shell fire and long-range rifle fire from front and both flanks, with absolutely no cover. Only seasoned troops, well led, could have stood it; but there we remained, drawing the fire and vigorously replying with long-range rifle fire and our pom-poms and, later, the two guns. Then General French pushed forward both his brigades.

Our artillery fire was good, and helped considerably to keep down the Boer fire, disabling at least one of their guns, all of which were at this time occupied with the regiment as a target. Two of the enemy's guns were 40-pounders, and they had pom-poms firing from the flank of their Klipriversberg position, from the high ground at Klipspruit, and from Klipriversoog. Meantime our guns cleared the Boers from Klipriversoog. The New South Wales Lancers' Squadron, which had gained the Klipspruit Farm, supported by A Squadron fire, cleared them from a farm on the west side of Oliphant's Vlei. Then the 4th Cavalry Brigade, coming round by Klipriversoog on our left, unfortunately masked the fire of our battery, enabling the enemy again to open fire with his Klipspruit guns, and so the terrific bombarding continued.

A further advance with cavalry only was impossible. Squadron Sergeant-Major Turnbull and Private Robinson of B Squadron were dangerously wounded by shell fire, both their horses being killed ; but the casualties during the day were few, and proved what little damage the Boer shell fire does. My frequent escape and that of most of the men seemed miraculous ; luckily the shells seldom burst, or I should many times have been killed. They seemed to pursue me this day especially, and often entered the ground a few inches from me, throwing up a cloud of mud ; once a 40-pound shell must have almost grazed my coat.

On three occasions I was ordered to send to neighbouring hills, which we had been vigorously shelling, to see whether they were still occupied. Each time I felt almost convinced that they were ; but it had to be done, and, reluctantly, I would select a young officer or N.C.O. with two men only, define the hill, and give the orders. Imagine yourself one of those men. How would you like it ? There is not a moment's hesitation. Away they cheerily go at a smart trot, in all probability, to death. Watch them through your glasses ; they reach the foot of the hill, commence the ascent—surely the hill is not now occupied—when, all at once, ping, ping, ping—such a fusillade ! The enemy are there still in great force. They have only been lying low and waiting till the small patrol is almost on them ; then they open fire. These men are, however, riding wide apart, so as to offer a smaller target ; they immediately turn and gallop back for dear life, zigzagging their horses to make themselves a more difficult mark. It is not easy, even for a Boer marksman, to hit a galloping

TWO POM-POMS FIRING AT BATTERY OF R.H.A. LIMBERING UP.
The flight of shells and escort of Inniskillings are shown in the foreground.

6TH INNISKILLING DRAGOONS ON TREK.

horse, and, thank God, on each of these occasions my gallant little patrols got safely back ; but each man had passed, for many minutes, through a perfect hail of bullets. Is not this facing death ? And how often our cavalry do it !

To the novice, artillery fire is always more alarming than rifle fire, but you soon discover that it is not nearly so dangerous.   One young subaltern, who had recently joined, went on one of these patrols, and returned with his mind quite made up on the subject. Often you *see* a little puff of dust at your feet, and only hear a distant *ping* : it is a bullet, aimed at you, which was within a fraction of taking your life, but you scarcely heard it. The shell that enters the ground close by is very alarming, but it was not aimed specially at you, and it would have been a great fluke if it had hit you ; in other words, the odds were big against the bullet, but immense against the shell hitting.

But to return. Our casualties for the day were not great ; amongst them was Major Mackeson, A.D.C. to General Dickson, who was wounded in the jaw by a piece of shell.

At evening, General French withdrew the cavalry behind the Klip River, the Mounted Infantry occupying the positions seized and commanded by the enemy's guns—positions that were anything but enviable next morning. However, they had been ours all day, and were bravely held. It had been an able reconnaissance in force by General French, and had thoroughly exposed the extent, disposition, and guns of the enemy on their strong positions in front of Johannesburg.

Next day we captured a postman with the last

G

copies published of the ' Standard and Diggers' News,' which reported the repulse of the British, that General French was wounded, that the British dead and the wounded were covering the veldt, that Boer ambulances were assisting the British ambulances in the humane work of collecting the dead and tending the wounded, &c.

At daylight the cavalry again advanced, but meantime General Ian Hamilton, with his column, arrived, and, after consultation with General French, it was decided that he should make the direct attack with his infantry, whilst General French turned the flank with the cavalry.   We now saw the, to us, novel sight of infantry—the gallant Gordon Highlanders—advancing with two big guns.   What a feeling of solid strength the infantry does give one !

May 29.
Capture of
Johannes-
burg
position.

As they relieved us, we proceeded rapidly to the flank, our 1st Brigade, as usual, leading, and on General Ian Hamilton taking up the direct attack with the Gordons, &c., we continued to turn the flank, driving the enemy before us all day with shell and rifle fire, many being seen to fall.   Our casualties were slight, but we much regretted the heavy casualties, 100, of General Ian Hamilton's force in the direct attack, especially of the Gordons in their gallant and successful assault in the centre, where poor Captain St. John Meyrick and other good men fell.

To us it was an exciting day, for at last we saw our enemy in the open and being pursued ; B Squadron Inniskilling Dragoons especially, in advance, knocked over a good many Boers.   We fought past Vogelstruis till darkness stopped us, then bivouacked

at Doornkop, the old site of Jameson's surrender,
below Florida, the horses much done. My squadron,
alas! now only numbered forty-six efficient. It was
strange to see several Cape carts out from Johannesburg watching the fighting, and the courage of the
Boers, who were waiting and helping their wounded
away, excited our admiration. Certainly some Boers
were worthy of Distinguished Conduct Medals that
day. It had been a hard day of good work by all
arms; but the brunt fell on the Gordons, who so
magnificently took the main position; and greatly
did we mourn their losses.

We marched again at daylight. The Mounted
Infantry stopped a train at Krugersdorp, coming
from Potchefstroom to Johannesburg with
200 Boers, who fled; but it was reported
that some were captured, amongst them a Commandant Botha!

May 30.

We moved through Florida and Roodepoort (finding the mines intact, and not, as we feared, destroyed
by the enemy) to Driefontein, to the north of
Johannesburg. The enemy shelled us feebly, and
were everywhere in flight. We picked up a few
dead, killed by our fire yesterday, whom we buried;
we also took several prisoners and one big gun, a
Norwegian 12-lb. long-range gun, and a wagon of
ammunition. These were captured by General
French's Mounted Infantry. We had a few
horses shot, which could be ill spared, as our
horses were dropping out daily under the hard work.
No news had reached us since leaving Bloemfontein
on May 6. In the saddle all day and half the night,
with little opportunity of ever washing, there had
never been a chance of sending or receiving a letter.

Loss of
horses.

G 2

That correspondents were nearly all with the main army accounts, in a great measure, for the little that was ever publicly known of the fine work of the Regular Cavalry at this time.   The main army reached Germiston, on the east side of Johannesburg, this day, and Lieut. Raymond Johnson, Inniskilling Dragoons, with six men, cleverly found his way, during the night, with General French's despatches to Lord Roberts at Germiston.   He had to elude several parties of the enemy, but returned safely, after a night full of adventures, his mission successfully accomplished.   He was accompanied by Mr. Paterson, the Australian poet and correspondent.

The following day we halted.   B Squadron (Major Dauncey) went out reconnoitring, and found

May 31.   many Boers in small parties.   One of his patrols had one man shot in two places and his horse in six, and he feared that another of his men, who was missing, had been killed.   These roving parties bolted before an equal force, but surrounded and killed solitary men, if they could, and were very cunning.   The halt this day was a great relief, and the opportunity for a good wash was a real joy.   We were now well round to the north of Johannesburg, with an extended outpost line, in order to prevent Boers slipping out of the town, as many were reported to be trying to do.

Up at 4.30 A.M.   A glorious sunrise, followed by another lovely and peaceful day : the weather was

June 1.   truly magnificent.   We marched to Waterval, north of the Dynamite Factory, without opposition, and reached our bivouac at 11 A.M. Johannesburg had surrendered the previous day.

Our march being again delayed, I rode with Major Allenby into Johannesburg—ten miles distant. We found all banks closed and shops barricaded. Many Jews were about. The town was full of stores and luxuries of most descriptions. We met a crowd of friends and heard much news—that Pretoria was not to be defended; that General Rundle had received a check, with the loss of 150; that the gallant Dalbiac and Orr-Ewing had met brave soldiers' deaths. We repaired to Frascati's restaurant and there obtained an excellent lunch; you could have imagined yourself at the Criterion. One waiter informed us that the times had been bad, as the Boers did not patronise the restaurant, but that now it was going very strong.

What a contrast to my first visit to the Rand, not so many years ago, when, with my friend and brother officer, Captain Mike Rimington, I got a few weeks' leave from Natal, where we were then stationed. He drove me up, in his Cape cart and four ponies, to inspect what was rumoured to be a new find of gold-fields. Then we found only a few tin huts, and now the largest town in South Africa; then we pegged out claims which would have made us millionaires, but a soldier's life took us away, and we lost all. Then there were no railways in the Transvaal, and we drove on to Pretoria and called on President Kruger, whom we found, in his shirt-sleeves, seated in his verandah, with his big pipe. A relation, who then introduced us, presented each of us with a share in one of his famous concessions, worth only the paper it was printed on. Our ex-host was now reported to have left Pretoria for Lydenburg, and our mission was to pursue. Of news of the world we learnt nothing, as no post or telegraph had yet been re-established.

Major Hunter Weston, with Burnham (the scout), and an escort of 9th Lancers and 16th Lancers, under Captains Willoughby and MacEwan, 200 strong, made a night expedition to destroy if possible, the railway to Delagoa Bay. They encountered large forces of the enemy at dawn, and had to retire with Lieut. Pollock and one man of the 9th Lancers killed, three officers and nine men wounded, and two prisoners. It was a hard fight, and the escort was skilfully extricated from a perilous position.

June 2. Major Hunter Weston's expedition.

CHAPTER VII

ADVANCE TO PRETORIA AND RELEASE OF THE WATERVAL PRISONERS

THE division marched at daylight nearly twenty-five miles across the Krokodile River to the Kalkheuvel Pass. At mid-day we saw the enemy moving across our front some miles off, and soon came into action. We shelled the hills, driving them back, and General French boldly pushed into the Kalkheuvel Pass late in the afternoon. The 1st Brigade, with Carabiniers and Inniskillings, were in advance. The 4th Brigade, who were advancing along the heights on the left, turned and followed into the pass; their orders I do not know, but a great jam ensued. If they had only pushed on along the flank, they would have cut off the enemy with a large transport; as it was, one of my troops under Lieut. Paterson, which was keeping communication between us and the 4th Brigade, found itself left alone and guarding the left flank which the 4th Brigade had abandoned. Lucky, indeed, that it pluckily stuck to those heights despite being fired on by our own men, otherwise the whole division would have been exposed to an awful disaster. The position appeared risky, but the enemy were pressed and retreated down the pass. We had now but this one troop in occupa-

Fighting in the Kalkheuvel Pass.

tion of the heights on our flank, with only a very rough road and no spaces on each side to manœuvre, as they were all bush and rocks. The enemy in the bush on our flanks suddenly opened a heavy fire on the Carabinier troop in the road to the front ; several (about seven) casualties at once occurred; two of the Carabinier troopers and several horses being shot dead in the road. Lieut. Rundle, with the advanced patrol of Carabiniers, had three horses shot under him, and Captain Johnson one. General French and Staff, riding well ahead, had narrow escapes and had to retire. It was not reassuring to see our General and his Staff galloping back, but it was the best thing he could do, and, thank goodness, he ran the gauntlet of fire safely. The head of the column was blocked by those checked in front, and there was great confusion— the natural result of the advanced guard walking into an ambush, and of the General himself, who was riding with them, being forced to retire. The advanced guard, however, under Major Hamilton, behaved most gallantly, and, despite the sudden surprise and their heavy losses, held their ground.

Major Allenby, who was next in advance with the Inniskillings, at once grasped the situation, and, although nearly overwhelmed by the horses galloping back on him from the front, he called loudly on the New South Wales Lancers and a squadron of Inniskilling Dragoons, who at once dismounted, took up good positions on each side of the road, and poured in a heavy fire ; this rallied all and prevented the panic which had appeared imminent. All credit for this must be given to Major Allenby, the New South Wales Lancers under Major Lee, and the Inniskillings supporting the Carabiniers. Meantime, General

French had sent forward two guns and a pom-pom, which were quickly dashed to the front, along the road; reinforcements from the 4th Brigade and Mounted Infantry in rear were also quickly galloped to the front, and a terrific fire was opened; the re-echo of the guns reverberating down the pass and causing a great roar.

The situation, as darkness fell, was: Carabinier Squadron checked in front; guns, Inniskillings, and Mounted Infantry supporting them; Inniskillings on both flanks; remainder of 1st Brigade and 4th Brigade in awful confusion behind, and crammed into the Kalkheuvel Pass. It was certainly alarming. An enterprising enemy could have wiped out the Cavalry Division, but probably General French knew well, before entering the pass at so late an hour and in such a random way, that such an enemy did not exist. Owing to the dense bush and the approach of darkness the casualties were not great, and firing was kept up by means of the flash of the rifles on both sides until long after dark. The division spent the night crowded up in this position—a desperate and critical one but for the fact that the enemy were in flight.

Lieut. Paterson, who was in advance on the left front, inside the 4th Brigade, with a troop of Innis-killings, did good service by sticking to the heights when the 4th Brigade turned into the pass, and was our only protection there. Gradually, however, a way was made, and the Mounted Infantry were got up from the rear to take up our positions. Of course, no transport was up, and we were glad to dine off a tin of soup and potted meat conveyed in our wallets. Then those not on duty threw themselves down,

worn out, to sleep soundly with a saddle for pillow.
Unfortunately, the ground was too rocky for our
poor worn horses to do the same.

Father Knapp, a Carmelite monk, who had only
just joined the Brigade and was attached to the
Father Knapp. Inniskillings, was most heroic in attending
the dying in the road under heavy cross fire,
and joined our bivouac party as if he had been accus-
tomed to such living all his life and thoroughly
enjoyed it.

We learnt later that the retiring force was the
Mafeking commando; also that our shell and rifle
fire down the pass killed and wounded many, amongst
them a field cornet, whose grave was pointed out
to us.

Next morning we continued our way down the
pass. The regiment (Inniskillings), in advance, had
Flanking Pretoria. June 4. hard work reconnoitring over the awful
country and hills; the head of the brigade
pushing fast along the road down the pass
made our task of reconnoitring properly quite impossible. We found several Boer wagons, with provisions and baggage, abandoned on the road; sacks
of mealies, of coffee, and of flour, and also female
garments, were strewn by the wayside, showing the
panic of their flight. They also showed that if the
4th Brigade had advanced on the left the previous
day, instead of turning into the pass behind the 1st
Brigade, the whole Boer convoy would have been
captured.

The enemy were viewed in flight and shelled, but
there was no reply. One hill shelled was occupied
only by Kaffirs, who had climbed it to see the fun.
We advanced without opposition and crossed the

bridge, intact, over the river near Hartebeest Poort, on the west of Pretoria. I received orders to push on with A Squadron Inniskillings, and reconnoitre Zilikatsnek (Nitrals Nek), which we found all clear, although the enemy was reported to have held it the previous day. If occupied it would have been an awful 'nek' to reconnoitre and almost impossible to force. The road approaching winds up through bush and rocks and then over a nek, which is a cleft in the range of mountains, the hills rising precipitously on each side to a tremendous height. A store by the side of the road was occupied by a Scotchman, who had some zebras that he drove in harness. It was with feelings of delight that I found my advance unopposed and could report 'all clear.' It was this nek where, later, occurred the awful catastrophe to Colonel Roberts's force of Lincolns and Scots Greys. They had neglected, because, it was said, a famous general on another occasion had neglected, to occupy the tops of these precipitous heights on each side of the nek. This was a point discussed as possible when starting on this dangerous enterprise.

The division bivouacked at Reiffontein. I was recalled, and the Scots Greys were sent on over Zilikatsnek to hold the drift on the far side.

June 5.

We heard the big guns near Pretoria during the day, and saw our war balloon on the hills to the south. At daylight we marched out of this lovely valley through Zilikatsnek into another lovely valley and on to Hartebeest Hoek. We met no opposition and found several Boers on their farms. The farms were surrounded with fine orange groves, which thrive on this north side of the Magaliesberg range,

but will not grow on the south (Pretoria) side. The
fruit afforded all ranks a welcome refreshment. Our
horses were terribly reduced ; only thirty in my
squadron that night were fit for any work. One of
our patrols brought in a New Zealander and another
who had just escaped from the Waterval Prison.

It had been a glorious and most peaceful day, with
no sign of an enemy. We heard that one of the
Pretoria forts had been taken, but no news of our
entry into Pretoria, and thought that the forts on this
side were still occupied. We were, however, quite
round Pretoria, and expected to advance to Waterval
next day, where it was rumoured our prisoners still
were.

At 6.30 A.M. the 4th Brigade (General Dickson)
marched to Koedoes Poort, on the Delagoa Bay line to
the east of Pretoria, occupying Wonderboom
Fort *en route*. A gallant captain of the 8th
Hussars was detailed to take his weak squadron for
this duty at dawn. He was quite dumfounded, as
he understood that the enemy were still in occupation ; he reported to his general, and asked how, with
such a force, he was to take a fort. The discomfit-
ing reply was, ' Do you want me to tell you how you
generally eat your breakfast ? '

Our 1st Brigade (Colonel Porter), which was very
weak, marched to Waterval, in order to release our
prisoners there, who numbered about 4,000. We met
some 100 of the enemy, who surrendered with wagons
and horses ; they were in rather a wretched state, and
some were wounded and glad of the services of our
doctor. On reaching Waterval the prison guard
surrendered, and the prisoners burst out, cheering and
frantic with delight ; several rushed off to the nearest

June 6.

BRITISH PRISONERS OF WAR AT WATERVAL, NEAR PRETORIA.

BOER PRISONERS OF WAR.

farms and returned with chickens, geese, young pigs, &c., remarking, ' Now, at last, we are going to have something to eat '—a case of counting their chickens before they were hatched, or at any rate cooked !

Colonel Porter had previously left two squadrons of the Greys behind at Honing Nest Krans, to cover our retirement on Wonderboom ; but opposition was not expected, and, owing to loss in horses, we were a very small force with two guns.

A Squadron of the Greys, under Captain Maude, after occupying the prison enclosure, advanced to the hills on the right front, and A Squadron of the Inniskillings, under Captain Yardley, occupied the hills on the left front, B Squadron, under Major Dauncey, guarding the right flank, as many of the enemy were visible in small parties. Captain Maude, on our occupation of the prison, informed me that many of the enemy were visible on the hills, and that something ought to be done ; so we at once occupied these hills to front and flank with our weak squadrons. The column was halted in rear for nearly two hours, waiting for a train expected from Pretoria to take away the sick prisoners. On arrival of the train the enemy opened fire on it with two guns which they had concealed in position, having evidently got the range to a nicety ; they also fired on our two guns—which at once came into action, but found themselves quite outranged—and on the prison laager, which was a dastardly shame, for it contained only helpless prisoners and sick.

It was some satisfaction that their late guard— now our prisoners—came in for a share of the firing, and their terror was very great. I fancy several were under fire for the first time ; to such, shell fire is always

alarming, but a very small experience soon teaches
men to treat it with *sang-froid*. This guard, for the
most part, did not consist of fighting burghers, but of
men who had been employed in high civil appoint-
ments in Pretoria.   Our released prisoners rushed
out and scattered in all directions, the enemy dropping shells amongst them.   The country was littered
with blankets and other effects which they dropped
in their flight, but occasionally an unconcerned man
might be seen calmly trundling his property in a
wheelbarrow.   With difficulty we headed all in the
right direction, to our rear.   I galloped to stop many
running blindly into country which was in occupation
of the enemy.   One officer in charge of prisoners,
whom I exhorted to try to collect his men, was too
scared to do anything, and, I should think, would
soon find his way into the hands of the Boers again.
With our few men we then advanced and kept back
the enemy, whilst the prisoners, officers and men,
scattered independently, and not unlike sheep, made
good their way to safety.

Our guns being outranged, Colonel Porter withdrew them, and Major Allenby was left to cover the
retirement.   He at once brought the remainder of
the regiment and the New South Wales Lancers to
reinforce us, and heavy firing took place. Affairs at
this juncture were critical, as, had the enemy dared
to rush us, we must have been overwhelmed.   At
Lieut. Paterson's suggestion, we attempted to utilise
the Boer Maxims and pom-poms placed, with plenty
of ammunition, at the corners of the prison laager,
but were disappointed to find our gunners had disabled them before withdrawing.   Undoubtedly the
guns ought to have been manned by the released

prisoners, or withdrawn, and we were sore on hearing afterwards that they had been left to fall again into the enemy's hands.

Under continuous shell and rifle fire, we kept a bold front until all the escaped prisoners were safely well away, and then, as darkness was coming on, we retired slowly after the main body towards Wonderboom Fort. We brought away with us all the prison guard, amongst them being the late Assistant Surveyor-General of the Transvaal, Von Gulich, a most intelligent, highly educated man, who owned a farm near Wonderboom, and was most useful as guide on a pitch-dark night to Koedoes Poort, where our orders were to bivouac. The enemy shelled us until we crossed the nek at De Onderste Poort, north of Wonderboom Fort. Here we halted till long after dark, and until the train, which had made a second journey out in search of prisoners, had safely passed back to Pretoria. The Carabiniers meantime followed our Brigadier, who, with the guns and Greys, had retired _viâ_ Pretoria for Koedoes Pass. Unable to find their way in the darkness, they did not arrive till the following morning. Under guidance of our Boer prisoners, we were more successful, and reached the pass about 10.30 P.M., our horses being clean done after a long day of over thirty miles—a cold bivouac, with no food. We were quite unable to find our way, although we knew the direction. I suggested a prisoner as guide, and thus we came to know Von Gulich.

His interesting conversation with Major Allenby and myself whiled away many dark hours that night as we led our weary horses along. He originally marked out the Portuguese boundary-line of the

Transvaal. He never uttered a complaint, although
the walk was terrible for a man of his age, without a
horse, often floundering in wet bog, and with a cheer-
less, supperless bed on the cold ground at the end.
Such, however, was also our portion ; for, the wagons
not being there, we had only the dry biscuits which
men and officers carried in their wallets. The usual
orders still were to carry three days' supplies for man
and beast on the horse, so as to be independent for
several days ; and the wagons joined us at the
bivouacs whenever they could. It was a cruel burden
on the horse, and often unnecessary, for the wagons
as often as not arrived. Some light two-wheeled
transport would have doubled our mobility ; and
what a saving in horseflesh there would have been !

Our few casualties included Lieut. Meek, Inniskilling Dragoons, who was mortally wounded, and died
during the night ; he was a most promising
young officer, whose loss we all deplored.
Just before the fighting commenced at the
Waterval many Boers had surrendered. Two or three
being seen on a hill, Lieut. Meek, accompanied by
Sergeant Broadwood, of his troop, rode out to them.
The sergeant galloped in front, waved a khaki woollen
sleeping-cap, and shouted in Dutch that it represented
a white flag. Their reply was that he should remain
motionless or he would be shot. Lieut. Meek, who
was following and had not heard, called on them to
lay down their arms, whereupon they fired. His
horse fell, and as it was down they fired again,
wounding Lieut. Meek in the stomach. Sergeant
Broadwood, who understands Dutch, was then dis-
armed and taken before Commandant De la Rey,
who remarked in Dutch, ' Why do you bring me

Death of
Lieut.
Meek.

prisoners ?   You know we do not want them.'   Then in English to the sergeant : ' If you like to take your chance, you can go back between the firing lines.'

Sergeant Broadwood said : ' In that case you will shoot me as I go.'

De la Rey then gave orders that he was not to be fired at, and said he himself would shoot any man who did so.   Sergeant Broadwood then walked back safely, his captor remarking, ' Any way, we have shot your pal.'   He himself gave me this account.

I have seen no details of the release of the Waterval prisoners in the English papers.   Opposition was not expected, and the 1st Cavalry Brigade, depleted of horses, was very weak.   General Porter wisely held the nek (Honing Nest Krans ?) over the range between Wonderboom and Waterval.   Whilst waiting for the train the able prisoners might have been collected under their own officers, the guns (Maxims) taken away, and stores destroyed.   On the enemy suddenly opening fire, the prisoners rushed in confusion all over the veldt, being shelled by the enemy.

The following fairly accurate account of the release of our prisoners at Waterval, by Mr. Paterson, who was with the 1st Cavalry Brigade, is taken from an Australian paper :

The capture of Pretoria was not attended with any very stirring fighting, but the release of the prisoners was one of the most pathetic incidents of the war.   French's Cavalry, including the two Australian cavalry squadrons, were not actively engaged in the Pretoria fight.   They went right round the town to Waterval, a place sixteen miles due north, where all the prisoners taken in the war were con-

H

fined.   The Dutch were reported to have all fled to
Lydenburg ; so the work of releasing the prisoners
did not seem to need a large force, and was entrusted
to the 1st Cavalry Brigade.   Owing to the great loss
of horseflesh, the brigade could only muster about
400 men, of whom about one-sixth were Australian
Horse and New South Wales Lancers.   So lightly
was the matter thought of that the battery of six
guns accompanying the brigade only took what
ammunition they could carry in the limbers, and sent
their wagons to the camp near Pretoria, where they
would meet them.   In order to release the prisoners
the brigade marched to Waterval, and found a huge
barbed-wire enclosure, with hospital and other buildings included.   As we drew near this place a mob
of the prisoners clambered over the wires, cutting
their hands badly, and came whooping, cheering, and
throwing up their hats, down to the advance party
of the brigade.   The Boer guards were still hanging
about the prison, but made no move to stop the
prisoners.   There was no sign of any Boer forts in
the neighbourhood.   The prisoners were in a deplorable state, having had nothing but mealie pap to eat
for months, except a very little meat, which was
issued twice a week ; and they had been sleeping four
under one blanket in the terribly cold nights we have
had here lately—nights when the ground was white
with frost and the wind cut like a knife.   They had
been trying to escape by various means.   Ford and
Whittington, of the New South Wales Lancers, got
away.   The 18th Hussars prisoners had dug a tunnel
that ran right under the fence, and had reached daylight on the other side ; but by the time it was
completed the British forces were so near that the
officers persuaded the men not to make any attempt
to escape, as it might only have cost them their lives
just as relief was at hand.   After the first few got
over the wires men were sent to cut the fences, and
the prisoners streamed out in a disorderly mass, and

for a while there was nothing but a batch of questions and answers, and recognition of friends between rescuers and prisoners, some of whom had been there for seven months. Then the news was flashed into town that the prisoners were released, and a train was sent out to bring them in. Meanwhile the prisoners said all their little belongings, rugs and so on, were still in prison, and asked for leave to go back to get them. This took some time, as the men were all talking and shaking with excitement. There was no order or method among them. A patrol of Scots Greys was sent up towards the heights overlooking the prison to guard against surprise, but no one expected any Boers would be found in the locality.

As soon as the train appeared a change came over the spirit of affairs. From a far distant hill the Boers opened fire at the train with a very long-range gun. They put the first shell right in front of the engine. It is marvellous how soon their gunners pick up the range, and before the train could move they fired another shell into the truck next the engine. The engine-driver put her full speed astern, and backed away out of range. The prisoners heard the firing and saw the train going back, and thought they were not going to be released after all. They swarmed out of the compound like bees, rushing hither and thither in every direction when the Boers started to shell the compound, literally sending one shell right in among the huts at the rear of the prison hospital. This sent the prisoners fairly distracted, and some of them started to run towards the Boer lines. Major Yardley, of the Inniskillings, in charge of the release, tried to get the prisoners' officers to stop them, but no one took any heed, except for himself, after all the months of prison life. The only idea was to get away, and get away quickly. A line of troops, consisting of the Inniskillings and New South Wales Lancers, Scots Greys, and 1st Australian Horse, formed between the prisoners and

H 2

the Boers. There was no longer any need to hurry the prisoners up in the departure. Some of them dashed over the barbed wire again rather than wait to go round by gaps that had been cut. The Boers continued to shell the compound. The Scots Greys' patrol reported the Boers were coming down with rifles, and asked for reinforcements. Captain Nicholson, with two troops of New South Wales Lancers, was despatched to their support, getting their horses under cover of the railway embankment. The heavy fire of the Boers checked the advance. If the enemy had only known it, they could have massacred a whole brigade of prisoners, as we were only 400 strong, while they had a commando of 2,000 men on the hills. Meanwhile the majority of the prisoners, carrying all kinds of red, blue, and green blankets, and dressed in all sorts of odd clothes, just like the prisoners taken at Cronje's laager, were streaming away to the train, while our battery replied to the Boers' guns, but was hopelessly outranged. The train took all it could hold, and the rest tramped alongside ; but about 100 sick were unable to move, and were left in the prison hospital, Surgeon-Lieut. Samuelson, of New South Wales, staying with them.

Nicholson and his men, on withdrawing from the railway line, told the rear-guard to bring along the Boer gaolers—about 100—who had been found in charge at the gaol. He told these men they could go to get their blankets. They were in abject terror of their own friends' shell-fire, and for the most part came away just as they stood. Every time a gun was fired they threw themselves down on their faces flat on the ground, and lay there till the shell had burst, while our men on the horses laughed at them. These gaolers had been ordered by the Boers to stay with the prisoners, and expected that the Boers would come down and capture the rescuing party ; but Nicholson got them all into camp safely, except that one of the Scots Greys was shot through the leg. Our gunners destroyed two Boer Maxims at the prison. These guns were mounted on sandbag forts just outside the wires to shoot at the prisoners inside if any disturbance arose or attempt to escape was made. Dr. Samuelson had an unenviable task in staying at the prison after all had gone, as the Boers were sure to come back when our men withdrew. At the date of writing he had not returned to the camp.

The prisoners were all camped outside Pretoria, and are not allowed to join their regiments for the present. They are too weak to do any useful work. The bulk of the officers were confined in a separate prison in Pretoria, and fared better than the men, and all seemed fit and well when released. The New South Wales prisoners all seemed well enough, though thin and weak. All the officers have to undergo a board of inquiry as to how they came to be made prisoners.

The bold front kept by the Inniskillings and New South Wales Lancers, under Major Allenby, when the other troops retired, aided at first by the Scots Greys Squadron and Australian Horse attached to them, kept back the large numbers of the enemy; gave time for the released prisoners to escape, and made an orderly retreat of what would otherwise have been a rout. I was much indebted to a small party of the Australian Horse who, at my request, remained to help me hold an advanced post which, save for the shelter of a stone wall, would not have been possible. Lieuts. Walton and Sullivan, R.A.M.C., who remained to attend Lieut. Meek and the sick, informed me that the enemy fired into the hospital and re-occupied the laager after our departure.

Lieut. Walton interviewed Baron von Dalwig, a German who commanded the Boer guns, and who _{Baron von} was very bitter against the English. Later _{Dalwig.} (August 30) we found the Baron at Waterval Onder, with one arm amputated, the other shattered, and three shrapnel bullets through his chest—wounds received from our guns in the battle of Machadodorp. He was a fine man and likely to recover. He must have had an iron constitution, but said he had been resigned to death, and piteously remarked, ' What use shall I be now ? ' He gave us to understand that he had a family to support, and that his pay from the Boer Government was a consideration.

During the retirement this day I made a valuable addition to my stud in the shape of a fine pointer. Seeing her ranging nicely whilst the shells were falling, I despatched my trumpeter to secure her. She proved a treasure, and never left me during the rest of my campaign. She showed high breeding, was well trained, and the fastest ranging pointer I have ever seen. Unfortunately the rules of the Board of Agriculture prevented her from embarking with me to England, and, before a permit could be obtained, she succumbed to the heat in Durban. It was often sad to see poor dogs and other animals left famishing and deserted by their owners at farms, as we swept the country.

The Boer prisoners, including our intelligent guide of last night, were sent to Pretoria, and the _{June 7.} 1st Brigade joined the 4th at Derdepoort, about four miles to the east of Koedoes Pass. At mid-day the enemy drove our patrols in, and the outposts were strengthened. The remnants of two of our weak squadrons were also ordered out to line the

neighbouring ridges, and our hopes of a day's rest
were dashed to the ground.   Major Dauncey's
squadron, whilst reconnoitring, located a large force
of the enemy at Pienaarspoort, returning just before
dark.

The horses unable to proceed were sent to the
sick depôt, thus reducing the number of horses in my
squadron to fourteen, and of those in the
whole regiment, including New South Wales
Lancers, to about 100 only.   Troops arrived from
Pretoria, and long-range artillery fire took place on
both sides.   The whole valley was full of soldiers
arriving from Pretoria, and it was cheering to set
eyes on infantry again, and on the big guns.   There
is a solid power of might that seems irresistible in the
advance of our infantry regiments, and which imbues
one with great confidence.   However, the sight was
not to cheer us for long, as their arrival meant our
departure.

June 8.

As soon as they were relieved, our small Cavalry
Division received orders and made a flank march to
Kamels Drift, about seven miles.   It was a lovely
spot for a camp, and pretty surrounding country,
but dreadful for cavalry work, being studded with
stones and rocks and scrub, very hilly, and the
roads only were fit to move on.   In the afternoon
about seventy Boers surrendered to us and reported
the enemy about 2,000 strong to the east, under
Commander Botha, and anxious to treat for peace.
Our orders were to stay operations, and General
French went to Pretoria, so the expected battle next
day did not take place.   As our numbers were so
reduced, it was necessary for the whole regiment to
be on picquet at night.   A heavy thunderstorm gave

us a thorough drenching, and quite destroyed our attempts to dine.

Lord Cowley passed us to-day, and informed me that he was nearly captured reconnoitring in the morning with a patrol of Compton's Horse.

The orders were not to provoke hostilities ; so we remained quiet, and delighted in a peaceful day and the opportunity of having a good wash. Our June 9. outposts were sniped at during the day. Three New Zealanders, foraging outside our outpost line, had their horses shot by a party of the enemy, but boldly attacked on foot and captured two of the Boers.

Our Roman Catholic chaplain, visiting Pretoria, told me that he met three French officers under French shelter of the priests there. He reported officers. them titled officers of the regular army, who had been fighting on the Boer side, and were now endeavouring to get out of the country and avoid being made prisoners of war.

On the following morning Major Allenby and I went a long ride into Pretoria, where we spent an interesting day. We found a nondescript crowd of soldiers (chiefly staff officers), correspondents, Boers, and British, all struggling for lunch at the club. We met a brother officer, Lieut. Ansell, who had, unfortunately, been a prisoner of war. His capture in the earlier part of the campaign has been narrated, and he was now rejoicing in being released from three weary months' confinement.

Lieut. Ansell afterwards did great service, and was promoted brevet-major. Apart from courage and personal prowess, his ability was undeniable, and Colonel Rimington, to whom, in the later stage of the war, he acted as staff officer, considered him his right-hand man.

He showed us round the Model School, where our officers were, at first, imprisoned by the Boers, and pointed out where Lieut. Winston Churchill escaped, and told us of the clever ruse by which Captain Haldane, D.S.O., Captain Le Marchand, and Sergeant-Major Brockie subsequently escaped. The story goes that another officer was to accompany Winston Churchill on the first occasion. There was then only a sentry at one end of a palisade which could be scaled. After Winston Churchill had successfully accomplished this, his companion, who was following him, stopped on the top of the palisading and exclaimed, ' Can I be seen ? ' The voice of the sentry replied : ' Yes, you fool; I can see you. Get down.'

Extra sentries and more stringent regulations made it much harder for the others. Their escape was effected by concealing themselves under the boards of the flooring ; here, for days, they worked, trying to burrow a way out, but water overcame them. Once they met underground another party of officers, who, unknown to them, were also trying to excavate a passage. Finally, the prisoners were ordered to be in readiness to be removed from the Model School to a regular prison. Captain Haldane and his party decided to remain under the boards, and escape when the rest were gone. They were fed by their brother officers. The Boers thought they had escaped, and their newspapers described how they had been seen making away on bicycles. Meantime, the order to remove was put off for about a fortnight, so they had to live in this damp, cramped position, fed by their

friends above.   Then came the removal, and they had
only to emerge when the guards had gone ; but
Captain Haldane, in a most interesting book, ' How
we Escaped from Pretoria,' has cleverly told their
adventures to the public.

On the wall of the Model School there is a
splendid map, executed by our officers while prisoners
—chiefly, I believe, by those of the Gloucester Regiment.   It is quite a work of art, and the Boers
preserved it.

We were shown over the regular prison, which the
Boers erected later, with a network of wire entangle-
ment and electric lights all round.   Here we were
introduced to the celebrated little monkey, ' Joko,'
which had been presented to the officers by the Boers
from the Zoological Gardens in Pretoria.   It had
been a source of great amusement to our officers.
Doctor Gunning, a Hollander, who was in charge of
the prisoners, was also manager of the Zoological
Gardens and Curator of the Museum.

On the capture of Pretoria places were exchanged,
and our officers made the late Boer guard their
prisoners, so that a group of them might be seen
playing with the monkey, in place of a group of
British officers.   Lieut. Ansell had now taken possession of this monkey, and for the rest of the campaign
it accompanied the regiment, generally riding one of
his ponies by day and sleeping near him at night.   It
was full of tricks, and caused infinite amusement :
often, at meals, it would slip round, pulling off every
officer's cap, and it loved to run in and pull violently
the tails of unsuspecting dogs, or drop suddenly on
them from the top of a cart when they were sleeping
by the side, and then bound away.   With some

BREVET-MAJOR G. K. ANSELL, INNISKILLING DRAGOONS.

THE CELEBRATED MONKEY, "JOKO."
Presented to the British prisoners of war by the Transvaal Government.

dogs it was very sociable, but when attacked it was generally a match for them, as it would box them in the face and always nimbly escape being bitten.

The prison itself consisted of a long iron shed, with rows of little bed-cots. In one corner Lieuts. Ansell and Haig had made a neat little partitioned room, secretly and ingeniously put on a wire from the electric light, and with a bottle and a pack of cards had cleverly devised a roulette table. Here great gambles took place, and the cheery Lord Rosslyn, who was one of the unfortunate prisoners, had good opportunity of testing systems, to be later perfected at Monte Carlo. Our officers also found another way of passing the time by bringing out a prison newspaper. All who had been in prison spoke well of their treatment on the whole, but complained of the bribery and corruption of the Boer officials, who made them pay enormously for small comforts received. All were unanimous in their praise of the American Consul, who had done so much, with great tact, to alleviate their lot.

An amusing story, doubtless exaggerated, was related to us. Just before our occupation of Pretoria, the Boers were anxious to take away the officers from the prison ; but they struck and refused to go. The Boers then threatened to fire into the prison. A Colonel, who objected to the proceedings, took refuge in the rafters above the ceiling, whereupon a precocious subaltern ran up and informed him that the Boers were going to fire first into the roof. In a hurry to descend, the Colonel slipped and both his legs came through the ceiling, and there he stuck, to the great amusement of those below.

Our officers certainly acted up to tradition and
with great boldness, and, instead of being taken away
prisoners, had the satisfaction of making their guards
prisoners.

We then went to inquire after Lieut. Haig, who
was most dangerously ill with enteric fever. I have
before mentioned the occasion of his being made
prisoner ; on that occasion he had a narrow escape.
After the party had been captured, a Boer, who was
enraged at the resistance they had made, appeared
very anxious to shoot Haig, and started putting his
rifle to his shoulder as if he was going to do so. Haig
shouted ' Foul ! ' and a Boer in authority knocked up
the man's weapon and put a stop to it, but it was a
near thing. He was then marched a long distance,
and probably on this occasion drank some bad water
which engendered the enteric. He now had another
wonderful escape, for the doctor had given up all
hope of his life. Colonel Rimington found him in
hospital very weak, indeed at death's door, but he
whispered, ' Get me some champagne.' This was
given to him, and he at once astounded every one by
rallying, and has now become the popular adjutant of
the Cheshire Yeomanry.

CHAPTER VIII

BATTLE OF DIAMOND HILL

THE division under General French marched in the dark at 5.30 A.M. over a rough country. The regiments were only the strength of squadrons (my squadron seventeen strong), with batteries of four guns only, as there were not sufficient horses to harness to the others. At 7.30 A.M., after crossing the drift at Kameelfontein and seizing the hill on the opposite side, we came to close quarters with the enemy, and fought till dark, gaining little ground. The first troops over had not seized this hill, but our Brigadier at once despatched B and C Squadrons of the Inniskillings to do so. Fortunate indeed was it that he did, for action was taken only just in time to forestall the enemy, who would otherwise have gained this hill and outflanked the remaining troops while crossing the drift. These squadrons, under severe fire, held this hill for eight hours against repeated attacks of the enemy, who were in large force and strong position, with good rock and bush cover. The whole division also was suddenly exposed to heavy shell and rifle fire at short ranges. Our guns were quickly in

June 11.

Fighting at Diamond Hill.

action, and, as usual, served magnificently, under
Major Sir John Jervis, R.H.A.

General French at once despatched the remainder
of our 1st Brigade to work round across the valley
and seize the hills on our left front.   Executing this
manœuvre over open ground we were a fine target
for the enemy's artillery, and, for once, their shrapnel
burst well.   Lieut. Gibbs, Lieut. Jervis, and a private
in my squadron had their horses shot under them,
but by our rapidity we forestalled the enemy successfully, taking the hills, which were weakly occupied.
We drove back the enemy and established ourselves
in a strong position, outflanking the Boer main position and so enabling the 4th Brigade to hold their
ground.   Lieut.-Colonel Sprot, of the Carabiniers,
also had one of his chargers shot.   General French
himself had narrow escapes.   Major H. G. Hathaway,
R.A.M.C., of his Staff, riding by his side, was shot
through the stomach ; he was conveyed to a house in
the rear by the drift, which the Boers, evidently expecting a fight, had previously barricaded.   He had
another narrow escape here, as one of the enemy's
shells came through the roof and burst in the room
in which he was lying.   Captain Kenna, V.C., on
General French's Staff, also had a wonderful escape ;
riding through the drift which the enemy, later,
commanded, he galloped through a hail of bullets
unscathed.

We bivouacked at nightfall, holding the hill to
the north-east of Kameelfontein ; the 4th Brigade
holding the hill to the east of Kameelfontein.   This
guarded the Kameelfontein Drift road, but was commanded by the enemy's guns.   General French
surprised them by seizing it on our advance, and held

it tenaciously despite their attempts to retake it.
The 4th Brigade were much exposed.   Amongst the
casualties Captain O'Brien, of the 8th Hussars, was
seriously wounded in the shoulder.   General Dickson
related to me that, in the darkness of night, he was
relieved to be able to stand up ; when he did so a
Boer shouted, ' British can't catch Boer,' then sang
' Rule Britannia,' ' God save the Queen,' and fired
in his direction.

Shell and rifle fire recommenced at daylight and
continued all day, but we were unable to advance
and could only hold our ground.   In the
June 12.
evening the enemy got two guns into position, from which they placed an accurate fire into
the 1st Brigade ; the movement had been reported
by our advanced scouts, preparations just made for a
move, and the artillery horses were ordered back
from watering.   It was short notice, but the horses
were galloped back from water, and our artillery,
T Battery R.H.A., under Major Lecky, came into
action very smartly, located the enemy's guns and
silenced them.   We found afterwards that seven of
the Boer gunners were hit, of whom six were killed.

We had the usual escapes—only three horses
killed and two men wounded.   One of the enemies'
shells burst in a bucket under a limber, which was
full of lime-juice ; the man behind was smothered
with the juice but unhurt ; those on each side were
wounded in the legs.   One shell nearly caught me
while saddling up my horse ; another shell burst in
the middle of the fire on which my native servant was
cooking our dinner.   He walked about picking up
bits of his cooking utensils, quite indifferent to the
fire, but most indignant that the officers' dinner had

all been spoilt.   He was a most useful and faithful
Indian, who accompanied me from a shooting expedition in India, and, probably through ignorance, always
looked upon shell-fire as a great joke ; but he could
never understand why we underwent such discom-
forts, and used to say : ‘ Master, this no country for
white man ; not right for officers sleep on bare ground,
eat bad food,’ &c.   He was always most willing
and cheerful.

It was necessary for all to be on night outpost,
and we spent another anxious, watchful night.   We
heard that the Infantry had taken the centre of
Botha's position, Gordon's Cavalry Brigade being
round the right flank commanding Witfontein, the
12th Lancers and Composite Regiment of Household
Successful
charges.
Sad losses. Cavalry effecting a successful charge, in
which they unfortunately lost those gallant
and good soldiers, Lord Airlie, Major the
Hon. Lieut. Fortescue, Lieut. the Hon. Charles
Cavendish, and sixteen men ; but all the news was of
victories, which was cheering.

To our surprise, there was only desultory sniping
this morning ; the enemy, 3,000 strong, was reported,
June 13. with twelve guns under De la Rey, to have
retired eastwards.   General French at once
pushed on over a very rough country, crossed the
Crocodile Spruit to Doornkraal, where we bivouacked
at sunset, without opposition.   On advancing, we
found some dead Boers, and heard that we had killed
and wounded a good many, those which our guns
killed being buried by a farm which we passed.

The Mounted Infantry led the advance this day,
over very rough country, our 1st Brigade following,
and the 4th bringing up the rear.   No fighting took

MESS WAGON AND CART, "A" SQUADRON AND REGIMENTAL STAFF.

OBTAINING FUEL, A SCARCE COMMODITY.

place, which was a change, but what a blessing it would have been to change our clothes and get a mail ! We had been without news for six weeks. It

June 14. was reported that the enemy had retreated to Bronkers Spruit, and we received unexpected orders to retire, so marched back to Kameeldrift.

Our small force had done well, with only twenty casualties in the two days : the fighting was severe, against great odds, in a powerful position which was strongly held. General Ian Hamilton broke the centre ; Colonel Gordon's Cavalry got round the right flank, and we repulsed the enemy on the left. The Boers on this occasion had strengthened their flanks in anticipation of our usual tactics. General French could not have done more with the small force at his disposal, and, had he not made a turning movement contrary to the direction the enemy expected, the result might have been a repulse to the whole army. In addition to the tactics he employed, it required a good deal of bull-dog pertinacity to hold the ground he did, and at the same time threaten the enemy, with so few casualties and with a force that was quite inadequate.

Our object, viz. to turn the Boers out of their strong position near Pretoria and clear the country, was thus effectually accomplished. The following is an account of the Diamond Hill battle by Mr. A. B. Paterson, the Australian war correspondent :

The capture of Pretoria does not appear to have ended the war. As we came into the town General Louis Botha and his troops moved out to the east, and established themselves on a line of rugged kopjes about ten miles out. They could see their city in English occupation, and their presence was a constant menace to the men who wished to give up their arms. Lieut.-General Pole-Carew's Division was sent out far enough to get in touch with them ; the words ' in touch,' within military parlance, meaning that General Botha was able to fire 15-lb. shells into the English camp, while Lieut.-General Pole-Carew retaliated by knocking clouds of dust off General Botha's kopjes with a ' cow ' gun.   This did not tend to any profitable result, so a move was made to force General Botha further back, and, if possible, capture his guns.

The advance was made in the three-fold style now usually adopted by Lord Roberts.   A large force of infantry made a direct march on General Botha's kopjes, while on his right flank Lieut.-General French's Cavalry made an attack, and on his left flank Lieut.-General Ian Hamilton's Mounted Infantry did ditto.   The cavalry were with General French, and the mounted infantry with Lieut.-General Hamilton.   The former had a rough experience.   Lieut.-General French was ordered, as he usually is ordered nowadays, to do an impossibility. He was told to march twenty-four miles on sick and tired horses before ten o'clock in the morning, and get right round the Boer position.   There were two reasons why the task was not feasible.   The horses could not possibly do it, and the enemy, who were now quite ready for this flank movement, were holding the hills in sufficient strength to stop three times the force French had.   The result was as follows.   After marching about six miles we suddenly came right up against a great frowning range, the hills of which were covered with a dense growth of thorn-bushes. Away on our left was a detached hill, separated from the main range by about a mile of open plain.   We saw about 200 Boers come out of the main range and ride across the open to the hill.   They were only about 3,000 yards off, and were riding across quite deliberately.

Lieut.-General French called up Sir John Jervis,

in charge of one battery of 12-pounder guns. 'There you are, Jervis,' he said; 'there's a treat for you.' One of our pom-poms was galloped into action, and the shells fell all among them, knocking their horses over and making them scamper off at a great rate. We were highly enjoying this when the Boers poured a heavy rifle fire on us at 800 yards. They had been putting men into the range in front while we were shelling this outlying party. Our guns were all up by this time and opened fire on the rocky range, and every available rifleman was dismounted and ordered to lie down and fire. Major Hathaway, of Lieut.-General French's Staff, was shot through the body while standing behind the guns, and for a while the position looked very serious. The bullets whistled past continually, and the gunners were working with the energy of despair to get heavy shrapnel fire to work before the Boers drove them from the guns. The pom-pom shook and swayed as belt after belt of ammunition was fired off, the empty shells jerking into the air as if the gun was some great machine manufacturing empty shells at the rate of 100 a minute. The Maxim hammered away as if some expert carpenter was driving nails at double speed, and the rattle of the rifle fire ran up and down the line unceasingly. All the time the 12-pounder guns were working methodically, as the guns always work, and all this volume of fire was poured into one little clump of rocks and trees on the top of a hill not 800 yards off, and in spite of it all the crack of the Mausers kept grittily answering. In every lull of our firing, man after man was carried to the rear, and more than once it looked as if the guns would go; but at last Lieut.-General French withdrew the 1st Cavalry Brigade, and sent them round to the isolated hill into which the 200 Boers had retreated. Their orders were to take it at all hazards and get some guns there, so as to enfilade the Boers who were so stubbornly holding the ridge in front of us.

CHAPTER IX

BATTLE OF DIAMOND HILL (*continued*)

HERON's troop of New South Wales Lancers were the first to go as scouts, and in the excitement and clamour the gunners mistook them for Boers trying to join the previous lot, and opened fire on them from one gun—the only one they could spare from the front attack. They burst shell after shell over Heron's head with mathematical accuracy, but the bullets, with which the shells were filled, all went on about 200 yards before striking the ground. The 1st Australian Horse, reduced in numbers to eight men and two officers, accompanied this movement, but they lost no men. They haven't many left to lose. The Lancers are only thirty-five strong now, the remainder having no horses, and the rest of the cavalry in the brigade are in the same plight. The skeleton of the 1st Brigade moved on to attack this outlying hill, and such of us as dared to lift our noses from the ground watched them go, expecting to see them get into a very warm corner; but the usual luck of the Australians stood to them.

The moment that the brigade's guns opened fire at a long distance the Boers left the hill and retired to the main range. The guns were pushed on to the position they had left, and opened a hot fire on the Boers on the main range. This drove them off the crest of the hill; but they opened a steady fire from the rocks at the back of it, and no advance

could be made across the open against such rifle fire.
All Lieut.-General French could do was to hold his
ground and trust to the infantry coming up in sufficient numbers to take the hill.   At the back of this
big main hill there stretched range after range of
hills, all occupied by Boers, and they had guns
enough and to spare.   They fired shells over the big
hill, and landed them in among Lieut.-General
French's Staff.   They advanced round the right flank
of our force, and shelled our convoy, including ambulances, with great spirit.   They shot the lamp clean
off one of Dr. Fiaschi's ambulances with a 12-lb. shell,
and put a fragment of a 50-lb. shell through an iron
building used as a field hospital, and then occupied
by the wounded. Lieut.-General French sent an
officer and two privates back to ask for reinforcements.   The Boers had stolen up to within range of
the drift crossing, which formed our only means of
getting back over the river, and they shot the two
men, but the officer got through.

Next day the same state of affairs continued.
Our artillery had nearly run out of ammunition.   A
constant stream of shell fire was sent at every part
of the camp, and our picquets were firing all day
long at parties of Boers, who moved backwards and
forwards on the distant hill, not daring to attack us,
but anxious to surprise and cut off any outlying party
they could find.   Just as evening fell they rushed a
couple of guns into action in front of the main range,
and put the first shell right in among the New South
Wales camp ; but all the troops were out on picquet
holding the hills, so the shells only startled the cooks
and camp followers.   Shell after shell followed the
first one, killing some Carabinier horses and wounding
some of the gunners, who at once went into action to
reply to the Boer fire.   Meanwhile the camp was
shifted up to a sheltered hill, and there never was
a camp shifted quicker in the history of warfare.
Horses and mules were harnessed at lightning speed,

while boom, boom, boom, the shells burst all about,
and pieces of iron went screeching and whizzing in all
directions.   After seeing a show like this, one can
understand how it was that Kimberley, Ladysmith,
and Mafeking suffered so little loss of life from shell
fire.   Here was a massed camp well in range, and
they had about twenty minutes' uninterrupted fire at
it, and only wounded two men and killed a few horses.
That night was spent on the kopje in expectation of
a daybreak attack, and before dawn all servants and
camp followers were called out to line the hills.   No
reinforcements had arrived, and the Boers had got
round us on three sides.

I for one was quite certain that French had at
last met his Waterloo, and that the brigades would
be cut up or captured ; but morning dawned and not
a rifle cracked from the grim line of hills.   The Boers
had all gone off east in the night—gone off in the
inexplicable way in which they always retreat.   Just
when a sharp advance would mean everything to them
they never attack.   We followed them up and found
one dead man that they had left behind, the graves
of several that they had buried, and a lot of lint and
bandages scattered round a building, showing that
they had been treating wounded men there.   We
saw no more of them, and came back to Pretoria to
refit and replace our crippled horses.   While the
cavalry fought on the left flank, the mounted infantry
were heavily engaged on the right.   They were about
ten miles away from the cavalry, making a similar
attack to ours.   They had to do the advance work
for Ian Hamilton's Division, and found that the
Boers had extended a heavy force to meet them.   In
fact, the flank movement business is always carefully
guarded against nowadays by the enemy.

Our Mounted Infantry, under Antill and Holmes,
were ordered to advance over a lot of open country,
and get possession of some kopjes outlying from the
main hills.   They made the advance in good style,

and got the hills on the first day (June 12) without much trouble, though they were well shelled as they went over. On the next day they were pushed forward on the extreme right, and had to charge against a steep rocky kopje and drive the Boers off it. So steep was the kopje that a horse could hardly be led up it. As they went across the open they received a heavy salute of rifle fire, but they gained the foot of the hill in safety. Then came the crucial point. They had got so far forward of the main advance that our own guns away on the left of Hamilton's force opened fire on them, believing that they must be Boers receding from the outlying hills. It was a curious thing that about the same time and the same day, but at a distance of ten miles apart, the two branches of the New South Wales forces were both under English shell fire. Not only did they get the English shells, but also those of the Boers on the top of the hill.

It was then that they lost two brave young officers, Harriott and Drage. Both these men— Harriott was little more than a boy—had shown bravery out of the common, and while the men were lying down among the rocks, crawling forward on their stomachs yard by yard, Harriott and Drage stood up, urging the men on, and calling them by name. The men implored them to lie down, but they took no heed. They actually got out their pipes and filled them while the bullets whizzed past and spattered in little grey splashes of lead on the rocks. Harriott was the first to fall. Sergeant Fleming (well known in Albury district in the peaceful profession of a solicitor) was by him as he fell, and Fleming proceeded to build a little wall of stones round him to prevent his receiving further injury. As he placed one stone in position it was knocked out of his hands by a bullet striking it. They managed to make a shelter for him, and the grim line of khaki-clad figures pushed steadily up the hill. Away a little distance Drage got his death-wound. He was shot right through the face, and the bullet came out at the back of his head. Even then he died hard. It took four men to hold him down, as he struggled half unconsciously to go forward over the rocks. Two troopers were also killed in this attack, going on to their death like brave men. Captain Holmes was shot through the arm by a shrapnel bullet, but went on with his men. This officer has earned the highest commendation in every affair in which he has been engaged. After a while the Boer fire slackened as the main advance pushed steadily on, and our men got to the top of the kopje and had the satisfaction of shooting at their retreating foes; but as the horses had been left at the foot of the kopje it was some time before they could pursue. They went on in open order, and actually got within range of Botha's main laager and poured some volleys into it ; but as we had 200 men, while the Boers had about 2,000, it was not practicable to advance further. As night fell the Boers withdrew altogether, and by dawn next morning their forces were away to the hills once more, and the New South Wales troops, with most of the others, were brought back to Pretoria to await the arrival of Baden-Powell and Buller. It is pleasant to think that in this critical engagement the men of the old colony have maintained the good name they have already earned all through the campaign.

We had received no mails for six weeks, and heard that some had been destroyed when coming up country, by the ubiquitous De Wet. Our war news was, however, satisfactory : that Baden-Powell and Mahon were at Rustenburg, and that a force was going to meet them ; that Ian Hamilton and Broadwood were off to Heidelberg, and that Buller was advancing.

From June 15 to July 9 the division halted at Kameeldrift, and were remounted. Sunday, the 17th, was a cold, wet day, with unusual thunderstorms. On the 18th the natives reported the enemy re-

June 20.
Cavalry
reorgani-
sation.

turning to the neighbourhood. We had a meeting at brigade headquarters to discuss the reorganisation of cavalry, a subject in which we naturally took a good deal of interest, and in which we were unanimous on many reforms. The latest war news detailed to us was not satisfactory.

Our Engineers destroyed about 20 tons of gun-

June 22.
Powder
manu-
factory.

powder at the Eerste fabricken manufactory close by. They commenced with dangerous explosions, but found it safer and simpler to throw the powder into the river.

This manufactory was in charge of Mr. Idle, the manager, who kindly placed his excellent lawn-tennis court at our disposal, supplied us with shot cartridges— a great boon—and was most obliging. His information of the enemy's movements was very vague, considering the number of natives at his command. Tennis, however, and not intelligence, was the object of our visits to this pleasant spot, but business combined with pleasure is always satisfactory, and trifles often lead to big results.

Forty good, but soft, remounts arrived for the regiment. Our patrols came across Boer picquets.

June 24-5.
Pretoria
news.

I rode into Pretoria, and found they were starting a newspaper there. We received news of the troubles in China, and that eight regiments of cavalry from India were being despatched there. We also heard with regret of Lord Kensington's death, and were sorry to find Captain

Milner, of the 2nd Life Guards, in hospital with enteric fever.

Captain Jackson now arrived from England with ninety-five more remounts for the regiment, in poor condition. No wonder that they were poor, for he had been continually employed with them *en route* on reconnaissance duty, and so was much delayed. He gave us the sad news of Sergeant-Major Harewood's death from enteric ; he was a capital sergeant-major of C Squadron, who had already earned the D.C.M. We invited Captain Jackson to dine at our squadron mess, and our chief dish was sucking-pig, captured that day. It was a very dark, wet night, and our rough shelter of boughs gave little protection for light to our feast. Daylight revealed the horrid fact that our sucking-pig was full of tapeworms, which discovery gave us a great shock. Such are the delights of campaigning, and, doubtless, our honoured guest fully appreciated them.

June 28.
Re-mounts.

Two Boers and a native, with arms, but no horses, gave themselves up to one of our picquets. One represented himself to be a schoolmaster. Passes were at once given them, and, after walking about our lines and taking stock of everything, they returned, probably with all information, to the enemy. The sight of them strolling about our lines and making their examination was, to say the least, annoying. These men were allowed to march off again with passes to the enemy's country, and meantime here we were being warned daily to expect attack. Why were they not sent under an escort to Pretoria ?

June 29.
Treatment of sur-renders.

Next day an A.D.C. arrived at 3.30 A.M. to say

Botha would attack at dawn, but again rumour was wrong.

The new month opened with another false rumour, but we commenced it with one improvement, viz. the relief of our picquets at daylight, instead of at other odd times of day—an invariable custom in the regiment, but one which the orders had hitherto discountenanced.

July 1.

A Carabinier patrol, under Lieut. Rundle, was captured by the enemy. Reconnoitring too far, they engaged a small party of the enemy, which proved to be the flanking patrol of a commando under Commandant Grobelar (?), advancing west. They killed two, but were themselves surrounded, several of their horses being shot and they themselves taken prisoners. One man escaped and brought back the news; next day dead horses marked the site of the conflict. The incident was unfortunate, as Lieut. Rundle was a smart officer, and the orders to patrols were not to engage the enemy; had he been able to avoid doing so he might have returned with valuable information.

July 3.
Disaster
to Cara-
binier
patrol.

Details of the 10th Hussars, about 100, under Second-Lieut. Bass, arrived, and were attached to the regiment. These were distributed amongst our different squadrons, and for many months to come served with us. They proved splendid recruits, and better fellows I do not wish to command. Other details for the 2nd Cavalry Brigade were attached to other regiments. This made us a regiment again, nearly 500 strong, but with horses unfit for hard work.

10th
Hussars,
under
Lieut.
Bass,
attached.

Two squadrons of Scots Greys left for Waterval,

and the rest of the Greys, to our regret, followed

July 4–6.
next day.   Scares of Boer attacks continued
to be frequent.

A patrol of 7th Dragoon Guards were attacked

July 7.
near Waterval, and had one horse shot and
a bullet through a man's helmet.

At mid-day on the 9th sudden orders to march
were received. It was a long, weary march south-

Move of
Cavalry
Division.
east to Grootfontein twenty-five miles.
It was again, unfortunately, necessary to
start with a very long march, thereby
knocking up our 'soft' horses, instead of being
able gradually to increase the length of marches
from ten to twenty miles a day.   Thus many
otherwise fine remounts soon became 'stone cold,'
and many had to be destroyed, unable to move
on.   The 8th Hussars joined the 1st Brigade, in
place of the Scots Greys.   We heard heavy guns

July 10.
cannonading during the day.   Next morning
we marched at 7.30 A.M. to Rietfontein,
about twenty miles, the regiment in advance.   We
found Generals Hutton, Mahon, Alderson, and other
forces engaged near Rietvlei in an artillery duel
only.   We heard that General Hutton had thirty
casualties the previous day when attempting a frontal
attack.

The regiment (Inniskillings) were ordered five
miles to the south-east, and bivouacked in a solitary
position in the dark.   The nights were now intensely
cold, and the water was frozen solid in the buckets.

At 4.30 A.M. we rejoined the brigade, and General
French directed a wide circle on Leeuwpoort Hill.

July 11.
The 8th Hussars, in advance, found the enemy
occupying it in small force.   We shelled

EFFECT OF LYDDITE SHELL.

A shell going through the tree trunk wounded four and killed five Boers sheltering behind, also blew the head off the horse.

[*See page* 125.

and took the hill at mid-day, and I held it with A

Taking Leeuw-poort Hill. Squadron Inniskilling Dragoons, the enemy shelling us all the afternoon, without effect. One of French's Scouts, attached to the 8th Hussars, was killed when taking the hill, and one horse was shot. This man rode on to the crest of the hill and halted to take a view, thus courting his fate. Had he only dismounted and crawled up, another life would have been spared ; but even bullets won't make some men learn this, whereas, to the Boer, such tactics are second nature—hence his superiority as a scout. With this slight loss General French secured this fine, powerful position, Several dead horses marked one of General Hutton's recent conflicts on this hill.

The 8th Hussars remained to hold the hill, and the brigade bivouacked below, at Olifantsfontein.

Effect of lyddite. The effect of one of our lyddite shells, fired by General Hutton's force a few days previously, was visible at the farm by the bivouac. It killed five Boers and wounded four who were sheltering behind a big tree, shattering the tree-trunk about 3 feet from its base, and going right through it, and also blowing one horse and saddle to pieces. Boer fingers and hands were lying about, and shreds of flesh were hanging high on the branches.

We sent escort with a convoy to Springs for supplies, and received the bad news that Colonel Roberts,

July 12. Disaster at Nitral's Nek. with the Lincolns, and Major Scobell's squadron of Scots Greys, had been cut up at Zilikat's Nek, or Nitral's Nek, and taken prisoners, the brave Lieut. Connolly, of the Greys, killed, Captain Maxwell dangerously wounded,

Lieut. Pilkington of the Royals (attached) killed, and many others. Major Scobell (now Major-General J. H. Scobell, C.B., commanding Cavalry Brigade, Aldershot) himself effected a clever escape ; as the prisoners were being marched away he gradually edged off and was not perceived till some hundred yards away. Then the guard opened fire on him ; but, luckily, without being hit, he gained the shelter of some trees, and so made his way during the night on foot to Pretoria. Thanks to the sergeant-major cutting loose the horses, they stampeded to the rear, and were all recovered.

The gallant behaviour of Major Scobell's squadron was, throughout, magnificent, but its position was a hopeless one. It was a sad affair ; but no blame attached to the gallant Greys, a magnificent squadron, commanded by one of the finest leaders in the Service, who had previously proved his title, and has since repeatedly done so. They were placed in a position no cavalry should have been asked to occupy—a narrow, rocky nek, studded with trees, in which horses were only a useless encumbrance, and, through no fault of their own, they were shot down like rabbits. Bravely they held out until ordered to surrender. Imagine the feelings of their proud leader as he effected his escape to Pretoria that night.

Presumably the cause of the disaster lay in the fact that the precipitous heights which rise abruptly on each side of the nek, and up which, it was thought, no Boers would scale, had not been occupied. The enemy by gaining these had the force at their mercy. It is a place I well know, having had to reconnoitre it on our first march north, and the question of whether those heights were occupied was then one of my chief concerns.

I held Leeuwfontein Hill—a twenty-four-hour outpost duty—with two squadrons Inniskilling Dragoons, including a troop of the N.S.W. Lancers, a force quite inadequate for the extent and the enemy in force all round. We worked hard, making sangars and good cover at the picquets, which had necessarily to be far apart. It was an enormous hill, being many miles round, and I could only furnish five picquets, with a support in the centre. This was one of those many occasions on which one could risk no sleep. In accordance with our custom when on these duties, we all off-saddled, except a messenger's horse, in order to give the horses more relief (otherwise they would always have been saddled up); also, our mission was to hold the posts, and men, in case of attack, are too often apt to think of getting quickly to their horses, an idea which we had now pretty well eradicated. The Boers were visible in force all round, and, in the middle of the night, there was heavy firing by my No. 4 picquet, which I felt certain was attacked. Galloping to the scene, the alarm proved a very mysterious and false one; it may have been caused by a party of Boers firing off their rifles, or by cartridges going off in adjacent grass-fire, but no bullets came, and we failed to elucidate the mystery.

At daylight my patrols had narrow escapes. One man, Corporal Duffy, made a good reconnaissance into the Boer lines, and escaped with a bullet through his helmet. He managed to get through a nek in the hills without being perceived by the enemy; leaving his horse secreted,

July 13.

July 14. Narrow escape of patrol.

he crawled round almost into a laager, counted the
number of men, horses and wagons, but was discovered getting away, and had a wonderful escape.
He said the bullet through his helmet was fired by a
Boer only about five yards off, as he jumped on his
horse and galloped away.   His orders were merely to
see if the hills were still in occupation at daylight;
but, having his patrol to assist him, he determined on
something more, and finally got away, covered by his
patrol's fire.   This shows the fine spirit of our men.

Major Duff relieved us with the 8th Hussars
whilst the firing was still going on.   Later we retired
to bivouac.

Our Brigadier, General Porter, had a fall to-day
and broke his collar-bone, for which we were all
sorry, as he had been a popular and careful Brigadier.

General Hutton sent information that the enemy
would attack next morning, so we strengthened the
outposts and made preparations.   This was
fortunate, as it was not, as was usually the
case, a false report, and at dawn the enemy
did attack, nearly rushing two of our picquets.   The
Carabiniers were on outpost; but the timely arrival
of Major Dauncey with B Squadron Inniskillings
and the New South Wales Lancers repulsed the
enemy's fierce attack and saved the posts.   Thanks
to this reinforcement, the enemy were driven back
and the remainder of the brigades hurried up.   Severe
fighting continued all day, the escapes from shell fire
being, as usual, remarkable.   The enemy endeavoured
to get round our right flank, but Major Allenby
extended the Inniskillings many miles, and frustrated
their attempt.   I took one advanced farm-house with
A Squadron, which we held all day, and from which

July 15.
Boer
attack.

we were firing till after dark, the Boers repeatedly trying to get to it by crawling under cover and through the long grass. The fighting continued till nightfall, the enemy being visible in large parties on the hills opposite, but with no heart to press home another attack. It was a wonderfully clear evening, and the enemy were so close that, through glasses, we could imagine we were really in the midst of them, dress and beard being quite distinguishable. Unfortunately we had no guns on our flank ; as the enemy were grouped in large parties of hundreds we should have had a fine target.

The regiment remained in position all night, fully expecting renewed fighting in the morning. In the middle of the night we took the horses many miles to the main bivouac for water and food, as they were suffering greatly ; but we returned at once. At daylight, however, it was evident that the enemy had no intention of attacking, and during a six-miles ride along my outpost line I saw only five Boers ; July 17. so at mid-day we returned to bivouac, the horses being much done for want of water, and from hard work. Save for six hours, most of them had been four days and nights with packed saddles on, and without a chance of off-saddling.

The enemy yesterday made a concerted attack all down the line, saying that they were going to take Pretoria. Our casualties were only three ; but General Hutton, fighting all day on our left, had thirty casualties and seventeen Australians taken prisoners. It is reported that fifteen dead Boers were found in one place alone, where most of his casualties occurred.

Again I commanded the outposts, with two

K

squadrons and two guns.   The enemy were active all
day, shooting on the picquets themselves and on any
July 18.   patrols that ventured out; so we were kept
alert, and I longed to use my guns, but the
orders were not to do so unless it was a necessity.
Once we saw the enemy in mistake fire briskly on
one of their own patrols which was returning to them.
It was difficult to see through our glasses whether
there were any casualties, but their unusual mistake
afforded us great satisfaction and amusement.

The 4th Cavalry Brigade, under General Dickson, having arrived, the 7th Dragoon Guards, under
Colonel Lowe, relieved my outposts, as he thought
it too big a line for even a regiment to hold.

General Gordon also arrived to take over command of our 1st Brigade in place of General Porter,
whose collar bone was broken.   The Scots Greys
too, to our satisfaction, rejoined our brigade.   In
General   company with General French, General Gor-
Gordon
takes   don visited our outpost line, and his keen
command
of the 1st interest gave confidence.   We were relieved,
Brigade.   in anticipation of marching at daylight.   But
this could not take place, owing to the supply convoy
not arriving, and on the 19th we sent all sick and
weak horses to the depôt at Springs, Lieut. Gibbs,
who was ill, accompanying them *en route* to Johannesburg Hospital.

It was reported that, through a woman's information, a dastardly plot had been discovered at Johan-
Plot at   nesburg.   Several hundreds of the enemy,
Johannes-   who had surrendered, were to attend the race
burg.   meeting with rifles under their cloaks, shoot
the officers present, and then attack the troops.

The Brigade stood-to at daylight, as usual; the

4·7-inch lyddite gun, or, as we called it, ' cow-gun,' because it was dragged by oxen, having been brought

July 20.

from General Hutton's force and placed in position on Leeuwpoort Hill, was fired, and stirred up about 100 of the enemy.   A German, who came to our outpost lines on Tuesday under a flag of truce, in conversation spoke of the enemy's terror

Effect of
lyddite.

of our lyddite shells.   He said that one shell the previous week took off a man's head near him and killed three others ; that the shock stuns all round and affects the nerves for some days, and that he himself was still suffering from the shock. This conversation arose from his hand shaking as he drank a cup of coffee.

A German commando, so called probably from being a foreign contingent composed of a good many Germans, was with the enemy, opposite our lines. Our chaplain, who went to the Boer lines to bury

German
com-
mando.

some of our dead, informed me that he met there the commandant, Baron von W ———, who was an officer in the German army, on five years' leave to travel, of which he had spent two years in England, subsequently taking part in the American-Spanish war, and now being with the Boers, with whom he was much disgusted.   Our chaplain added that the Boers were most reverent, attending his funeral service and joining most devoutly at the graveside in singing a hymn.   Conversing with one of them, who wore a mourning band, he remarked :

' I fear you also have suffered a loss.'

' Yes,' he said, ' I have lost my father ; he was not killed, but he was an old man, and the war caused his death.'

In further conversation our chaplain remarked that we admired many of their generals very much, but especially the late General Joubert.   The answer was :

'Oh, I am glad to hear you say that : he was my father.'

Strange that, without knowing it, he should have been conversing with General Joubert's youngest son !

CHAPTER X

THE CAPTURE OF MIDDELBURG

WE received orders to march at 5.45 A.M. next morning on a big combined scheme on Middelburg, our Advance on Middelburg. 1st Brigade, Gordon's, to be the flank column, and to get round *viâ* Vlakpan, Leeuwfontein due north of Bethel, and Paardekraal; then the 4th Brigade, Dickson's, *viâ* Dieplaagte, Steenkoolspruit, Rietpan Station; then Hutton's Mounted Infantry, *viâ* Witklipbank, Bankfontein, Rhenosterfontein; and the main army along the railway, our mounted troops finally combining to strike the line beyond Middelburg and cut off the enemy's retreat. Owing to the failure of the main army to advance rapidly along the railway, and to General Hutton also having received a check, the times and distances could not be kept, and General French had eventually, by orders from headquarters, to give up the original plan and combine much sooner on the flank of the railway. The distances marked for each day were great, and we arranged to carry five days' forage and supplies on packhorses. Lieut. Ansell, Inniskilling Dragoons, invented a good plan for carrying corn-sacks on the ordinary saddle with stirrup-leathers and reins. We thus dispensed with wagons on our flank column for four days at least.

It was also proposed to march with regiments on a very extended front, covering many miles, which proved too extensive and scattered when it came to be practised.   All ranks were very cheery and confident.

The start was, however, delayed.   It was a dismally cold day for standing-to ready saddled, and

July 21-22.   we enlivened it with some mule races.   Postponement occurred next day again, owing to telegraphic instructions from headquarters.   On the former day about 800 of the enemy were seen opposite our picquets, which the 4·7-inch gun opened on, and at last, at 5.45 A.M. on the 23rd, we started in the dark on an extended front.   Thick mist, which was long in clearing, interfered, and the troops got much scattered.   One of my patrols of three men lost themselves, and I feared that they were captured. Eventually they found their way to Springs, but it was weeks before we saw them again.   I was guarding the right flank, and found it necessary to ride fast for six hours.   After covering quite twenty-five miles we reached Dieplaagte, and came into action, which was chiefly an artillery duel; and we bivouacked, holding the position, 800 of the enemy falling back from the Hekpoort ridges.

Amongst the few casualties, Captain Ebsworth, of the Australian Horse, attached to the Scots Greys,

Death of   was killed.   While standing by his horse and
Captain
Ebs-   spying the enemy through his glass, a chance
worth.   bullet, fired quite 2,000 yards off, struck the glass and penetrated his brain.   There was heavy firing; several dead and wounded Boers were picked up and nine captured.   After the hard day on horse-flesh, I was glad to find myself in possession of a pony we captured from the Boers.

AWAITING ORDERS TO MOVE.

THE MIDDAY MEAL.

We marched at daylight; Inniskillings right advanced regiment, with orders to march on Steenkool Spruit to Wolverkran. The 4th Brigade came behind us, so the original programme of marches was already abandoned. This was apparently caused by the check to the main army, and, after starting, a halt of about two hours, caused presumably by getting communication from General Hutton, wasted precious time.

July 24.

On meeting the enemy the Inniskilling Dragoons were ordered to advance and seize the hill from which the Boers were shelling us whilst our guns replied. Major Allenby at once extended the regiment and galloped down a valley, taking the hill from front and flank with great dash and skill. The enemy had got their gun away, and were flying everywhere. Major Allenby at once rushed the regiment on, and we took the hills beyond, driving the enemy before us. I came across several fine farmhouses, which were well stocked with forage, and some beautiful Cape carts; the Boers occupying them invariably escaped on horseback, only stopping to fire at us when they could obtain good cover. It was reported that General Botha had been here the previous day, going round the farms.

Dash of Inniskillings.

With our advanced parties we came upon the whole Boer army, retreating with their guns on Middelburg. Lieut. Paterson, with a small troop, opened fire on their main body at short range, causing the enemy to bring a Creusot gun into action and shell the ridge from which our small party were firing. Further advance with our few scattered squadrons was impossible. It was sunset and our horses much done. It was unfortunate that the brigade had not pushed on rapidly after us with the guns, when great execution would have been done.

Escape of Boer army. As it was, our reports found the brigade too far back to act, and the Boer force escaped in the dark, the regiment being recalled some miles back to bivouac.

July 25. We stood-to at daylight, but did not march till 9 A.M., the 8th and 14th Hussars being attached to the 1st Brigade. It was a long, slow march over a bleak, barren country, and the weather was bitterly cold.

Seizing drift, Olifants River. Advancing with great precaution, we seized Naauwpoort drift over the Olifants River unopposed, and occupied the heights beyond. This would have been a very strong position for the enemy to have opposed us from. The river, which is deep, runs through the nek at Naauwpoort, and the only very bad drift is completely commanded by the heights on the east side, our approach from the west being from a gradually sloping, undulating country.

Bad weather. We bivouacked in torrents of cold rain, spending a terrible night. One officer died afterwards from the exposure.

July 26. At 7 A.M., with the Inniskilling Dragoons in advance, we marched on Hartebeestfontein to Sterkwater and seized the hills. The Boers opposed on our left front, but we soon drove them off, and their shell fire was harmless. They were evidently a protecting flank guard to the enemy in full retreat. My advanced troop, under Lieut. Jervis, rode down and captured a wagon with a fine team of oxen.

It had been a hard day's work, and a cup of tea

with Major Hunter Weston and Captain Abadie, of
General French's staff, in a barn, which they were
going to make headquarters, was a luxury.   Then I
got thoroughly wet rescuing a trooper's bogged horse,
and had to go straight on in the dark—being officer
commanding outposts—in order to select the line,
place picquets and guard during the night.

Only those who have tried it know the difficulty
and almost impossibility of doing this in a rough
country by night.   It means miles of floundering on
tired horses, getting touch with regiments taking up
the line on other flanks, and a great deal of imagina-
tion in fixing the best spots for picquets; but the
responsibility is great, and the cavalry on active
service require iron constitutions.   Everyone soon
learns to look after himself; but it often entails the
men going day and night sleepless, with only the
scraps of food and rations they carry on them.   Some-
times a farm which has been passed has provided a
feast of ducks or chickens, to be cooked on picquet,
or a sheep is collared close by, or a pig is run down
with sword or lance ; otherwise the ration of beef is
produced from haversack and cooked in mess tins, or
the ration may be tinned meat and biscuit, all ready.

At this time our squadrons usually had small
Cape carts, which would generally find their way
out to the outpost line and afford the officers a
more or less good meal at their picquets, or one's
faithful servant would ride out with necessaries.
Unless carrying some days' rations, a man would be
left at the main bivouac to get the rations on arrival
of the wagons and bring them out to the outpost line.
General Baden-Powell, in his useful little book on
scouting, says that if a good scout is given a sheep he

should consider himself lucky and well rationed for many days, and the soldier on active service soon discovers this.

All officers who have been on active service will acknowledge how very little one really requires, and what thousands of our young bloods have had their eyes opened to this fact. It was a shocking sight to behold the tons of useless articles and stores brought out by the first Imperial Yeomanry regiments and other corps, most of them to be left on the quays in Cape Town or elsewhere as they progressed north. Luxuries and mobility will not combine on active service, for the former hinder the latter, and Brother Boer is an exponent of mobility. Personally, like most of our officers, I effected the maximum of both when possible.

My kit consisted of a pony and a pack-saddle, on which was packed my valise and a small tente d'abri that weighed only a few pounds. The valise contained my bedding, and in saddle-bags I had a change of clothes and luxuries. The pack-pony was generally up when I wanted it ; but, failing that, I was equipped as one of my men, except that I carried a small saddle-bag on my charger, holding pocket lantern, razor, soap, and a penny looking-glass. Whenever we halted, the men would make a tente d'abri out of blankets with a sword at each end as poles ; but, to compete with an enemy like the Boer, our system of a man carrying everything necessary for some days on his horse is ridiculous. He must ride like the Boer, with his saddle and ammunition only, and light, two-wheeled transport should be provided to fall back on.[1]

Service kit. (margin note)

---

[1] This the columns adopted, in most cases, in the later stages of the war.

AN OFFICER'S BIVOUAC TENT

OFFICERS TRY ON THE GIFTS SENT BY KIND LADIES AT HOME TO THE
TROOPS AT THE FRONT.

After this digression, I must return to our doings. The night passed quietly, and, as usual, I saw my patrols off before dawn. They returned at daylight, reporting all clear for four miles. The division then advanced at 10 A.M.; the Inniskilling Dragoons, with a section of guns, a few miles to the left front. We seized Erfdeel Drift, on the Klein Olifants River, and occupied the hills on the other side, where we engaged the enemy. The 8th Hussars and others were also engaged more heavily on our right. Our guns were rapidly pushed forward and the enemy driven back. The enemy fired a big gun from the railway at a range of 10,000 yards with black powder, which made a great explosion, but which did no damage. They had this gun on a railway truck, and so ran it back just in time, as an 8th Hussars patrol nearly succeeded in damaging the line, and so preventing them from getting it away.

July 27.

Capture of Middelburg.

The Inniskilling Dragoons, with two guns, bivouacked at Groenfontein, holding the ridges to the east of the river, which necessitated a long line of outposts, the main body being at Erfdeel. General French rode into Middelburg, on our left rear, which had just been occupied by the Mounted Infantry. It was reported there that a great rabble of the enemy, many of them being drunk, including many foreigners —French, Germans, and Italians—had passed through the town on the previous day with eleven guns. There was a large quantity of stores of all descriptions in Middelburg. The inhabitants reported that the water in the district engendered tapeworms. One of our officers learnt this in a curious way when getting stores. He had secured a barrel of salt herrings, and

another dealer, with whom he was bargaining for
some flour, noticed the herrings on his cart, and was
at once anxious to know how they were obtained,
as he thought there were none in the place. He
remarked, 'They would be so good for my worms.'
Then came the explanation to our puzzled officer ot
the complaint, cause, and imagined remedy, which
resulted in a satisfactory exchange of herrings for
flour.

On the 28th we halted. With a brother officer
I visited a large farm a few miles off, as usual carrying my shot-gun, and picked up a few brace of
partridges. The farm was occupied by a Hollander
and some ladies, who professed great friendship. In
the farmyard I discovered one of her Majesty's
branded troop-horses, simply worn out and quite
incapable of moving; but, doubtless, it recovered,
and later mounted one of our enemies. The farmer
said he was only a guest, and was anxious to know if
they would be allowed to keep any of our worn-out
horses which they had picked up, so that they might
convalesce. We were treated to coffee, and bought
three couple of chickens for our mess, which, as we
left, were handed to us alive, tied by the legs. We
rode off with a great cackling and much hampered by
our live stock, so, directly we were out of sight of
the ladies, we decided on slaughter; and, believe me,
if you have not previously tried it, wringing the necks
of half a dozen chickens is no easy matter. One
escaped, and the gun had to be brought into requisi-
tion. Riding home in the dusk, we tried to circum-
vent a mounted man whom we rightly took for a
Boer scout, but, after a long chase, he eluded us in
the darkness.

Our detachment joined the division at Erfdeel, being relieved at Groenfontein by infantry, which had been brought up along the railway.   At
July 29.
midnight I received orders to send a Cossack post about four miles down the river, in view of the enemy being in that direction.   The strength of the regiment this day was 25 officers, 485 N.C.O.s and men, and 415 fit horses.

CHAPTER XI

NEXT day the division advanced, the Inniskillings, with a section of Royal Horse Artillery, under Lieut. Staunton, to Koppermyn, the 14th Hussars to the right, 8th Hussars to the left, and 6th Dragoon Guards (Carabiniers) supporting. Officers' patrols went about twenty miles in all directions and reported the country clear except to the east. A patrol of the 8th Hussars, under Lieut. Vanderbyl, found the enemy in strength beyond Wonderfontein Station, and had three of their horses shot. One of the men, whose horse had been shot, found his way on foot to our lines, and was under the impression that his patrol had been annihilated. The cheering news of the surrender of 5,000 of the enemy, under Commandant Prinsloo, to General Hunter was announced.

The Inniskilling Dragoons, with three squadrons 14th Hussars, under Major Brown, V.C., a section R.H.A. and a pom-pom, all under Major Allenby, marched to Strathrae, at which place there was a store; we suspected the Hollanders who occupied it of treachery, and one of them slipped away in the night. At a large farm which we passed near Grootpan our advanced patrol discovered a huge

July 30.

August 1.

quantity of geese, turkeys, and poultry, in addition to forage, secreted in a loft, but all taken were duly paid for.

We fully expected hard fighting, but saw only a few of the enemy. General Gordon, supporting, bivouacked at Grootpan, with the Scots Greys near Wonderfontein Station.

The enemy commenced firing at daylight on our outposts, and continued all day. One patrol, under Lieut. Terrott, found the enemy in strength

August 2.

near Goedehoop Farm, but got back with their information under heavy fire. We had a tremendous line to hold, but kept off the enemy, our pom-pom being very useful. Sergeant McCubbin, Inniskillings, was shot through the thigh, but rode back under the impression that he had only been hit by a stone. Corporal Quinn, Inniskillings, with his sword drawn, charged three Boers single-handed ;

Outposts.

surprised, they were about to surrender, when they perceived that he was alone, so they picked up their rifles and fired at him ; he had to gallop away, luckily unhit. A patrol of the New South Wales Lancers, under Lieut. Nicholson, discovered the enemy in force to the north-east ; they surprised one commando at breakfast and did some execution. Second-Lieut. Bass, of the 10th Hussars, attached to us, was lost yesterday, with his troop, when reconnoitring, but rejoined us to-day. We feared he had been taken prisoner ; but he had cleverly avoided the enemy, and made a Boer farmer make his party comfortable for the night.

At midnight I received orders to reconnoitre at daylight next morning to the Komati River with A Squadron Inniskillings. A thick mist delayed

our start till 6 A.M.   Major Allenby supported the
reconnaissance to the Goedehoop heights, and A

Recon-
naissance
by A
Squadron
Innis-
killings.
August 3.
Squadron (only thirty men) pushed on, meeting with great opposition.   The thick mist,
which kept rising and falling before it cleared
at mid-day, enabled us to cross the heights
and push on down the gradually sweeping
slope towards the Komati Valley and river.   At one
time we crawled cautiously to within a few hundred
yards of a party of Boers, and for some time there
was a deadlock, as to show oneself was to be shot.
Outflanking them, we caused them to retire, and
again pushed on over a series of ridges.   Coming on
to one of these my advanced scouts suddenly found
themselves in the midst of large numbers of the
enemy, who had been collecting to oppose, and were
received with a fusillade at close quarters.   Following
a few hundred yards behind, with the few men with me
well extended—having placed the remainder on our
flanks—I at once dismounted and covered the retirement of the scouts, who came galloping back on us,
with as rapid fire as possible.   I myself was using a
sporting rifle that my servant always carried for me
in cases of emergency, and this time it came in very
useful, for I checked a nasty fire from the left, and
must, luckily, have got the range of the Boers
concealed in long grass there.

Corporal Fenton's horse galloped back through us,
riderless, mad with three bullet wounds; another of

the scouts who was wounded fell with his
horse on him, pinning him down by the leg;
and a third scout galloped back wounded.   We were
ourselves, meantime, under heavy fire, bullets raising
little puffs of dust all round me.   On my calling for

some one to go to the aid of the fallen man, Corporal King, of the 10th Hussars, attached to my squadron, Corporal King. at once vaulted on his horse and galloped, under heavy fire, the 200 yards out, got the man up, conveyed him to the rear, and at once galloped back to me with the request that he might go out again and try to find Corporal Fenton. To do so was madness and certain death, as the Boers were all over the ground on which he fell and were now getting all round us.[1] All the others being safe away, I ordered the mount, and we galloped back to the ridge behind, which we at once lined and from which we kept back the enemy.

At this time Major Allenby, from the Goedehoop heights, advanced his guns, and sent the New South Wales Lancers to support us on the flank. This gave us the upper hand. The enemy retired and we again pushed on. Later in the afternoon, under heavy fire, we gained a valuable point, which was obtained in the face of great opposition and with slight loss, and from which we obtained a good view of the valley and river. It was impossible to advance further, as the enemy, to the number of several hundreds, were holding the drift at Witkloof ; but our reconnaissance was valuable. We retired at night on Goedehoop, where Major Allenby had taken up an extended line of outposts, and said ' Good-night ' to the Boers, who had been following us up, with several rounds from a pom-pom which Major Allenby had left to cover our retreat.

On our later advance we searched the ground on which Corporal Fenton had fallen, and were much

---

[1] For this gallant conduct Corporal King received the Distinguished Service medal.

L

chagrined to find he had been removed by the enemy :
I fear, mortally wounded, for we never heard of him
again (a court of inquiry has since reported him dead).
He was a Royal Reservist, attached to my squadron,
and a splendid fellow, daring but cautious, and, I fear,
must on this occasion have been deceived by one
of his men riding into the Boer ambush in front
of him.   He was a gentleman in every sense of the
word, and a great loss.

Our horses were much exhausted, and the escapes
remarkable.   One man was shot through the top of his
helmet ; another had a curious escape : a bullet was
diverted by his sword-hilt, and, passing down through
the fleshy part of his calf, was found in his stocking.

Advancing in the morning, we were fired at from
a farm ; on rushing it, several Boers galloped away,
and we found a good many Boer women in it who did
not understand English.   Returning by the farm, I
gave the men leave to take what ducks and poultry
they liked, and gave the women a written notice to
the effect that if there was any more firing from the
farm it would be burnt or shelled by our guns—this
because I knew that their men were likely to return.
We took up an outpost line close by, however, and
the following morning one of our patrols, with a man
who understood Dutch, visited the farm.   One of the
women inquired, ' Where was the nice captain who
visited them yesterday and gave her a receipt for the
ducks ? '   She produced my notice, which she fondly
imagined was a receipt to enable her to obtain pay-
ment from the British for her ducks.   This shows
the spirit that prevailed.   The men would always
leave their women in the farms, well knowing they
would be protected, act as spies, make money out of

THE LATE LIEUT. KIMBER, IMPERIAL YEOMANRY,

CAMP WHERE BRITISH PRISONERS WERE CONFINED AT NOOITGEDACHT

the British, and be ready to receive their men again
when our troops had passed. The foregoing is a
good specimen of one of our small reconnaissances.

During the night Privates Kimber, of the Duke
of Cambridge's, and Hely, of the Middlesex Yeo-
Privates
Kimber
and Hely
of I.Y.
escape. manry, walked in, having escaped from
Nooitgedacht, on the railway, where the
enemy held our prisoners. They took five
days and six nights coming, marching by
night and hiding by day. They effected their escape
by mingling unobserved with their officers on a Sunday church parade, and then walking into the mountains at night. The officers, being on parole, were
unguarded. They reported a rough, precipitous
country, and that they had heard guns in the direction
of Ermelo, which, we presumed, was General Buller
advancing. Whilst hidden, they had watched our
engagement the previous day, and then gained our
lines in the dark. They said there were about 400 of
the enemy at the Witkloof, and that they were longing to rush out and warn us of this fact when I was
doing the reconnaissance, fearing we should fall into
their midst. Their escape was a very fine performance, and we hoped to be able to get them attached
to the regiment. They were both very nice fellows,
of the right sort, and Kimber was well known to me.
Their thrilling adventures would make a good narrative, and they had certainly weathered them remarkably well, and proved their ability. Hely had been
with the late Major Dalbiac when he was killed while
boldly charging a Boer position. He carried as a
memento a piece of Dalbiac's serge, with medal
ribbon on, which he cut off when he was lying dead.
Poor Kimber was killed later in the war, shot

L 2

through the heart, when heroically attempting to rescue one of his men.

The 14th Hussars who had been attached to us rejoined their regiment, stationed at Grootpan.

General Gordon rode over and approved our outpost line, reinforcing Major Allenby's small force of the regiment, two guns and a pom-pom, with 100 of the Carabiniers, under Major Hamilton. Sniping went on at the outposts, and a picquet of the 14th Hussars, to our left rear, was attacked.

<small>Aug. 4.</small>

From August 4 to 18, with this small force, under Major Allenby, we held a line of about eight miles at Goedehoop; the enemy were very aggressive and in strong force all round. The greatest vigilance was necessary, and the incessant outpost duty proved very trying to officers and men. For this purpose the regiment was formed into six small squadrons of forty men each. It was a fine performance to hold this line with so few without disaster, and well merited the praise bestowed on the regiment by General French. Again during this period, as so often during the war, our signallers proved their great value, both with the heliographs and flags by day and with the lamps by night. One great drawback, however, that we had to contend with, and which was a great trial to regimental and squadron commanders, was the constant calling on regiments by generals and staff for our signallers and their apparatus. This is not right, and squadrons should have the entire control of their signallers, whom they have trained in times of peace. As it was, both when reconnoitring and on outpost duties, we were constantly being deprived of our best trained

<small>Good work of the Inniskillings.</small>

men and signalling apparatus at a time when they were so essential to us.

The following is a brief summary of this last fortnight:

On the 5th a party of the enemy, as they were attempting to crawl through the lines in the dark, Aug. 5. stumbled across one of the picquet sentries. The picquet, luckily, had no light, and the enemy received a surprise when the sentry fired into them, springing up all round and rushing away. In the afternoon I shot four and a half couples of snipe in the bog by our horse watering-place. About sixty of the enemy tried unsuccessfully to cut off a patrol, and the usual sniping continued all day.

Our sangars and trenches were strengthened all round; these were invariably occupied by every avail-Aug. 6. able man before dawn, and everyone was Outposts. always ready at a moment's notice to occupy them. The pom-pom and Maxim were most useful during this fortnight, thanks to our signalling, being always brought rapidly to any threatened point.

On the 8th a determined attack was made on one of the picquets, but was repulsed; the pom-pom was rapidly brought up and the enemy scattered. A farmer, having obtained the information through a native servant, reported that a commando of the enemy, 400 strong, with two guns, was on the hills to the south-east. This farmer had surrendered after hiding for two days with his cattle, in fear of both the enemy and ourselves. Leaving his wife on his farm in the enemy's line, he slept out at night with the cattle to prevent their capture. After our departure he was made prisoner by his own countrymen

and flogged.   On taking Barberton, where we found
him in jail, we released him.

At night one of my Cossack posts on outpost
reported to me that there was a small fire about a
quarter of a mile below his post and figures moving
round, which he believed to be Boers.   Quickly
raising volunteers, I made dispositions to surround
them, and we crawled off with our rifles in the dark.
We found the light a will-o'-the-wisp, for it turned
out to be the light by a Kaffir kraal nearly two miles
off, so we had a long, exciting crawl for nothing.
Lights are very deceptive at night, but the post
should not have made such a mistake.

A patrol of six men, under Lieut. Harris, was
pursued on returning.   In the usual endeavour to cut
Aug. 9.   them off, one man was taken prisoner through
his horse falling.   Again next day a patrol
of the Carabiniers was pursued by about 150 of the
enemy, and had one man wounded and two missing.
Another patrol found the Boers still in strong force ;
they were all round our front and flanks, and their
guns could be heard shelling Wonderfontein Station.

There was a good deal of sniping during the night,
and a furious gale made things unpleasant, blowing
Aug. 11.   cups and plates bodily away when we were
trying to breakfast.   At this time the cold
with hard frost at night was severe.

The usual patrol sniping and pom-pom practice
continued.   We received news of an extraordinary
Aug. 12.   plot in Pretoria to kidnap Lord Roberts and
murder other officers, which later resulted
justly in the execution of one Cordua.

The Boer women in two farms outside our outpost line were notified to be ready in the morning

for removal to Pretoria, as they were in the habit of harbouring and signalling to the enemy at night. At daylight, however, it was discovered that they had all gone in the night to the enemy's lines. This Major Allenby had expected, hence he requested that we might remove them without warning; but, in accordance with our too lenient policy, the orders were otherwise. One of these women we had designated 'the wicked widow,' for, whilst being agreeable, we well knew she signalled to the enemy at night and had communication with them.

CHAPTER XII

DURING the afternoon of the 14th Captain Harrison, 11th Hussars, Intelligence Officer, rode in from General Buller reporting his force of 15,000, with two cavalry brigades and many guns, advancing. At the same time their advanced scouts came in touch with our outposts. This we antici-

<small>Arrival of General Buller.</small> pated, as orders to make a reconnaissance in force to discover their whereabouts had been cancelled. General Buller's army bivouacked at Twyfelaar, about six miles south-east of our outposts, in one huge camp, covering a very small front. We were glad of the kind opportunity to replenish our larders from the large quantity of stores they carried with them. From all accounts they had an easy march north, occupying Ermelo and meeting with slight opposition. Their arrival cheered us much.

Sniping continued at our northern picquets. General Buller visited our main bivouac with General Hutton and General Gordon. General Sir

<small>Aug. 15-16.</small> Redvers Buller lunched at our squadron mess. We had little to offer; our only drink at this time consisted of ration rum, and we thought ourselves lucky to have that. The General, fortunately, was in possession of his flask: but, on offering his

orderlies (troopers) rum, they replied that they did not drink rum, but would take whisky. It was condescending of them not to request champagne. 'British warm' coats (a sort of khaki pea-jacket) were received for the first time and issued to officers and men. They were badly needed, and proved the greatest benefit throughout the rest of the war.

The 8th Hussars moved up on our right rear, which considerably relieved our long line.

Next day Captain Harry Deare, of the 8th Hussars, brought us a welcome present of a bottle of whisky, and together we rode over and visited General Buller's camp at Twyfelaar Drift, only about six miles off. It was a huge camp of 15,000, and, after holding such long lines with our few troops, it surprised me to find them all crowded together and covering such a small front. Their march north on a similar plan had, from all accounts, not done much to clear the country, as the Boers quietly marched away until they had passed. We waited now while General Buller's large convoy of wagons proceeded to our railway to re-ration his force. As regards stores and luxuries we found the force, however, decidedly well off. I found a relation, who commanded a brigade of artillery, like a good many others, luxuriating in a tent.

August 17.

On the 18th the Inniskilling Dragoons moved on to the ridge in front of the Goedehoop Farm; the 6th Dragoon Guards to the right, in connection with General Buller's army; General French and General Gordon, with the Scots Greys and headquarters, to Goedehoop. The enemy were still aggressive on the ridges opposite us, and our reconnoitring patrols were unable to advance further.

August 18.

A patrol, under Lieut. Amphlett, reconnoitring to Blesboksspruit, was severely fired on.   Private Sykes, 10th Hussars (attached), showed great gallantry in rescuing a comrade, his horse being shot whilst doing so.   One of the Carabinier picquets was temporarily driven back with a few wounded, and, from one of our picquets, with a Maxim we effectually got into a party of the enemy pursuing a patrol, only four out of nine of the enemy getting back.   Sniping, by means of the flashes of the rifles, continued till after dark.

The cavalry with General Buller consisted of the 5th Lancers, 18th and 19th Hussars, under Colonel Brocklehurst, and the South African Light Horse, Strathcona's, &c., under Lord Dundonald.   Time was found for an impromptu polo match between our respective forces, our opponents, luckily, being in possession of some polo sticks.   And we were told many good stories of the dash and daring of the Strathcona scouts.   I repeat one of them for what it is worth.

A small skirmishing party had one of their number wounded and then shot in cold blood.   They effected the capture of the four Boers who had done the deed, got some rope from a farm, and at once strung them up.   A staff officer suddenly arriving remonstrated in horror, but was glad to gallop off when they remarked that there was enough rope for one more if he made any objections.

On the 20th General French, with his staff, rode round the outpost line.   With his usual daring he General French. exposed himself in order to get a good view of the ground, and had a narrow escape of being shot.   The horse of a staff officer from General

Buller's force, who was accompanying him, took fright at the firing, bolted, and conveyed him back several miles to his camp. All thought the horse had been shot ; but the bullets had only frightened it, and no doubt he came in for a good deal of chaff.

The enemy appeared to be making entrenchments, and we could see one lady in a habit boldly riding on their outpost line.

A general advance, in conjunction with General Buller, now took place in the direction of Belfast. General French's cavalry moved a few miles to the north, to Blesbokspruit, whilst General Buller advanced on Witkloof and the ridges opposite us. These were taken after some stiff fighting and a good many casualties, chiefly among the 18th Hussars and the Gordons, six of the latter being killed. The strength of the opposition appeared to us, who knew the ground, to be underestimated. The ridges were not previously shelled, and the direct advance caused many casualties.

August 21. Advance with General Buller on Dalmanutha.

The advance was continued to Geluk, about eight miles from Dalmanutha. When taking the Geluk Hill General Buller had a great many casualties, and eighty of the Liverpool Regiment, advancing too far, were cut off and taken prisoners. The infantry, on this occasion, seem to have been doing the work of cavalry, and were caught whilst reconnoitring on foot. During the next two days, in bad weather, we remained halted alongside General Buller's army, and a good many casualties occurred to his forces ; amongst them Captain Savory, of the 4th Hussars, with the South African Light Horse, was killed. The whole force was much crowded under shelter of the hill, which the enemy

Death of Captain Savory.

commanded with their guns. Shells were falling into
the middle of General Buller's headquarters and into
our bivouac. We were altogether huddled into an
uncomfortably crowded position. Riding round the
outposts, which were almost on us, I was struck with
the care and improvement shown by all ranks in
taking cover. Ladysmith experience had not been
without its advantages.

Our patrols were unable to advance much beyond
the outpost line, when they were heavily engaged.
Captains Hamilton and Jackson's patrols of Inniskillings, endeavouring to push on to Dalmanutha,
had one man and five horses wounded. Colonel
Henderson, of the Argyll and Sutherland Highlanders, General Buller's very capable Intelligence
Officer, kindly let us have a few stores from his small
stock, which were much appreciated   Colonel Payne
also, commanding the Inniskilling Fusiliers, sent us
from his officers, as an *entente cordiale* between the
regiments, a case of stores, which were a great treat.
Two Natal friends of old days, Messrs. Henderson
and Streuben, surprised us by a visit. Old colonists,
they were now giving assistance as guides and in-
terpreters on General Buller's Staff: another proof
of how Natal has given its services. Their feelings
on the subject of the war were strongly expressed,
and they were emphatic that we were not nearly
severe enough.

Aug. 26.
Flank
march of
General
French's
Cavalry
Division.
These last few days appeared to us un-
satisfactory, so it was with no regret that the
1st and 4th Cavalry Brigades and Royal
Horse Artillery, under General French, re-
ceived orders to march at 4 A.M. on the
26th. After marching to Belfast, which was occupied

by General Pole-Carew's Division, we made a wide circle in rear of the town to avoid observation, and then advanced north. The regiment, Inniskilling Dragoons, under Major Allenby, with Captain Griffin's pom-pom attached, was sent a few miles to the flank, through an intricate country, almost impracticable for horses, in order to attack the hills on the left. The enemy everywhere occupied the broken, bushy kopjes, but we gradually pushed them back, and nightfall found the regiment still fighting and holding a long, scattered front throughout a cold night. It had been a long day since 4 A.M., with fighting at close quarters all the afternoon, but the casualties were slight and chiefly among the horses, several of which were shot. Escapes were remarkable, but the enemy's firing was not good. Some of them were dressed in khaki, with helmets, and were riding big horses. It was impossible at first to distinguish them from our own patrols. The pom-pom, under Captain Griffin, which was worked skilfully and continually at close quarters, and so saved us many casualties, proved exceptionally useful in driving the enemy out of their many rugged positions.

Early in the afternoon Lieut. Harrison, of the Scots Greys, in advance of our main body, was mortally wounded, shot through the neck from behind a kopje. He died a few days later: a good officer, sadly missed. I viewed the sad occurrence through my glasses from some miles off, a small party of four or five Boers, who were lying behind a kopje, being distinctly visible to me. An officer, with his men extended, advanced reconnoitring. If only I could warn them! Then, pop-pop-pop; and the Boers, running down behind

Death of Lieut. Harrison.

the kopje, mounted and galloped away. I heard later the sad news that one of the fatal 'pops' betokened poor Harrison's death. How many have met their fate in the same manner! And I fancy few junior officers or men could relate the numbers of times they have narrowly escaped it. Reconnoitring like this, which is a daily duty of the cavalry, is a perilous mission.

That night was a trying one; after working and fighting hard since 4 A.M. the previous day, we had to be on the alert in isolated positions, which were bitterly cold, without food or extra clothing.

At daylight we drew in to the main body near Laken Vlei, got some food for our famished men, and continued the march. Yesterday our artillery silenced one of the enemy's guns, but they managed to get it away. We bivouacked at Vlakplaats, the regiment being selected to take the last hill, which was successfully done, with slight opposition. Several horses were bogged in a long deceptive valley we had to cross. The hills opposite were strongly held; a good deal of long-range fire took place, and our guns came into action. Heavy firing was taking place from the army advancing on our right. This proved to be General Buller fighting his successful battle at Dalmanutha.

Aug. 27.

In the morning General Pole-Carew's column, consisting of the Guards, &c., came up on our right rear. The regiment, Inniskilling Dragoons, under Major Allenby, was again selected to take the ridges opposite, which were occupied by the enemy, who were reported in force, with two guns. It appeared a desperate enterprise, and we expected heavy losses. On our advance long-

Aug. 28.
Arrival of
General
Pole-
Carew.

range fire soon commenced. Major Allenby used his
guns opportunely and, as it proved, with good effect;
then we (Major Dauncey's and my squadron) rushed
the main ridge, from which the enemy fled. From
rags soaked in blood we found traces that our
fire had been effective; we also found some ·303
sporting-cartridge boxes by Holland & Holland.
General French at once pushed on rapidly, seizing
the range of hills at Wakfontein without opposition.
It was a tremendous position, from which the enemy
had just removed two big guns, leaving shovels, tent-
pegs, and other signs of their hurried retreat. In
one of their large gun-emplacements an amusing
letter was pinned up, to this effect:

'Dear Mr. Khaki,—So sorry we cannot stay, but
don't feel very well this morning, or should have given
you a warm greeting. Hope we shall meet next
year,' &c.

The spelling was very bad and illiterate.

From this commanding view we could see that
Machadodorp was in General Buller's possession, and
the enemy everywhere in retreat.

At 5.30 A.M. we continued the advance in rain
and thick mist, descending the steep mountain pass

Aug. 29. into a terrible country of precipices, closely
followed by General Pole-Carew's column.
The Inniskillings led the advance, seizing the heights,
which were then occupied by the Mounted Infantry.
A small force could easily have harried our progress,

Touch but there was little opposition. At mid-day
with
General we reached Helvetia, where we met General
Buller. Buller's Cavalry advancing from Machadodorp. The enemy, retreating north on the Lyden-

burg road, placed a belt of pom-pom shells almost into the brigade, one lot bursting a few feet in front of me. It seemed a great piece of cheek, and was another fine instance of the bold and admirable way in which the Boers could fire their guns and then rapidly get them away safely. On this occasion it was to their cost, for it brought the immediate fire Prowess   of all our guns on their retreating forces, of Naval General Pole-Carew's naval guns from guns.   the rear being the first brought into action. A very pretty shelling took place, which, it was discovered later, caused the enemy considerable loss.

Leaving General Buller's force at Helvetia, General French pushed on to the heights above Waterval Boven and Waterval Onder ; a good many of the enemy were scattered about, and continued firing was kept up on our picquets as we bivouacked.

In the morning we marched to Waterval Onder and occupied the heights overlooking the town on Aug. 30.   the west. A steep road wound down to the Capture of Waterval town itself, which is situated in a gorge Onder.   1,000 feet below, through which runs the Crocodile River and, along the further bank, the railway to Delagoa Bay. Colonel Sprot, with a squadron of the 6th Dragoon Guards, occupied the town and railway station at daylight, being fired on whilst doing so. The town of Waterval Onder con-sists of only ten to twenty houses, with tin roofs, and the railway station. Both here and at Waterval Boven there were, however, a good many stores and luxuries, such as liqueurs, which were, doubtless, *en route* to Pretoria from Delagoa Bay.

About 1,500 of the enemy were visible in the

open country, above the precipitous cliffs on the opposite side of the valley, and a good many were hiding in the cliffs, from which they commanded the town and drift over the river. These latter were reported to be men chiefly of the Italian commando. Our artillery shelled the heights and searched the kloofs.

Italian Commando.

President Kruger was reported to have been at Waterval Onder the previous day, and General French was anxious to obtain news. So B Squadron of the Inniskillings, under Major Dauncey, was ordered to descend to the town and bring away the prisoners we had taken, among whom was a wounded soldier of our own. The enemy, hidden in the rocky kloofs and bush beyond the town, completely commanded the drift and approaches, and also the town itself. The squadron gained the town, galloping over the exposed ground through a hail of bullets. Lieut. Lawlor, at the head of his troop, was mortally wounded, shot through the body. He was a fine officer and a great loss to the regiment, and died cheery and brave to the last. Major Dauncey himself, charging in advance of his squadron, with Lieuts. Lawlor and Johnson, was grazed by two bullets, but the town was reached. In it none could show without being shot, so cover was taken in the buildings, and the prisoners were not brought away till darkness ensured a safe return.

Death of Lieut. Lawlor.

General Pole-Carew, meantime, arrived with his column, but, we understood, did not feel justified in risking the loss that would be incurred by clearing the kloofs and heights beyond the town with his infantry ; and, as it was an impossible country for cavalry, General French ordered the 6th Dragoon

M

Guards and the Inniskilling Dragoons, occupying the town, to bring away the prisoners when dark. Mr. Bennet Burleigh, the well-known *Daily Telegraph* correspondent, went down there to seek information, and ran the dangerous gauntlet of fire, luckily unhurt ; but, like others, he would not attempt the return journey till dark.

Lieut. Lawlor, to the great grief of all ranks, died that night. He was carried into a house which the Boers were using as a temporary hospital, where also was Baron von Dalwig, whom I have before mentioned. The latter was recovering from the terrible wounds and mutilations he received whilst commanding the Boer artillery at the battle of Machadodorp. He discoursed of friends of poor Lawlor's whom he knew in Germany, and how he hoped soon to be able to return there.

General Pole-Carew's column remained to occupy Waterval Onder, the Cavalry Division returning to their last night's bivouac above Waterval Boven.

Owing to our occupation of Waterval Onder and General Buller's advance north, the enemy released Release of all our prisoners at Nooitgedacht, a few miles prisoners, Nooit- down the railway line, telling them that for gedacht. certain reasons they found it advisable to do so, and requesting them not to loot the farms on their way. Late in the afternoon they wandered in to General French's outposts, and we made them as comfortable as possible with our small stock of supplies and clothing. They included our Yeomanry taken at Lindley, and also Lieut. Rundle of the Carabiniers, whom I have previously mentioned as being captured with his patrol—a dashing young officer, destined, later in the war, to die fighting for his country.

There was some talk as to whom the credit was due for the release of these prisoners. The general advance had compelled the enemy to evacuate Nooitgedacht. Being unable to take their prisoners with them, the Boers directed them to our nearest force.

The Cavalry Division proceeded to Machadodorp, a wretched little place of about twenty houses. As August 31. it had a great name, and had for some time been used by Mr. Kruger as the capital of the Republic, I expected something a little larger; but most of the Boer towns consist of only a few houses with tin roofs, a store, and a church. More desolate spots cannot be imagined, and any adornments, such as gardens, round these wretched buildings are usually utterly ignored. Truly, it is an uncivilised country.

Next day Lord Roberts arrived by special train, and proceeded with General French to Waterval Sept. 1. Lord Roberts. Boven, the railway being intact there and the cog line luckily not destroyed. At this spot there is a tunnel and a very steep gradient— so steep that the novel device of a cog line has to be employed, for which special engines are necessary. To have destroyed these and the tunnel would have been a serious blow to our line of communications, and, although the Boers did enormous damage in blowing up bridges and communications, they were often neglectful and, despite their practice, certainly not adepts in the art of demolition. Their usual method of blowing up bridges, for instance, was to insert the charges of dynamite at the top of the piers,

M 2

and so blow up the roadway.   If, however, the
charges had been inserted at the foot of the stone
piers, the foundations would have been blown away,
and this would have made the work of reconstruc-
tion greater.

CHAPTER XIII

A WIDE TURNING MOVEMENT—CAPTURE
OF BARBERTON

GENERAL FRENCH's task now was a wide turning movement, *viâ* Carolina, on Barberton, which was brilliantly accomplished in the face of great difficulties. It was a hard task, and one of the most brilliant performances of the war. Our armies were practically held up, unable to advance : General Pole-Carew unable to push on from Waterval Onder, and General Buller, in difficulties, advancing on Lydenburg. In order to enable a general forward movement, General French undertook to make a wide turning movement through most difficult mountainous country, and boldly to attack Barberton : this, when cut off from any reinforcements, with no base of supplies to fall back on, and through a country full of the enemy. Any retirement on his part would have been dire disaster ; but retirement was not one of General French's mottoes, and he successfully executed a task that few generals would have cared to undertake. Certainly supplies and support were promised from General Hutton's forces from Kaapsche Hook ; but General Hutton found himself, like the other armies, unable to advance, and, further, that he was in such a precipitous country

that his efforts to advance supplies were futile ; so,
like the rest of our armies, he sat on the top of a hill,
and all waited for French to do or die. To give
General Hutton his due, he had volunteered to go to
General Pole-Carew's help. He successfully cleared
the country round him and then took up a position
on Kaapsche Hook, where he was a powerful factor
in protecting one of General French's flanks from
attack.

On September 2 our 1st Brigade, under General
Gordon, marched to Zevenfontein. The regiment,
Inniskilling Dragoons, with a pom-pom, was
sent on in advance to clear the way. Pushing
on rapidly, we drove back small parties of
the enemy, reconnoitring a wide extent of
country, and occupied Welgelegen ; then
returned and took up a line of outposts in front of
Zevenfontein, the enemy in some force sniping from
the hills to the east.

On the 3rd the 4th Brigade followed. The enemy
on the hills to the east had a pom-pom and a long
gun in position. To hide the latter from our
view, it was covered up with blankets, which they
removed to extinguish a sudden grass fire ; so the
gun was exposed. Our artillery was placed in
position, but neither side opened fire. The Boer
guns were laid on us, and we had our guns concealed
at close range. Momentarily we expected the enemy
to open fire ; but, strange to say, they did not do so,
and I can only imagine that they were short of
ammunition. The arrival of the 4th Brigade appeared to give a grand chance to capture their guns ;
at any rate, we longed to see our artillery open on
them, but the orders were not to attack. The last

Sept. 2. General French's march to Carolina and Barberton.

night had been a hard one for me, arranging the outposts in the dark; and, when going round this
morning, the atmosphere was so clear that I could
see every movement of the enemy on the hill opposite. One Boer, out of bravado, as it was too far for
effective rifle fire, waved and fired his rifle at me.

We had an unexpected feast to-day, and tasted
fish for the first time during the war. A native was
captured with a haunch of venison and a fish from
the Komati River, which were being sent by one of
the Boers to his wife, who pretended to be most
friendly, and lived at their farm just inside our
lines. She came to see Major Allenby as we were
breakfasting, and eyed the fish longingly. She
was sure, if we would let the native go back with
a note from her, her man would come in and surrender. Meantime, she utilised her opportunity to
sell us poultry, and doubtless, on our departure, husband and wife reunited had a hearty laugh over the
silly English and the good business they themselves
had done.

Captain Jackson, of the Inniskilling Dragoons,
with a small patrol, reconnoitred at night to Bonnefoi,
across the Komati River, and discovered that a commando of the enemy was in that neighbourhood. It
was a difficult and dangerous reconnaissance well
executed.

The brigade advanced beyond Welgelegen, the
Inniskilling Dragoons, with two pom-poms attached,
again in advance to clear the way. We met
Sept. 4. the enemy in a difficult country with the
regiment much extended. The New South Wales
Lancers Squadron and Captain Hamilton, Inniskilling Squadron, seized an important hill which

commanded the Komati River, with only a few casualties—one man (New South Wales Lancers) was mortally wounded in the abdomen, and Lance-Sergeant Curley (Inniskillings) severely wounded. My squadron raced for a hill guarding the left flank, and gained it just in time to repulse the enemy with some loss.   We were fighting till dark, and remained holding the advanced positions.   It was 10 P.M. ere our outpost line was fixed.   Taking up an outpost line in the dark, through bogs and rocky hills, was again a difficult, wearisome task, and, with the enemy in such close proximity, it was necessary to be extremely alert.   That the sentries were alive to this was proved by a shot at midnight.   Rushing to the place where the sound came from, I discovered the shot to have been fired by one of the sentries at a horse galloping on him.   Receiving no answer to his challenge, he fired and killed the horse.   It proved to be a loose horse and, further, an officer's charger; its owner was, naturally, highly indignant, but I could not help being pleased at the alertness of the sentry and his good shot.

At 4 A.M. on the 5th we lined the heights.   The 4th Brigade relieved and had a few casualties, one

Sept. 5.

man and horse went down, shot as they were taking up our position, whilst we pushed on over the Komati River, and all bivouacked at Bonnefoi, the 6th Dragoon Guards occupying the heights in advance without opposition.   Just after taking up our bivouac we had one of our many narrow escapes from a veldt fire.   The long grass at this time of year is dry as tinder, the slightest spark will set it in flames, and at once one is surrounded with a prairie fire, which is a most serious affair, and

stampedes the horses and burns up saddles and all
one's kit and accoutrements. Some one carelessly
throws away the end of a lighted match, or the cooks
do not properly clear the grass before starting their
fires, and the country, in a minute, is a blaze of fire.
Everyone seizes his blanket and does his utmost to
beat it out. This evening it was only by the united
efforts of every officer and man that we saved the
bivouac, and the flame of fire swept away over the
country. The grass fires by night are a lovely sight.
The Boers generally fired them when retiring, in
order to destroy the grazing for us, and that we
might offer better targets when advancing over the
blackened space ; so every night the country for miles
around was a blaze of light that illumined the lurid
skies. Just before dark I shot three guinea-fowl
and a hare, which were a welcome addition to our
squadron mess.

Next day we had a stiff climb up these heights,
and marched over an open country to Carolina, with
only a few snipers about. One man was
Sept. 6. treacherously shot from a farm flying the
white flag, and I was told that General French, on
hearing this, ordered a gun to be turned on it.

We took up a large outpost line round the
town. The Suffolk Regiment arrived, and next day
(7th) General Mahon's force joined us, consisting of
Mounted Infantry, Imperial Light Horse, Lumsden's
Powder Horse, &c. We destroyed a well-built
magazine powder magazine at Carolina, which must
at
Carolina. have been erected before the war—another
proof of the way the country had been arming.
We lost some horses here from eating tulip-grass ;
five of our artillery horses and also one of Colonel

Gordon's chargers died from eating it whilst out grazing. This tulip-grass, which comes up with the first
Tulip-   young grass and has a small yellow flower,
grass.   grows in most parts of South Africa. Horses
will eat it ravenously, and it is most fatal to them ;
they should never be grazed where any is seen about.
The specimen illustrated I picked at Carolina.

The combined force—viz. the Cavalry Division,
Mahon's mounted column, and the Suffolk Regiment,
Sept. 9.   all under General French—marched for
Barberton, the 1st Cavalry Brigade (Gordon's)
on the right, Mahon's Brigade on the left, 4th Cavalry
Brigade (Dickson's) in the rear. At mid-day we reached
rough, mountainous country, and engaged the enemy,
who made a good resistance, at Roodehoogte. The
1st Cavalry Brigade on the right and Mahon's Imperial
Light Horse on the left were pushed forward on the
flanks, engaging the enemy in rough country. The
latter were disputing our advance down the road to
Buffels Spruit, but their flanks were threatened and
our artillery was in a commanding position. The
Suffolk Regiment, which was now brought up, made
a fine attack in the centre, the enemy being repulsed
and retiring fighting. On the right our 1st Cavalry
Brigade descended through rough, broken country,
fighting till dark, the Inniskillings a long way in
Lieut.   advance to the front. Lieut. Paterson, with
Paterson. his troop, galloped on to a big hill, and
climbed the precipitous sides just in time to forestall
the enemy and drive them back, giving us this commanding position. It was a fine piece of dash, and
fairly surprised the Boers. They had one long-range
gun and a pom-pom, with which they made accurate
practice, our artillery being unable to locate them.

TULP GRASS (*Homeria pallida*).

The regiment (Inniskillings), pressing a long
way in advance of the 1st Brigade, bivouacked at
night on the ground gained.   The enemy, turning
their guns on us, placed their shells well into
my squadron, but luckily without damage.   Our
casualties, considering the close fighting, were small :
one of the Suffolks killed, and amongst the wounded
three of the Imperial Light Horse.   Four or five of
the enemy were known to have been killed, and many
were wounded.   They retreated during the night,
going south.   Fighting after dark, a long way ahead
of the main body, Major Allenby decided to hold
the ground we had won, and we settled down to a
wretched night of watchfulness, without food.   It
was, however, a day to be remembered, and with
which General French must have felt satisfied.   The
successful attack of the Suffolks in the centre, the
work of the Imperial Light Horse on the left, and
Allenby's fine advance of the Inniskillings wide on
the right, movements all executed with slight loss
in most difficult country, made a good start of the
advance to Barberton, and proved most demoralising
to the enemy.

At 6.30 A.M. our forces united and marched along
the Buffels Spruit to Koppie Aleen.   The enemy
had got their big gun away ; the cleverly
Sept. 10.   concealed position from which it had been
firing the previous day was revealed by the gun
tracks, behind the top ridge of a small kopje, from
which it defied observation.   Only a few snipers
were about.   The country was very rough and impracticable for cavalry, the hills on each side of the
valley, along which the awful road ran, being rocky
and covered with bushes.   Our transport was too

big, rendering progress very slow. In such a country infantry would have been more useful, as they could travel as fast as mounted troops, and would not have required the huge transport necessary for horses ; the latter also were only a target for the enemy.

With the regiment, Inniskilling Dragoons, again in advance, we marched on the 11th to Hlomo Hlom,
Sept. 11. where we crossed the Komati River at the drift.   Here   the   forces   bivouacked,   the Inniskilling Dragoons advancing two miles and throwing out a line of outposts at the foot of the mountains which rise beyond. We expected great opposition, but the enemy could be viewed everywhere retreating, and only a few remained to snipe. With my advanced squadron I captured a wagon loaded with Martini ammunition, and also secured yesterday's Barberton mails at Hlomo Hlom, which is a post office. The place consists, however, of only the one building.

After leaving the Komati Valley here the road winds up a precipitous range of mountains and through a nek (Nelhoogte Pass) on to the high plateau to the south-west of Barberton ; it was a range and nek that appeared impregnable, and it could easily have been rendered so by the enemy. General Hutton was expected to aid us from Kaapsche Hook by threatening the left from Tafel Kop, and also getting supplies to us. He, however, reported afterwards that the country was impracticable.   Our advance appeared impossible ; a retreat would have been disaster. General French determined to force the road, the 1st Brigade attacking on the right.

It looked hopeless to get animals up the precipitous, broken mountains by any way but the winding road. However, the orders were to go at it. Accordingly at 3 A.M. on the 12th the Inniskilling Dragoons, with two squadrons of the 6th Dragoon Guards and a pom-pom, under Major Allenby, started in advance, General Gordon, with the rest of the brigade, supporting. Crossing the branch river of the Komati River in the dark, where several horses came to grief in the rocky bed, we somehow floundered through and commenced the ascent, along steep tracks, through a chaos of heights and precipices. The pom-pom we could not get along, and we led our horses where it was impossible to ride. At dawn we were a long way up, having successfully wound our way through apparently impossible places. With squadrons of the Inniskillings and Carabiniers in advanced line, in touch as near as possible, we rushed up and kept crowning each height above us. Suddenly, at the top of one which we had rushed up on foot, Lieut. Paterson's Inniskilling squadron in advance saw about 100 of the enemy bivouacked. Quickly volleys were poured into them, effecting a grand surprise. The Boers had evidently slept there with no look-out, and were just getting ready to take up position. Our sudden fire from such an unexpected quarter completely routed them, and they fled, leaving many articles behind, only one or two stopping on the further heights to fire back. We estimated that many were wounded.

This fine dash of the Inniskillings and squadron of Carabiniers quite decided the situation. On we rushed, on horseback where we could, otherwise dragging horses up the rocks, and gained the ridge

(Margin note: Sept. 12. Night march successful.)

next to that commanding the right flank of the road through the nek. From this the enemy gave us a heavy fire, but we got cover and brought our Maxim into action. It was only possible to approach this position by a narrow ridge of kopjes on our left. Lieut. Paterson's troop advanced some way along this ridge, but was stopped by the shell fire of our own people as well as the enemy. The former, not expecting us so soon on these heights, were preparing this ridge for an infantry attack. Meantime General French, advancing at daylight along the valley below, with Colonel Mahon's force in front, brought his guns into action, and most effectively shelled the ridge; but still the enemy held on firing. Then General Gordon, supporting us, with the Scots Greys and Hussars, got up our tracks two guns and a pom-pom. To get guns up those precipitous heights, through rocks that horses could scarcely climb, was a marvellous performance that the Royal Horse Artillery may well be proud of. Major Lecky was in charge of the guns, with Captain Griffin in charge of the pom-pom. Colonel Jeffries was present directing.

Good work of the R.H.A.

With these guns opening fire on the flank, we were enabled to get round the exposed nek and seize the final height commanding the road through the pass, about 1,500 feet above our original starting-post. It was about 2 P.M. when half a battalion of the Suffolks, having climbed up from the valley below, joined us on this ridge and took the final position, the Boers not waiting after they got within 300 yards of them. General Gordon heliographed down to General French that he commanded the road; the infantry from the centre climbed up to us and

continued the fighting; our big guns cleared the
heights on the left of the pass; the Imperial Light
Horse dashed on by the road through the nek; and
we had taken this impregnable position with scarcely
any casualties. The enemy had two long-range guns
and a pom-pom, which they removed early in the
day, and from which they opened fire again at a long
range. We saw them for miles retreating over great
mountains in the direction of Steynsdorp, driving
before them huge flocks of cattle and sheep. I estimated that I saw about 1,500 mounted Boers, and
that only a few hundred remained to oppose us, in
order to give time to the others to get their stock
away. We captured a good many; also large
numbers of cattle and sheep, and twenty
wagons laden with supplies. We bivouacked at
dark—men and horses quite done. Three more
horses in my squadron died to-day from
exhaustion. We had, however, done a great
performance in terrific country, suitable only for
goats. We heard afterwards that the Boers had
reckoned that it would be quite impossible for us to
make an attack from the flank.

Captures.

Loss of
horses.

It was long after dark before we reached our
bivouac, but at 3 A.M. on the 13th we again advanced; the orders being for the 1st Brigade
to seize Barberton, General Mahon's force of
Imperial Light Horse, &c., to continue the pursuit
of the enemy retreating by the road through the
mountains to Steynsdorp, and the 4th Brigade and
infantry, under General Dickson, to hold this range
and guard our transport, which the Engineers estimated would take some days to get up. General
French himself accompanied the 1st Brigade. It was

Sept. 13.

General Gordon's wish that the regiment should
again lead the advance; but, after doing this hard
work for so many consecutive days, the horses could
scarcely crawl, so the post of honour was allotted to
the Scots Greys, to be supported by the Carabiniers and then ourselves. This, alas! instead of
a rest, proved to be the hardest task of all for the
Inniskillings.

Barberton was reported by our guide as eighteen
miles direct by a track down the mountains; thirty-
five miles by the only road. We found the track
impossible for our guns, so the Inniskilling Dragoons
were ordered to escort them round by the road, the
remainder of the brigade, with General French and
Capture of General Gordon, going direct on Barberton,
Barberton. which they surprised and occupied without
resistance. Some of the enemy escaped to the hills;
about 200 surrendered. The town was full of Boer
women. Many of the British residents had been
turned out of their houses for the women whom
Lord Roberts had previously sent over to the enemy
from Pretoria. There were large quantities of stores
in the town, especially flour, the goods station being
crammed with it; also thirty locomotives, slightly
disabled by the removal of driving-pins. Twenty
wagons and a Cape cart also were captured. The
cart was escaping with about 1,400*l.* in specie, and
was taken by Major Scobell, of the Greys, who was
in advance and entered the town with only thirty
men, as all had to lead single file down the mountain
track. Much of the specie, however, proved to be in
Government promissory notes.

So as not to be quite out of it, we sent an officer
with the advance to purchase some food and neces-

BARBERTON.

saries. Thus I secured an excellent pair of K boots
—a great boon, as many of ours, not for the first time
during the war, were almost soleless through footing
it up the rocky kopjes. About 400 of our prisoners,
including Colonel Roberts, of the Lincolns, Captain
Egerton Green, 12th Lancers, &c., were found in the
prison and released.

Meantime, the Inniskillings, in ignorance of what
opposition might be met, escorted the guns the
thirty-five miles round by the road, an arduous task.
We marched along a high plateau which overlooked
the valley in which Barberton is situated ; then we
descended by what is called the chute, the road
winding for miles down some places which are almost
perpendicular. The wheels of the guns and transport
had to be tied, and all the horses except the wheelers
in the guns taken out. We got the guns down
safely, however, and, except for a little sniping in
the morning, met no opposition. We travelled the
valley till dark, crossing the Queen's and Concession
Rivers by fairly good drifts, and then, the horses
being quite done, bivouacked six miles from Barberton, B Squadron Inniskillings in advance only going
on to the town.

Everywhere there were signs of the enemy's
retreat : great tracks of cattle and sheep, dead oxen,
lambs with their throats cut, and many alive and
only just born. At mid-day we obtained helio-
communication with General Hutton from Kaapsche
Hoop. He reported the country impossible for
wagons, that he had had two slight engagements
with the enemy, who on our approach had abandoned
their position, leaving three guns—the latter capture
was not afterwards confirmed.

N

At daylight we escorted our guns into Barberton, which is situated under steep heights. From these some snipers fired into the market square, wounding one man. General French at once issued notice that if there was any sniping the troops would be withdrawn and the town bombarded. This effectually stopped it. The following is a copy of this notice :

Sept. 14.

TO THE INHABITANTS OF BARBERTON.	AAN DE INWONERS VAN BARBERTON.
——	——
This is to give notice that if any Shooting into the Town or Sniping in its vicinity takes place, the Lieutenant General Commanding will withdraw the Troops, and shell the Town without further notice.	Hiermede geschiedt kennis dat indien eenig schieten in het dorp of in de nabyheid plaats vindt, de Luitenant Generaal in bevel de troepen zal onttrekken en zonder verder kennis het dorp bombardeeren.
By order	By order
D. Haig Lt. Col.	D. Haig Lt. Col.
Chief Staff Officer to	Chief Staff Officer to
Lt. General French.	Lt. General French.
Barberton,	Barberton,
Sept. 13, 1900.	Sept. 13, 1900.

The regiment, Inniskilling Dragoons, took up a big outpost line round Barberton. Being in charge, I used up three horses fixing and riding round it. The weather was intensely hot, and, like many others, I felt utterly worn out with our late exertions day and night. Several of the enemy came in to give up their arms. General French held a ceremonial parade and hoisted the British flag. Communication by helio and wire was established with Lord Roberts, who congratulated General French on his smart work.

Sept. 15.

After dark Major Allenby received orders to march at daybreak with the regiment, Inniskilling Innis-killings. Dragoons, and a pom-pom, taking two days' supplies, and to seize the Sheba Mine, 1,600 feet above, and fourteen miles from Barberton. The enemy, with two guns, were supposed to be in occupation. We had looked forward to a sadly needed rest; but it could not be, and our night was spent in handing over the outposts, which I had just withdrawn, to a night line. At 3.30 A.M. reveille, and at 5 A.M. on the 16th we started in the dark. Speaking of reveille, I may mention that no bugles or trumpets were ever used for this purpose; in fact, they were entirely discarded by the cavalry until the closing scenes of the war as doing more harm than good. Further, until I was lying wounded in hospital, I never heard a military band, and then it was a treat.

To continue my narrative: a guide accompanied us, by name Cooper, a daring fellow who blew up the Komati Poort railway bridge some time ago. He was then captured and sentenced to death; but President Kruger remitted the sentence to penal servitude, and we released him from the jail here. He remained with us till I left, and proved of great service. He was a splendid Swazie interpreter, knew the country well, obtained valuable information, and would go out for days by himself, always returning with horses and cattle, which he obtained from the enemy through his knowledge of the natives.

CHAPTER XIV

AT EUREKA CITY—THE SHEBA MINE

AFTER leaving the valley we marched through the Elephants' Kloof, a deep gorge with precipitous bushy sides, and only the one possible narrow road to move along ; gradually we climbed the 1,600 feet up to Fairview. This is a kloof into which the hunters used to drive the elephants, and from which they could not escape. Some years ago highwaymen held up the secretary of the Sheba Mine at this spot, robbing him of 2,000*l*., which he was conveying for wages, and the bones of his horse, which they shot, are still lying by the side of the road.

Inniskilling Dragoons march to Eureka City.

It was a relief to find that the enemy did not oppose, as our task would have been murderous ; about a dozen rifles could have stopped the column ; luckily for us the Boers had retired, taking their guns. Panting and blown, we gained the top ; advancing along the neks and ridges until we occupied all the heights over the Sheba Hill, we made our head-quarters in Eureka City. Captain Griffin, R.A., with the aid of our men, managed to drag up the pom-pom—a great achievement, as it takes fifty oxen to drag vehicles up. There are a great many houses scattered about on the sides of the mountains,

AVOCA BRIDGE, WRECKED BY THE BOERS SEPTEMBER 15, 1900.

THE EXPLOSION WHICH WRECKED THE AVOCA BRIDGE,
AS SEEN FROM SHEBA SIDING.

and several stores, which were fairly well stocked. We took several Boer prisoners and were welcomed by a large number of English inhabitants, managers of mines, and employés, who had stuck to their posts during the war. Around, on the sides of the mountains, are the mines—the Sheba, Bon Accord, Joe's Luck, &c. These were undamaged. Mr. Leggitt, the acting manager of the Sheba, who was throughout our stay of great service to the troops, informed me that everything was in order to start working; that the Boers had seized the mine, tried working it for a short time, and then deserted it, sending the natives over the border; that the natives were quite willing and anxious to come back; and that he could start in about six weeks. Yesterday the enemy had blown up the railway bridge over the Kaap River at Avoca. Mr. Holman, of the Royal Sheba, gave me the accompanying photograph of the explosion, and regretted that we had not been a day earlier, or that he had not had a few armed men with him, who, well placed in the hills, would, he considered, have scared the enemy from effecting the explosion.

Mr. Leggitt.

Mr. Leggitt piloted an officer (Lieut. Harris) down on the Sheba tram and light railway; he returned, reporting fifty-two locomotives on the railway and few of the enemy about. At my suggestion Major Allenby at once ordered a troop of the N.S.W. Lancers, under Lieut. Nicholson, to proceed down by the railway, occupy Avoca, and guard the locomotives, which were found to be intact. This was successfully done; they kept off the enemy, took several prisoners, and held the place until the arrival of reinforcements a few days

Capture by Inniskillings of 52 locomotives.

later; 1,400 tons of coal and engine oil were also secured. We established helio communication with Barberton from a post at Fairview.

From September 16 to October 2 the regiment, Inniskilling Dragoons, remained in occupation of the mines, the squadrons being scattered four miles apart, from Fairview to Eureka City, on almost inaccessible heights; the country all round a broken-up chaos of mountains—mountains tumbled about in heaps. A ten minutes' walk in any direction meant about an hour's climb back; such a spot was certainly unique for a cavalry regiment—even cows could not be kept on these heights. Water was a great difficulty; but the mines helped us to secure a sufficiency. The horses had to be led, single file, down precipices, to the various little springs or spots where water was pumped out of the mines. Food supplies were sent out from Barberton by rail, and then got up by means of an aerial tram, and later by the Sheba tram

Mr. Leggitt, Mr. Metcalf, Mr. Holman.

and pack donkeys. Mr. Leggitt of the Sheba, Mr. Metcalf of the United Reef, and Mr. Holman of the Royal Sheba especially, gave valuable aid and information. Mr. Leggitt supplied materials and skilled labour for the deviation of the railway line at Avoca over the river, which Major Hunter Weston, R.E., came out to superintend on September 17.

That night some of us dined with Mr. Metcalf, and it was indeed a treat to behold once more a tablecloth and a nicely arranged dinner-table. He fired my enthusiasm with the accounts of his great experiences, big game hunting in South Africa, and of how, in earlier days, he fought for dear life, with elephant guns, against hordes of savages; and of the

VIEW OF SHEBA MINE FROM ONE OF OUR OUTPOSTS AT EUREKA CITY.

PACK DONKEYS WHICH BROUGHT OUR SUPPLIES UP TO EUREKA CITY.

big game that was to be procured now, within a day or two of us. This gentleman placed his steam aerial tram at our disposal for getting up stores. This consisted of a steel wire that ran from the top of the mountains for some miles to the railway in the Kaap Valley below, which carried buckets large enough to hold a man. It shows how precipitous the side of the mountain was. Thus we got up our stores sent out from Barberton, nine miles by rail. He suffered much from the wanton destruction to his property near Avoca by some of our own troops, when they advanced along the Kaap Valley, and they also, to our great inconvenience, damaged the aerial line.

Major Hunter Weston required, amongst other things, 1,500 natives to construct the deviation to replace the Avoca Bridge. The mine managers did their best, and many were secured ; but, meantime, the infantry all set to work as navvies—a trying, hard, uninteresting work, that fell so often to their lot during the war. Brilliant Guards and other regiments all had to take their turn at this work, generally under a broiling sun, and often within sniping range of the Boers. Yet the rate at which they got the lines back into working order under the direction of the Royal Engineers was marvellous. The Suffolks, under Colonel Mackenzie, were now hard at this work.

Major Allenby acted as Governor of the district, and issued the latest proclamations, which were to the effect that all who surrendered would be made prisoners of war, but would not be sent out of the country unless they had committed unmilitary acts. He interrogated the prisoners and collected the arms, many of which were of obsolete patterns. The Boers, on occupation, seized all the mine arms and left many old weapons in their place. The following is a specimen of a proclamation :

V.   R.

NOTICE.

TREATMENT OF THE INHABITANTS.

The following orders of the Field Marshal Commander in Chief, contained in telegram No. C5065, dated Pretoria Sept. 28th, are promulgated.

By order.

D. HAIG, Lt. Col.,

Barberton,   C.S.O. to General French.

Oct. 1, 1900.

As it seems to me advisable to insure uniformity in the treatment of the inhabitants of the various districts of the Transvaal or Orange River Colony, the following instructions are hereby published to assist General Officers Commanding in carrying out the conditions of recent proclamations issued by me.

1st. By Military Secretary telegram No. C4825, dated Sept. 20, General Officers Commanding have been empowered to promise that Burghers who surrender voluntarily will not be sent out of South Africa provided they have been guilty of no acts other than fighting against us which should debar them from this privilege ; this concession does not apply to those who have taken prominent military or political part in the war, nor to those who have broken their oath of neutrality, nor to foreigners. In the event of a military or political leader enquiring as to terms of surrender, the question is to be referred direct to Army Head Quarters.

2nd. All stock, supplies etc., of those on commando or of those who have broken their oath are to be taken and no receipts given.

3rd. In cases where some members of a family who all live on one farm have broken their oath and gone on commando those remaining are to be warned that unless the former surrendered within a reasonable period all stock, supplies etc., will be taken and no receipt given.

4th. In cases of sniping, leaders of bands are to be informed that unless it ceases, their (leaders') houses will be burned; a few days should be allowed for this to become known, notices being sent to the resorts of the leaders and to their wives; in the event of its being necessary to burn the farms, further notice should be issued stating why this has been done and giving a list of other houses that will next be burned.

5th. All stock, supplies etc., of snipers are to be taken and no receipt given.

6th. Protection is to be given to all inhabitants who have kept the oath of neutrality, remaining quietly at home and taking no further part in the war. Any stock and supplies taken from them are to be paid for, or receipts in full given for them.

7th. Wives and families of men who are prisoners of war are to be protected and receipts in full given for anything. When a man surrenders, a protection pass is to be given to his wife.

8th. Widows of men killed in the war and all lone women are to receive protection passes, and to be paid or given receipts for anything taken.

9th. Burghers are to be informed that as soon as their Leaders submit and when every cannon has been surrendered peace will be declared, and all prisoners of war will then be sent back to their homes. Exceptions only will be made in the cases of members of the Governments of the South African Republic and Orange Free State who are responsible for the War and its present disastrous prolongation, and of those who may be proved to have been guilty of acts contrary to the customs of war.

The way having been cleared by General French, General Pole-Carew's forces advanced along the Kaap Sept. 18. Valley and bivouacked four miles beyond General Pole- Avoca, engaging a few of the enemy and Carew. making some captures. The Imperial Light Horse also passed Eureka City, reconnoitring towards French Bobs on the Swazie border, where the mountains are terrific—a duty we expected the regiment would be ordered to undertake. On this day also General French and staff visited the Sheba, expressing satisfaction with the arrangements.

Owing to the destruction of the aerial tram we

were now cut off from our food supply at its
terminus, Joe's Luck Siding, on the railway below,
_{Sept. 20.} and another way of obtaining it had to be
_{Avoca.}   devised.   Accordingly I was sent down with
Mr. Metcalf to make arrangements.   We had the
supplies sent on by rail to Avoca, thence by the
Sheba light railway round the north side of the
mountain up to the Sheba mine.   From there it was
conveyed by pack donkeys up to our camp—a slow,
tedious process.

At Avoca I saw Lieut. Nicholson, in command
of the New South Wales Lancers, who had been
guarding the place and locomotives.   He described a
clever capture, on his first arrival, of three Boers on a
neighbouring farm.   Visiting the farm, he found only
a woman, who assured him that she had not seen her
husband or any of the men for many months.   He
noticed, however, that she was cooking a large meal,
so, saying ' Good-bye,' he and his troopers hid in the
vicinity, and, very shortly, in rode the husband and
two other Boers.   Surrounding the place quickly, he
cleverly captured and brought them back prisoners.
Noticing small details is one of the arts of scouting,
and in it our colonial brothers excel.   Lieut. Nicholson
himself was a fine specimen.   Though getting on in
life, he was capable and worthy of a much higher
command ; but on the war breaking out he cheerfully
undertook the duties of a subaltern.

Whilst at Avoca, General Ian Hamilton's force of
Royal Scots, &c., was passing *en route* to Komati
Poort, and, the need of the New South Wales
Lancers as a guard for the place being over, I was
glad to be able to obtain the order for their return to
the regiment.

Lord Roberts was reported at Nels Spruit, and the utter rout of the enemy confirmed. Mr. Metcalf's

Sept. 21.

son, who was in the Imperial Light Horse, returned with his corps, *en route* to Barberton, from their expedition to French Bobs, and they reported the Boers utterly demoralised and routed everywhere, having destroyed their big guns and run the locomotives from the railway line into the river at Komati Poort. The Kaffirs, who are wonderful for getting intelligence, which they shout from hill-top to hill-top, further reported that the Portuguese had requested our blue-jackets to come from Delagoa Bay to Komati Poort in order to keep order there from the Boer inundation.

Lord Kitchener visited Avoca. We heard that he was much pleased with the capture of the fifty-

Sept. 22.
Lord
Kitchener.

two locomotives, for which we certainly deserved the credit that, I fear, we never got. A trooper yesterday, sitting by me and carelessly handling a revolver, nearly shot me. The bullet, however, went through his own thigh and he suffered great agony, and repeatedly asked God why he was ever born. I bandaged him up and got a doctor. For some days he was in a critical state, but eventually he recovered. Anyone reading the daily casualty list during the war must have been struck by the number of 'accidentally shot.' Carelessness with firearms, especially with such weapons as Mauser pistols, was generally the cause, and this is only one instance of many I myself saw.

Generals French, Gordon, and Staff, including

Sept. 25.

Colonel Haig, Captains Bingham, Abadie, and Algie Lawson, rode over from Barberton, glad, I think, to visit our cooler heights. Whilst here they received the news through our heliographs that our troops had occupied Komati Poort, the enemy retreating and throwing their big guns into the river; further, that General Pole-Carew had recovered fifteen of their guns. The railway from Barberton to Pretoria was opened for the first time, the deviation at Avoca being completed.

Sept. 27.

Captain Prince Alexander of Teck, who rendered good service when attached to the regiment in the early part of the war and was most popular with all ranks, came out from Barberton with Captain Deare, of the 8th Hussars, to spend the night with us. They reported the heat there great and several suffering from fever, but all was quiet.

Sept. 28.

We accompanied them over the Sheba Mine, which is a wonderful sight and different from other gold-mines. The whole mountain is auriferous and the main reef 100 feet broad, so enormous caverns have been excavated for removing the gold-bearing quartz in the centre of the mountain, and these, when lit up with innumerable lights and by occasional openings in the side of the mountain, have an imposing effect. The cyanide process for collecting the gold after crushing was also of great interest. You can get on to the Sheba light railway and run down the hill for many miles, winding through lovely valleys until you reach Avoca. Strong brakes only are required, but it seems perilous. For the ascent very strong little locomotives are used, which can take only light weights. From the end of the line to the top of the Sheba Hill, which is called Eureka City, pack-donkeys must be used. Wonderful to say, they

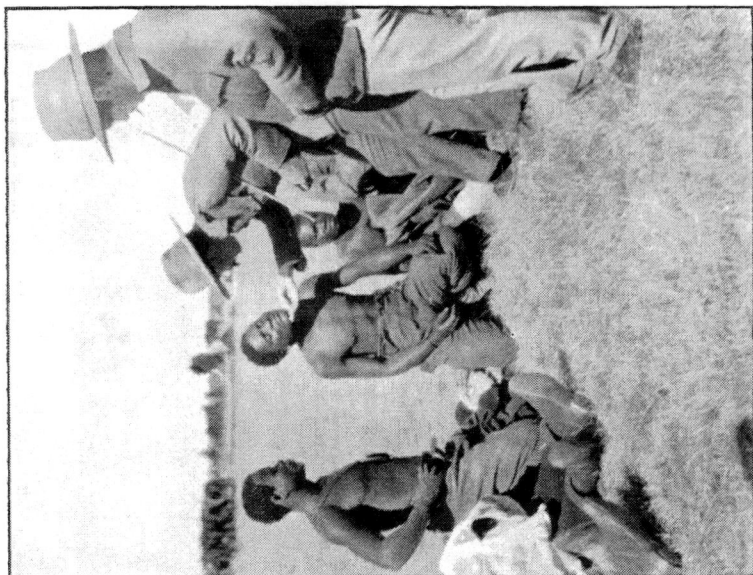

OUR DOCTORS EXAMINING SICK KAFFIRS.

A DIFFICULT TONGUE TO DIAGNOSE.

have a racecourse at Eureka City. The track winds
along the crest of the hills, and the only thing to
mark a racecourse is a wooden scaffolding, on which
is a small platform. This, you learn on inquiry, is
the judge's box. The course itself is full of steep
gradients, and in many places, if you were to run out,
you would not be seen again alive. The scaffolding
was, however, a cheering sight, and, doubtless, if we
had possessed horses that could gallop we should have
made use of it. Another remarkable thing was a
lawn-tennis court, cleverly levelled in the side of the
hill and enclosed with netting; on this we were permitted to enjoy some capital recreation.

At Avoca we found fresh arrivals, viz. the
Colonel and Staff of the 20th Company Rough
Riders, including Colonel Colvin, Major Anderson,
and Viscount Maitland (Adjutant). They received
us hospitably and took charge of our guests, who
eventually spent a rough night getting back to Barberton, whilst we returned by the light railway to the
top of the Sheba Hill.

On October 1 one squadron proceeded to Avoca
to escort transport from there to Kaapsche Hoop,
and on the 2nd the regiment received orders
to retire to Barberton, pass through the town,
and bivouac four miles to the west. During our
stay at Eureka City we had managed to get a few
Cape carts up from Barberton with squadron mess
stores. Getting them down was more dangerous
than up, as, if a brake gave, there was dire disaster.
My squadron cart, unfortunately, met its fate. While
we were waiting anxiously for it that night at our
bivouac, in dark and drenching rain, the messman
arrived on foot to report the cart totally wrecked and

Oct. 1.

all our stores gone ! Luckily, another kind squadron mess that had been more fortunate saved us from starvation. It was a dreadful night of raging thunderstorms, but we were fortunate in not being exposed to them on the Sheba heights, as the lightning was most dangerous.

CHAPTER XV

FROM BARBERTON TO MACHADODORP

ON the morning of October 3 the Cavalry Division, under General French, commenced a march to Machadodorp in a terrific thunderstorm, which had raged all night and lasted throughout the day, rendering progress slow. Two men of the Royal Horse Artillery, several horses, and seven mules were killed by lightning. Many of us also received shocks, having our arms or legs numbed, as if from a severe blow. One flash burnt my cheek, and the lightning fairly ran along the ground among us. Some of the effects were ridiculous. One man standing by me was indignant, thinking someone had given him a most violent kick behind. After proceeding about twenty miles we bivouacked at the foot of the Devil's Kantoor. Luckily, the night was fine, and we managed to get a limited supply of wood for a fire to dry our clothes, but most of the men had to walk about all night to keep warm.

In the morning we commenced the long ascent, but were obliged to halt as we found our transport, which had left Barberton on the 2nd, stuck in the mud all along the steep road, many beasts being dead. In the afternoon we

Oct. 3. March from Barberton to Machadodorp. Difficulties of country and weather, but no opposition.

Oct. 4. The Devil's Kantoor.

climbed to the top, and our Royal Horse Artillery, by continual double-spanning, got their guns up. Colonel Alderson, with Mounted Infantry, was in occupation at the summit.   Captain Charlie Beatty was his A.D.C., and lamenting Colonel McCalmont's fine stud of race-horses that he ought to have been superintending at Newmarket.   The old Kaap Gold-fields are there, where a 50-lb. nugget was once found, the owner making a good profit by exhibiting it in Barberton at 1s. a head.   There was a lovely view of Barberton from the summit of the Kaapsche Hoop over the volcanic valley below, that looked like a mass of huge green ant-heaps.

Oct. 5.   Next day the orders to march were can-celled, and the day was spent in getting the transport up the mountain.

Oct. 6.   Then we marched to Goodwan Station, where we drew supplies, General French himself proceeding by rail to Machadodorp.

Having sent the baggage by rail, we made a long, hot, dusty march of quite twenty-two miles, that

Oct. 7.   rendered our eyes painfully sore, through a deep gorge with great mountains on each side, past Nooitgedacht, where is the wire enclosure in which our prisoners were confined, to Waterval Onder.   There we drew rations, and thence made the steep ascent out of the valley, bivouacking at dark on the heights above.   At Waterval Onder we visited the grave of our old comrade, Lieut. Lawlor.   The Scots Guards, who occupied the place after we had formerly left, had, with their usual kind feeling, erected a nice cross over the grave, for which we all felt a debt of gratitude.

We completed the march to Machadodorp, where

MAJOR DAUNCEY AT LIEUTENANT LAWLOR'S GRAVE
AT WATERVAL ONDER.

we found the South African Light Horse and other troops being broken up, General Buller being *en route* to England. There was a universal opinion that the Boer resistance was quite at an end. Lord Dundonald, amongst others of General Buller's commanders, was returning; most of the irregular corps were arranging to depart; and the South African Light Horse were disposing of everything and preparing to proceed to Natal for disbandment. Our Intelligence Department at this time was certainly at fault.

Oct. 8.

To give an idea of how matters were proceeding at another theatre of the war, the following letter, entitled 'A Boer Drive,' was forwarded by Colonel Rimington[1] at this time. Although Colonel of the regiment (Inniskilling Dragoons) which he dashingly led in person for a considerable period of the campaign, he was then commanding a column in the Orange River Colony, his position in the regiment being ably filled by our second in command, Major Allenby[2]:

A Boer Drive.

It is difficult to think of a better way of illustrating the extraordinary state of affairs in the Orange River Colony at this date, October 11, 1900, than by giving an account of how we spent the day before yesterday.

A sergeant and six men had been chased back when on the right flank patrol of an escort to a convoy. This must be looked into, and it was proposed to send out a small force early, before daylight, to investigate the matter.

But, on mature consideration, it was thought a

[1] Now Brigadier-General M. F. Rimington, C.B., Commanding Cavalry Brigade, Curragh.
[2] Now Colonel E. H. H. Allenby, C.B., Commanding 5th Lancers.

O

good sporting drive of Boers, in which the guns would be represented by a part of the infantry garrison—viz. two companies, assisted by seventy men of an Irregular corps and some thirty Yeomanry, with five hundred odd of the M.I. acting as drivers—would be more likely to give a good result.

Orders were given to the troops to parade at 3 A.M., about one hour and three-quarters before daylight.

So we had breakfast—chops and jam, bread and tea—at 2.15 A.M., and hurried down through the cold air to the rendezvous. No sooner there than we were off, and, after riding about half an hour, we halted and the plan was explained: how the M.I. were to march from the east, extending their left arm some eight miles from the road, and pushing the Boers west towards our line of infantry on the left and Irregulars on the right. These would also cover a front of nearly seven miles.

The Irregulars' only preparation was twenty extra rounds and a couple of biscuits in their pockets.

Blue overcoats were now folded up, and khaki was predominant.

Our furthest post on the right, under an experienced Colonial captain, moved off, and an hour later a very good line had been taken up, but not without some stir amongst the Boer farmers, whom we could plainly see, after we had crept up to a slight rise, galloping from farm to farm and going up to the kopjes to get a better view. Another party of two or three Boers began driving in their horses at a gallop, but a few shots from the Irregulars soon put a stop to that, and a lull followed.

Hullo! What is that dust, just in the eye of the sun, almost on the horizon? Is it Boer cattle, the M.I., Boers, or what?

With the aid of glasses—Ross or Zeiss—we can only say it looks most like cattle, and there are men riding at a fast pace near it. Now all is excitement as to which way they will turn. Our men get under the cover of the rocks and lie close and watch the Boers (I had almost said birds).

Then we cannot make head or tail of what happens, except that there is a sound of musketry, and we see mounted figures galloping and bullets striking up the dust near them. Occasionally the mounted men stop and fire a shot or two back. Then they disappear behind the fold of a hill; they look just as if they were riding straight up to us.

We keep our heads down. Looking up later we see that a party of four Boers, each with a led horse, are bearing away from us, as though they were going straight to the infantry on our left. But, whether these showed up or what, certain it is that the Dutchmen are keeping near the river and away from the infantry. With our glasses we can see them get clear away over the road. A non-commissioned officer and six men who are sent after them are only able, after a long gallop, to get some long-distance shots into them, with probably no effect.

A horseman comes riding up to us, and the men are anxious to shoot, but are restrained, and he turns out to be a messenger from the right, who reports 'One Boer and horse captured, one Boer wounded, and two mules captured.' Riding down we have a look at the bag, and find a fierce-looking yellow-bearded Boer, Theron by name, on a good-looking though thin horse. He had ridden up to the Kaffir kraal where our Irregulars were posted, and never had a suspicion till the officer stepped out, and then Theron immediately threw up his hands.

The Mounted Infantry now appear on the scene, and they have taken a prisoner or two and had a few shots at flying Boers; but they think some have slipped away to our right, which turns out to be correct.

We now view a lot of cattle near a neighbouring

o 2

farm and determine to round them up. One strong party of twenty-five men go to get them.

But, as it has been noticed that Boers show on the outline of a hill called Spion Kop, near the farm, a support of another fifteen or twenty men makes a demonstration nearly on the right rear of the cattle-lifting party. Nothing happens for some time ; but soon a message comes to say that a prisoner taken in the farm alleges that he had measles, and so the doctor is sent to vet him. Having got the cattle in hand, the support retires, and is three-quarters of a mile on its way home, when several reports are heard, and we at once turn and canter back. More shooting is heard at the farm and our pace is quickened.

As we near the farm the brave little doctor gallops up to say that the officer in command recommends our going to the right, and says the Boers have rushed a kraal near the farm and are firing heavily into the farm. We then line a cactus hedge, with an excellent ditch, and fire at the kraal.

Our commanding officer posts an outlook on our right, to prevent our being flanked. Then he proceeds to the farm, and his decision is that if the prisoner, who, it turns out, has been causing great delay (no doubt to enable his friends to rescue him), does not come along at once, his escort is to shoot him. This bloodthirsty threat has the desired effect, and a minute after all are on the move and making good their retreat.

A dropping fire from the hills is checked by dismounted fire, and we regain our own hills.

We now hear that the men at the farm were regularly charged by the Boers in most audacious style, and Young, the man on look-out duty, just managed to escape with a bullet through his coat, the sight of his carbine shot off, and a bullet wound in his horse's belly. One amusing incident occurred.

Harris, an Irregular, had shot at a Boer, and, on seeing his man drop, ran out from cover, calling out, ' I've got him, I've got him ! '

A bullet had hit a stone at the corner of the house, splashing in the captain's face. One man jobbing his neighbour's horse with his carbine, the latter had gone off, killing his own private horse. And so we ride home to a late lunch, after being out nearly thirteen hours.

A lie-down and sleep after lunch, and we wake up, have a cup of tea, and attend a concert in the town-hall, the joint effort of the Irregular corps and the English townspeople.

Few but English are left in the town, and some fifty of them make an appearance on the scene. The hall is lighted by the aid of the abominable double-wicked ration candles.

Some excellent songs are sung. The song of the evening is decidedly that by Young, who had so narrowly escaped being shot when look-out in the morning : ' There'll be razors a-flying in the air.'

But when the Chairman calls on Mr. Burton (the man who shot his horse) for ' The Arab's Fare-well to his Steed,' the call is not responded to, and so we sing ' God Save the Queen ' and ' Rule, Britannia,' and off to bed after a long day.

The next few days were spent by us in remount-ing and refitting, General French making arrange-ments for a fresh expedition to clear the country *viâ* Carolina, Ermelo, and Standerton to Pretoria. It was even contemplated to extend one of our columns from Ermelo to Piet Retief. Then it was expected that the *rôle* of cavalry as a division would be ended, and flying columns alone required.

General French's Column consisted of the 1st Cavalry Brigade, Greys, Carabiniers, and Innis-killings, and T Battery R.H.A., under Colonel

Gordon ; the 8th and 14th Hussars, with M Battery, under General Mahon ; the 7th Dragoon Guards,

March from Machado-dorp to Carolina, Heidel-berg and Pretoria.
Lumsden's Horse, and 500 of the Suffolks, under General Dickson.   Lieut. Elphick and nineteen men of Kitchener's Horse, who expected to be disbanded at Pretoria, requested to be attached to the regiment to see service. This was granted, and they were posted to B Squadron, and certainly had their desire fulfilled. They were fine, bold fellows, and most efficient.

This force had to carry a fortnight's supplies, so was much hampered by an enormous convoy ; the oxen also were very poor.   The information was that there were a few hundred of the enemy between Machadodorp and Carolina, and a commando of about 1,000 in the Lake Chrissie district ; but much opposition was not expected.   To avoid unnecessary transport we even dispensed with an extra ammunition train.

On October 12 General Mahon's force (8th and 14th Hussars and M Battery R.H.A.) moved off

Oct. 12.
towards Belfast to make a right flanking march on Carolina, in conjunction with General French's direct advance there.

CHAPTER XVI

THROUGH THE EASTERN TRANSVAAL TO PRETORIA

AT 4.45 A.M. the next morning General French moved, our 1st Brigade in advance, direct on Caro-

Oct. 13.
Engage-
ment of
General
Mahon.

lina. General Dickson's force followed, escorting the transport. At daybreak the sound of guns in the far distance informed us that General Mahon was engaged. Pushing on past Welgelegen, news of his serious engagement was received. We were about to cross the Komati River; but General French at once directed us to the west, seizing the hills and threatening the flank of the enemy who were attacking General Mahon, and who were reported to be moving in our direction. They turned off south, however, and, with the aid of glasses, could be viewed, evidently retreating to Witkloof, for the Twyfelaar drift over the Komati River, on Carolina. It transpired that the enemy, consisting of the Ermelo commando, 800 strong, with three guns, had attacked General Mahon's small force at dawn, their guns being laid on the bivouac and a bold rush being made on the outposts. Such an attack was not expected, the proximity of this commando being entirely unknown to the Intelligence Department.

Machadodorp apparently had been living in a

fool's paradise.   The position was a big one for so
small a force as General Mahon's, but a gallant stand
was made.   The fighting was severe and the
casualties, forty-eight, heavy.   The 8th Hus-

Casualties.

sars especially suffered.   Colonel Clowes himself had
a narrow escape, receiving a bullet through the water-
bottle at his side.   Lieut. Jones, Adjutant, a most
capable and popular officer, when going to his aid,
was shot dead through the head.   Lieut. Wylam was
also killed with most of his picquet, and Major Duff
and Lieut. Gilmore were wounded.

The 14th Hussars had two men killed, nine
wounded, five horses killed, eleven wounded.   Major
E. D. Brown brought a sergeant and trumpeter out of action on his own horse, one
after the other; he himself then remained

Major E.
D. Brown
earns V.C.

under heavy fire to assist Lieut. J. G. Browne to
mount his horse, which was restive.   For these
gallant deeds he received the V.C.

M Battery R.H.A. also suffered heavily.
Captain Taylor, commanding, was himself
killed, one officer wounded, and eleven men

Death of
Captain
Taylor.

killed and wounded.

An ammunition cart was lost; the guns at one
time were in jeopardy; and General Mahon's advance
was checked temporarily, his wounded being sent
back to Belfast.   Meantime General French determined to push on to Carolina and, if possible, inter-
cept the enemy.   The transport had steadily moved
forward, and at dark General French's column had all
crossed the Komati River and reached Bonnevoie,
where is Everard's Store.

At 3 A.M. our 1st Brigade commenced the ascent
of the hill, and, hurrying forward, we occupied Caro-

lina without resistance. Our patrols at once pushed on and reported about 300 of the enemy retreating south with a 15-pounder and a pom-pom, and about forty to the south-east, who retired sniping. Three wagons were captured a few miles out trying to escape, their owners being armed with passes. One patrol brought in from a well-stocked farm a written authority that nothing was to be taken, which was evidently a forgery, bearing the signature of a provost-marshal who was not in the country on the date.

Oct. 14.
Occupa-
tion of
Carolina.

'Boer
slimness.'

Being Sunday, our chaplain held a voluntary evening service in the deserted Dutch church, which I attended with Lieut. Swanston and his great friend. We were only a small gathering of soldiers who could get a brief respite from duty, and perhaps a foreboding of death made it a singularly impressive little service. Lieut. Swanston's fine singing of the evening hymn, 'Abide with me,' especially struck me. Alas! Two days later he died a soldier's death, killed on the battlefield, holding a desperate position and gallantly trying at the time to save a comrade.

Immediately we had occupied Carolina the Carabiniers, under Major Garratt, moved to Twyfelaar Drift to prepare the way for General Mahon, being strengthened at dawn on the 15th by two of our squadrons of Inniskillings and two guns. This was successfully accomplished, General Mahon arriving, and all joining General French at Carolina. The enemy had only moved out of Carolina on our approach, and many parties were still hovering round. Lieut. Bass, with a patrol of Inniskilling Dragoons, had one man, Private White, badly wounded in three places. Another man of B Squadron on outpost mistook a small party in the dark night for a picquet. They proved to be a patrol of the enemy, who, taking him several miles, relieved him of his arms, boots, and 27*l.* he had in a belt, and, with two hearty kicks, sent him back barefooted to tell us they were quite ready when we came on.   He reported that they spoke with an Irish accent.

A New South Wales Lancer, whom we left badly wounded at Carolina on our last occupation, died a few days ago ; the inhabitants reported that the enemy had buried him most reverently, numbers attending the funeral in tall hats and frock coats.   We found his grave beautifully decorated with flowers.

On the 16th General French directed an advance on Ermelo by different routes, the columns being widely extended to sweep the country.   Our 1st Cavalry Brigade, under General Gordon, took the left, *viâ* Tevreden and Lake Chrissie ; at daylight we moved off, the Inniskillings being advanced regiment, with Major Dauncey, Captain Yardley, and Captain Hamilton commanding the advanced squadrons.   We drove a good many snipers out of the farms, and early in the afternoon reached the Tevreden Hills.   Advancing along these, our advanced scouts surprised the Boer main laager and at once became heavily engaged ; supporting them, we reported and awaited reinforcements.   Unfortunately the brigade had suddenly changed its direction, halted, and was making arrangements to bivouac !

Oct. 16.

Fight at Tevreden, near Lake Chrissie.

Meantime the enemy, about 1,000 strong, with two guns in position behind their laager, rallied.   Our advanced scouts exhausted their ammunition.   The enemy got our range accurately with several belts of

pom-pom and shell from their guns ; one man was
horribly mutilated, a pom-pom shell bursting full in
his stomach. Under cover of this fire about 600
made a bold attack ; our advanced scouts were driven
back, galloping, mixed up with the enemy, who were
firing at them from their horses. Major Allenby at
this juncture, coming to the firing line, informed me
that the hill must be held, otherwise the enemy
would rush the bivouac. Major Dauncey, with a few
men of B Squadron, was holding the centre, whilst
I was holding an advanced position on his right,
with Lieut. Swanston and nine men only of my
A Squadron. I considerably checked the enemy's
rush, which came direct on my post, for some time
stopping it altogether, and enabling the advanced
scouts to get back clear, whilst reinforcements and
two guns at last got out from the brigade to support.
Finally my small party was overwhelmed, the Boers,
with Commandant Smuts at their head, getting right
amongst us.

I ordered those who could to escape being made
prisoners, and fired my last shot at the Boer leader,
who sprang from his horse as I pulled the trigger.
Men and horses were falling fast under a hail of
bullets, but I seemed to bear a charmed life. Private
Garlick, a short way to the rear, was on the ground,
shot through both legs, still holding the reins of my
horse, of his own, and Lieut. Swanston's. Garlick's
horse having been shot, Lieut. Swanston, a fine,
Heroic powerful young fellow, gallantly lifted him
death of up and placed him on his own horse, but,
Lieut.
Swanston. alas ! it was a fatal attempt, for this horse
was shot. Private Bisset, who had just mounted unscathed, rushed up and said, ' Here, Sir ; place him up

behind me.' This was effected and Bisset galloped off; but a storm of bullets brought them down, the horse shot, Private Bisset severely wounded, and Private Garlick with two more bullets through him. Lieut. Swanston himself was shot dead.

Vaulting on my horse, which, like myself, bore a charmed life, I galloped twenty yards off, and then pulled up to see if anyone was left. Immediately I did so I was shot high in the thigh, the bullet passing through me and just missing the spine. Gripping the pommel, I galloped away, my clothes riddled with bullets; but the one only had struck me. I found Major Allenby leading the regiment on, supported at last by two guns, and one squadron preparing to charge. The enemy almost reached the guns, which were firing case, but they were driven back, and our old positions were reoccupied. All our men whose horses had been shot, and who would have been taken away prisoners, were rescued.

My wound and loss of blood prevented my taking further part. Lieut. Walton, A.M.D., came to my aid, and, still mounted, I reached an ambulance. Hard galloping was the only way to do it ; walking or trotting would have finished me, and my fear was a cut artery.

The gallant little band with me had consisted of Lieut. Swanston and Private Garlick, killed ; Privates Bisset, Stinchcomb, Turner, and Brooks, who were all severely wounded, and whose horses, I think, were nearly all shot; Squadron Sergeant-Major Baxter, whose horse was shot and who was made a prisoner and escaped ; Corporal Hartland, Privates Hills and King.

Major Dauncey's post was also overwhelmed and

had to retire under a storm of bullets at 40 yards range. Amongst his casualties, Sergeant Hunter (Kitchener's Horse), Corporal Mullins (10th Hussars), attached, and Corporal Porter (Scots Greys) were killed.

The death of Lieut. Swanston was a bitter grief to us. He was a splendid young fellow, who had only recently joined the regiment, and the previous year had been rowing in the Cambridge Eight. Already he had endeared himself to all. He had been my special care, and this day in particular I had kept him with me, as he was a young soldier, and I knew his gallant, daring spirit. Truly he sacrificed his life trying to save another, and died an heroic death. Private Bisset's conduct, also, was a fine piece of gallantry, well worthy of reward.

Another of my squadron, Sergeant Farrell, successfully brought out of action, under heavy fire, Gallantry of the Innis- killings. Private Mann, who was horseless and wounded when with the advanced party, supporting him behind him on his horse. Many other gallant deeds were done, especially with the advanced scouts. Lieut. Paterson behaved with great dash, being slightly wounded as he galloped, unfortunately unarmed, alongside Commandant Smuts himself. Lieuts. Terrott and Gibbs were ridden over by the enemy, sticking to their advance posts. Lieut. Parker, with a troop of the Scots Greys on the left, also behaved gallantly, aiding to hold that flank. The enemy were unable to make any prisoners, as we drove them so rapidly back again, and we held the ground till dusk, sniping and being sniped. Our losses were severe—eight killed and twenty-five casualties—nearly all in two weak squadrons.   Lieut. Harris was among the wounded, being shot through the foot as he was galloping with a message to Major Allenby.

About 600 of this commando, under Commandant Smuts, made this bold attack with great dash.   Several

Incidents.   were riding barebacked, as they had been surprised in laager and only just caught their horses.   They were well mounted on horses in good condition, with neat-coloured saddle-cloths, and many native servants were riding after them with spare horses and rifles.   Some of the Boers shouted as they advanced, 'Where is General French?   Where are the guns?'   One of our men reported that two of these armed natives attacked him when he was left with his horse shot.   One fired at him, but missed. Drawing his sword, he rushed at them as the other native fired; the bullet broke his sword-blade at the hilt, leaving him unarmed, but the natives fled without waiting to see the effect of the shot.   Another man said that he saw a Boer shoot one of our wounded in cold blood, whilst another said that a Boer, coming on him as he lay wounded, was greatly distressed and propped him up with every kindness.

This day was a sad loss and disappointment to the regiment.   We surprised the enemy, and, if reinforced, should have gained a great victory.   We were very weak, one squadron having been left on the Carolina outpost line to follow later, and we were covering a wide front in hilly country.   The bivouacking of the brigade, with its advanced regiment in ignorance of what was going on and several miles forward, was an error, as guns and supports could not be supplied in time.   As it was, the gallantry of the Inniskillings alone saved the column from disaster.

A HEAVY PULL UP.

A TONGA.

Lieut. Swanston and our other dead were buried at sunset at the foot of the Tevreden Hills, close by where I lay wounded with Lieuts. Paterson and Harris. The sadness of it all I shall never forget, with no feeling of victory to cheer the heart—only regret.

As darkness set in, General Gordon moved the brigade south-east in the Ermelo direction, in order to get more in touch with the centre column, under General French. Owing to the intense darkness and the rough country, the brigade wandered about for four hours, getting a few miles to Witkrans. It was a rough jolt across country for the wounded. We bivouacked at 11 P.M., horses having been under saddle for sixteen hours, and moved off again at 4 A.M. My conveyance was a tonga, a small two-wheeled Indian cart, supplied by Danjheeboy, for which our Army Medical Corps was indebted to the Indian Government, and which proved of great service. Stretched out in this, with a native Indian driving the two ponies, I was jolted along in pitchy darkness till midnight : no road, and over the roughest country and watercourses. It was an agonising drive. All things have an ending, and at last that memorable day was over, and I was lifted on my stretcher into one of the few tents which the Hospital Corps had. It was but for a few hours, during which groans were chiefly heard, as at 4 A.M. we were lifted back into ambulances, and once more, in the dark, the jolt commenced.

Dense fog, however, delayed a real start for several hours. After very slow progress, with many halts, owing to threatened attacks, the enemy attacked

Again attacked.

Oct. 17.

boldly in the afternoon, but was driven off, with loss.
We who were wounded had a twelve-hour jolt in the
ambulances, under which Sergeant Blevin,
Deaths. Inniskilling Dragoons, and Private Garlick,
a Royal Dragoon Reservist, my servant, succumbed
to their severe wounds, and were buried together
whilst we made a short halt.   Both were a great loss.
Horses had been under saddle since 4.30 A.M., but it
was dusk before we reached Mooiplaats, only about
seven miles, when, taking up a night outpost line,
the Carabinier picquets were fiercely attacked, but
we rapidly reinforced them and drove the enemy off
with loss.

We started again at 4.30 A.M., and marched to
Ermelo. The enemy continually harassed us. The
Inniskilling Dragoons were advanced and
Oct. 18. left flank guard. Desultory fighting took
place all day on the left flank, but nothing serious.
There were no casualties in the regiment, but one of
the 6th Dragoon Guards was wounded. This night
all the Inniskilling Dragoons were on outpost duty.

The enemy had a good temporary hospital and
doctor in Ermelo, where one of our feared hopeless cases was left (Private Marshall, Inniskilling
Dragoons). This man had his arm amputated there
and recovered, being afterwards permitted to return.
He had been most dangerously shot through the
abdomen and also slightly grazed on the arm ; the
latter wound was thought trifling, but, owing to
having rubbed the bandage off, dirt set up blood-
poisoning in the arm, and his case was considered
hopeless.

With all his forces united, General French marched
again at 4.30 A.M. in the direction of Bethel. The

enemy reoccupied Ermelo as we evacuated it, and harassed the column all day. Major Allenby, with the Inniskilling Dragoons, two guns, and a pom-pom, fought a fine rear-guard action, the regiment bearing the brunt of the fighting. Captain Stevenson-Hamilton's Squadron did good work; also the New South Wales Lancers. The latter, which worked as a squadron of the regiment, consistently rendered excellent service. They were a very fine lot of men, and their officers, especially Major Lee, Captain Cox, and Lieut. Heron, were hard to beat anywhere. Captains Staunton and Griffin, attached, fought their two guns (Royal Horse Artillery) and pom-pom with great skill and daring. The casualties in the brigade were twelve, the regiment having one killed (Private Corliss, 10th Hussars, attached) and five wounded. Several of the enemy were killed, amongst them a Field-Cornet, who was killed by one of our pom-pom shells.

Oct. 19.

Our immense convoy, with poor oxen that were daily growing weaker, owing to the lack of any grazing, was a great hindrance to us. When the country permitted it we marched in three parallel lines of wagons, but they covered many miles, and it required great skill to protect them against our foe. Our ambulances had necessarily to move with the convoy, but were always placed in the safest position possible. Had the Boers possessed many guns we could not have complained of their shelling the Red Cross flag. This, doubtless, had often been done during the war when it was unavoidable.

Our casualties this day were slight, but included Second Lieut. Calvert, of the 6th Dragoon Guards, missing. He was another fine young officer who,

P

two years previously, rowed in the Cambridge Eight with the late Second Lieut. Swanston. It transpired later that he was killed by the Boers under

Death of Lieut. Calvert.

suspicious circumstances. Private Dival, Inniskilling Dragoons, riding with Captain Jackson, was seriously wounded, a bullet passing through both cheeks and carrying away all his front teeth. It was a very dangerous wound, but he afterwards made a wonderful recovery.

Next day, starting at 4.30 A.M., we did not reach Bethel (fifteen miles) until dark, followed by a night of drenching rain. The enemy sniped

Oct. 20.

all day, one of the Royal Horse Artillery being killed. Captain Russell, A.M.D., attached to the Scots Greys, proceeded, under the Red Cross, with four bearers and a tonga (small cart) to bring in a wounded man. The enemy, under Commandant Smuts, deliberately fired on them, made them prisoners, and threatened to shoot them

Treachery.

because a farm had been burnt. General French sent word that, if they were not released at once, he would burn Bethel and all farms; so, having deprived them of everything, the Boers permitted them to return. Two more of our dangerously wounded died during the day. The poor

Deaths.

fellows had little chance under the rough travelling, despite the indefatigable care and attention of Majors Johnson and Thurston, A.M.D., who were in charge of the sick and wounded. Lieut. Paterson, shot through the thigh at Tevreden, pluckily returned to duty; but this inflamed the wound, and, later, he was invalided home in consequence.

During Sunday the column halted at Bethel. In the morning a sergeant of the 6th Dragoon Guards was treacherously killed. Seeing three men on the outpost line dressed in khaki, exactly like our own men, he rode out to them. They waited till he approached them, then suddenly dismounted and shot him dead.

Oct. 21.

General French decided to send his sick and wounded, under the protection of the Red Cross only, direct to Standerton, which was the nearest field hospital. Considering the temper of the enemy, we felt that we were embarking on 'a risky proceeding. The General himself visited the wounded, quite cheering everyone up. Further, he addressed the troops, thanking them for the good work done. He said it had been a hard and trying time; but a little more and a good rest at Pretoria awaited them. He was certainly a General in whom all had the fullest confidence, and for whom troops would go anywhere; always successful, kind, dashing; possessing bull-dog determination, and none of that abomination—fuss. It was a great regret to me to leave his command and the brilliant Cavalry Division.

Sick convoy. Enemy.

At 4.30 A.M. our convoy of eighteen ox-wagons, containing seventy-eight wounded, of whom I was one, under charge of Major Copeland, A.M.D., started for Standerton. At the same time General French, with the column, continued his march to Heidelberg. Their guns came into action, and heavy firing commenced soon after we cleared the town. Many of the enemy were on the hills around, and our little, unarmed procession fairly puzzled them, as, with our convoy of wounded, we took no arms or horses. After slowly advancing three miles along the Standerton road with our poor

Oct. 22.

oxen, the enemy at last rode down on us. They consisted of a small commando under Field-Cornet Janse. He at once selected eight of the best wagons and oxen, ordered our wounded to be moved from them, and, with our own native drivers, sent them off to his laager. These natives were then released and sent back to us. At the same time, he ordered that we should 'rejoin our commando'—viz. return to General French. This, Major Copeland pointed out, was an impossibility with our poor oxen, and, with our wounded crowded up, a barbarous cruelty. Still he insisted, and professed great anger at the burning of farms. Major Copeland, point-blank, refused to attempt it, and threatened General French's return. Field-Cornet Janse was extremely nervous, and continually surveyed the situation with his glasses ; possibly he feared that our convoy was some trap. Many of his commando rode off to take part in the fighting which was taking place close by, and our oxen were outspanned and a deadlock occurred.

Meantime the fighting grew more distant. Several of the enemy passed, having given up, and two Cape carts arrived containing Boer ladies ; and another commandant rode up. Captain Feilden, of the Scots Greys, who was with us, being ill with fever, was in my wagon, but able to get about. At my suggestion he undertook to discuss the situation with Field-Cornet Janse. Being gifted with great tact, he persuaded him to be more reasonable, and finally induced him to give Major Copeland a pass to Standerton, on the condition that we reported nothing we might see. Poor Feilden, later in the war, was killed in action.

Commandant Janse said that our oxen were scarcely worth taking, and that he had never known the country so dry, with no grazing, at this time of year. Many of this commando were fine, intelligent-looking men ; one only was dressed in khaki. They evinced no curiosity or desire to speak or look at us, and did not search the wagons or attempt to take anything we might have—not even the two horses that our doctor and conductor were riding. In the first instance, however, they continually rode down the wagons, looking carefully for marks and names on them, anxious to discover whether any were wagons previously captured from themselves or friends which they could recognise. One thing I had kept with me was the pointer dog, whose capture I have previously mentioned, and which had faithfully followed me through the war. This I feared would be taken, so I had her put into my wagon and covered up alongside me. An occasional growl as they rode along made me fear she would be discovered, but, luckily, the noise was not noticed, as they never looked inside. To do this commando justice, I think the majority of them were men that would have let me keep her, unless, perchance, her former owner had been amongst them. Directly permission was granted, we inspanned our oxen and moved off, fearing another commando might arrive and counter-order the permission.

Owing to this detention, we could only reach Topfontein, twelve miles, by night. We saw no further signs of the enemy, the country being quite deserted.

The following day we were successful in hiring
Oct. 23.
another wagon at Denmark Farm to relieve our crowded wounded. We met a patrol of the 13th Hussars from Standerton, but, as our

oxen could only crawl, we were compelled to halt eight miles off that place.

Next morning we met a troop of Captain Wiggins's squadron of the 13th Hussars, which escorted us into Standerton, where we were carried into the field hospital. The comfort and arrangements of this field hospital were excellent. Under the splendid management of Sister Russell, as chief matron, it had justly gained a great reputation, and, after our many days' and nights' jolting, was to us a Paradise. My bed was in a most comfortable Indian marquee. A military band, the first I had heard during the war, played in the grounds. Everything we wanted was obtainable, and a feeling of perfect peace, rest, and comfort reigned supreme. Lieut. Stubbs, an Electrical Engineer volunteer, occupied a bed in my marquee. He was covered with wounds and still in a critical state. He had been wounded recently on a locomotive, with an old friend of mine, the late Captain Paget of the Rifle Brigade. They were reconnoitring the railway near Vereeniging and fell into a Boer ambush, when all the party, including poor Paget himself, were killed or wounded. His description was that, advancing cautiously, they saw some dynamite on the rails, so pulled up, and Stubbs, dismounting, proceeded to remove it. As he stooped to do so he found himself looking down a row of Boer heads and rifles pointed from behind some rocks at the side of the line. Immediately he ran back to the engine and climbed up amidst a hail of bullets which spattered all round him ; metal splinters tore awful wounds through his flesh as he climbed the engine. He then fell senseless, Captain Paget falling by him, shot dead on the engine. Death and destruction were also dealt to the Rifle Brigade company in the single truck behind.

These railway reconnaissances were amongst the many perilous duties our soldiers and Engineers had continually to be doing during the war. What easier than for a small party of the enemy to lie in ambush in some of the terrible country through which the lines run, and then to mount their ponies and dash away? Train wrecking is another of the brutalities of war in which our enemies became adepts, thereby causing the deaths of even innocent women and children. The following week I nearly met a similar fate, when being moved from the field hospital at Standerton to Howick. The Boers wrecked a train at Waaschbank, in Natal, looted and burnt the railway station, which was a mass of flames as we arrived in the following train. The enemy had, of course, fled. One plan adopted to minimise this was to make some of the leading Boer inhabitants of a place we had taken travel as prisoner passengers on the train.

To return to Bethel. On our arrival there the telegraph was open, enabling General French to communicate with Lord Roberts and also with Standerton, that he was sending his convoy of wounded there. Directly afterwards the wire was cut. General French also addressed the troops, praising the work done and the splendid behaviour during a harassing time, which would shortly be over.

As our convoy of wounded cleared Bethel, on the 22nd, General French moved off for Heidelberg, leaving some of the 1st Cavalry Brigade to effect a surprise. This was successfully done, the enemy suffering a heavy loss.

Terrible thunderstorms, with hurricanes of hail and rain, were encountered. So violent were they Terrific storms. that the horses would not face them, and for some time the whole force had to halt and turn their backs to them. Two Kaffirs and three horses were killed by lightning. These awful storms continued for the next few days, and also swept over our field hospital at Standerton, where we had two men killed by the lightning—one soldier and one native.

There was constant sniping and fighting every day, the enemy hovering round and making vain Oct. 26. attempts to attack the convoy until Heidelberg was reached. At dawn of the previous day, in driving rain, a Boer patrol of ten men unexpectedly met face to face Corporal Mitchell, Inniskillings, who was detached with three men as a Cossack post. The corporal rushed at one of them, wrenched his rifle out of his hand, and galloped back to his men. The Boers were so astonished that they did not immediately fire, and the corporal got safely away into the mist with his men and the rifle before they opened fire.

General French brought into Heidelberg about seventy Boers and refugees, taken chiefly at Ermelo and Bethel.

Here a three days' halt was made. Major Lee, with his New South Wales Lancer Squadron, now left on Oct. 27-29. their return to New South Wales, greatly to our regret. Captain Cox, second in command, afterwards returned as lieutenant-colonel of the New South Wales Mounted Rifles, and rendered admirable service for twelve months under Colonel

OFFICERS, 1st CAVALRY BRIGADE AT PRETORIA, NOVEMBER 1900.

Rimington. Lieut. Elphick, with his troop of Kitchener's Horse, which had requested to be attached to the Inniskillings at Machadodorp, and fought gallantly with us throughout the march, also left the column.

General French now continued his march to Springs, where the Commander-in-Chief, Field-Marshal Lord Roberts, came out, inspected and addressed the troops. Then, in perfect deluges of rain, day and night, the march was resumed to Rietfontein *en route* to Pretoria.

Oct. 30.
Oct. 31.
Nov. 1.

The regiment was detached at 4 A.M. with orders to capture Field-Cornet Pretorius at his farm, three miles east of the line of march, destroying all stores and forage; then to proceed three miles north to bring in the Van der Walts. We expected to get well sniped during the operations; but the awful weather was in our favour, as it was impossible to see anything more than a mile distant. So the objects were accomplished without opposition. The occupants were brought in in a mule wagon, Field-Cornet Pretorius himself driving his old mother in a Cape cart.

Nov. 2.

The day before our transport mules had been allowed to graze on the bright green grass in some artificial canals, most tempting-looking stuff, but very deadly; there were also green fields of young oats on which they had gorged. Regaining the column we witnessed the dire results. Mules were lying all along their route. We counted sixty along the portion of the road after we struck it, some dead, many lying kicking in agony, their stomachs distended to a great size. All found alive were mercifully shot.

After another night of continuous rain the column arrived at Pretoria. So ended the great march of French's Cavalry Division to Barberton and back.

Nov. 3.

This last march of General French's from Machadodorp to Ermelo, Bethel, Heidelberg, and Pretoria was successfully accomplished in the face of great difficulties; but the results were disappointing. Few prisoners were taken; the various commandos under General Smuts and Hans Botha were not broken up; and their losses probably were no greater than our own—about 150 casualties. Owing to the great distance to be covered, it was necessary to carry a fortnight's supplies, for which an enormous convoy was necessary; the line of wagons was great, being about nine miles long; the oxen were poor, and there was no grazing; the mortality amongst them was terrible, quite 500 falling out exhausted; and several wagons had to be burnt to prevent their falling into the hands of the enemy. When travelling with the convoy it was sad to hear the constant reports of revolvers putting an end to the miseries of worn-out horses, oxen, and mules.

Notes on the march.

The regiments being very weak, the force was only about 1,500 strong. At the outset, the check to General Mahon's force caused a delay at Carolina, and the distance to be travelled, away from supplies, rendered it impossible to halt and take the offensive. The enemy everywhere were extremely bold, being informed by their leaders that General French, having been defeated and driven out of Barberton, was attempting to escape out of the country. Their continual harassing and attempts to attack the long convoy were only prevented by the greatest skill, and retaliation was impossible.

My wound was too severe to permit my taking further part in the fighting, and I was removed to hospital at Howick, where I spent some weeks. This gave me fresh insight into the splendid way our sick and wounded were cared for during the war. Large wooden huts were erected for the sick and marquees for the convalescent. The whole station was skilfully commanded by Colonel Quill, with Major Glynn as his Adjutant : most trying posts for officers keen to be at the front.

Nothing could have exceeded the kindness shown me in the delightful, loyal, go-ahead little Colony of Natal. Formerly I had spent ten years' service in this Colony with the Inniskillings, during three of which I was A.D.C. to the Governors : first the late Sir Charles Mitchell, and later Sir Arthur Havelock, G.C.M.G. Consequently, my present visit was to a land of old friends. General Dartnell, one of the chief saviours of our army in Natal, Colonel Sir Albert Hime, Sir David Hunter, and a host of others, many of whom have since been distinguished for their great services, gave me a right hearty welcome.

The improvements I saw in the Colony, after a ten years' absence, were vast, but nowhere more so than in Durban, which has sprung into a city of great importance.

Times and places change, but all were for the better here, and my sojourn in Natal helped me on well towards recovery. After being most hospitably entertained by Mr. Charles Hitchins at Durban, that splendidly arranged hospital ship *Simla* conveyed me to England.

It was a great regret to me to part from my faithful dog, which followed me to the ship. Here I learnt that, owing to the laws of the Board of Agriculture, I could not embark her until I had obtained a written permission from England.

A further disappointment was in store for me at Cape Town, when I learnt that valuables to the extent of several hundred pounds, which I had left there on going to the front, had been stolen by burglars. The police could give me no redress, and many others in this city had suffered like me.

CAPT. C. G. JACKSON, 7TH DRAGOON GUARDS.
Attached Inniskilling Dragoons.
Killed December 16, 1899. (*See page* 9.)

LIEUT. A. J. GRANT MEEK.
Killed, Waterval, June 7, 1900. (*See page* 96.)

SECOND-LIEUTENANT OLIVER.
Killed, November 30, 1901. (*See page* 297.)

SECOND-LIEUTENANT A. W. SWANSTON.
Killed, Tevreden, October 16, 1900. (*See page* 203.)

SECOND-LIEUTENANT F. N. DENT.
Drowned, Orange River, Norvals Pont,
March 15, 1900. (*See page* 33.)

LIEUT. J. LAWLOR.
Killed, Waterval Onder, August 30, 1900.
(*See page* 161.)

CHAPTER XVII

THE MAGALIESBERG TREK AND B SQUADRON TREK

ON arriving at Pretoria the regiment encamped near the racecourse, being for the first time for eight months under canvas again. A rest was truly welcomed and sadly needed, but the halt was not of long duration. On November 15 orders were received to march south, about twenty-three miles, to Kaalfontein; next day, in pouring rain, about fourteen miles, to Elandsfontein; and on the third day, about fifteen miles, to Klip River Station, which was held by Spencer and 200 men of the Rifle Brigade.

Nov. 3, 1900.

Nov. 15. Kaalfontein, 23 miles.

Nov. 16. Elandsfontein, 14 miles.

Nov. 17. Klip River Station, 15 miles.

During a reconnaissance to the west the Boers were encountered and driven off. Two Cape carts, two mules, two ponies, and a span of oxen, also kits and a quantity of dynamite, were captured from them.

Nov. 18.

The regiment then moved six miles to Vark-fontein, three miles north-west of Meyerton Station, and remained there twelve days, constantly expecting an attack.

Nov. 20. Vark-fontein, 6 miles.

Information being received that about 400 Boers had congregated at Losberg, about twenty-two miles west of Meyerton, the regiment, under command of

Major Dauncey (Major Allenby being on short sick leave), took part in a combined movement by four columns to surround them. On the third day's march, during which a Frenchman only (one of thirty) was captured, the Losberg was reached. The other columns—Babington's from the west, Douglas's from the south, and Hart's from the north—did not arrive simultaneously. After watching the Losberg all day, the northern column appeared, and commenced shelling the bare hill, which we could see was unoccupied! The Boers had all escaped to the west. This little expedition took five days, after which Major Allenby again resumed command of the regiment at Meyerton.

A 'provisional regiment,' consisting of B Squadron Inniskillings and Captain Maude's Squadron Scots Greys, was formed, under command of Major Dauncey, and proceeded to Taaibosch, *en route* to join General Bruce Hamilton's column, in order to escort a large convoy to Hoopstad and Bultfontein, in the west of the Orange River Colony.

After their departure news was received of General Clements's disaster in the Magaliesberg, so headquarters, with the remainder of the Inniskillings, under Major Allenby, marched the same day in great haste with the 1st Cavalry Brigade to his assistance.

Having reached Vlakfontein Farm, near Houtkop, a lamp message was received to move on at 3 A.M. and join Colonel Gordon at Jaroosfontein. This having been done, the brigade moved on by Van Wyk's Rust to the Roodepoort mines, and by another night march to Krugersdorp. Being Dingaan's

Day, it was expected that the Boers would attack Krugersdorp.

Dec. 18.   The 14th Hussars joined by rail from
Dec. 19.   Heidelberg, and the brigade marched at 3 A.M. with the 14th Hussars, Scots Guards, and Dublins in support, to co-operate with General Clements to the north-west. We heard his guns firing heavily all the morning. Near Zeekoehoek we came on the flank of some 2,000 to 3,000 Boers, under De la Rey, falling back west before Clements. Unfortunately we were too late, and they got away with some casualties. Bivouacking at Vaal-
Dec. 20.   bank, we started again at 4 A.M., but only succeeded in slightly engaging the Boer rear-guard, which was retiring south-west. Colonel Gordon was now appointed to command the whole force, Colonel Hamilton, 14th Hussars, taking com-
Dec. 21.   mand of the brigade. Next day General Clements, supported by Alderson's Mounted Infantry, attacked Naauwpoort Hill, to the west of us. Captain Mosley, with a squadron and a half Inniskillings, advancing eight miles south-west, got in touch with the enemy, killing one, and then Gordon's force marched to Vlakfontein, driving back the Boers.

Dec. 22.   General French left for Krugersdorp, and
Dec. 23.   Gordon's force now moved near Welver-diend.

The Inniskillings, reconnoitring to Varkenskraal on the Mooi River, found a large Boer laager and
Dec. 24.   many wagons and cattle. The enemy attempted to work round our flank, and a patrol of the 14th Hussars on our left lost three killed and two wounded. Our casualties were *nil*,

but Regimental Sergeant-Major T. Wood was taken prisoner on his return from taking a despatch five miles across country, owing to the brigade having moved during his absence. He was released with the loss of his revolver and field-glasses only.

The men got Christmas beer at Welverdiend, Dec. 25. and in the afternoon we moved eight miles to Dec. 26. the north, halting without water. At 3 A.M. the advance was continued to Rietfontein, and Dec. 27. next night to Wolverfontein on the Mooi River, in pursuit of Commandant Beyers. Slight sniping only took place, Beyers himself with the main body getting away before we could engage him.

1901. A convoy of supplies having come in from Jan. 2. Ventersdorp, the forces moved again on Jan. 3. January 3 to Rietfontein. The Inniskillings, one squadron 14th Hussars, four companies Scots Guards (all under Colonel Pulteney, Scots Guards) in the centre, Colonel Gordon with the rest of the force on our right, Colonel Kekewich on the left, and General Babington in rear.

The Inniskillings, in advance, engaged the enemy on the ridges south of Zandfontein all morning, Jan. 5. being relieved by the Scots Guards at noon, when the Boers fell back. The Scots Guards had two men wounded, and the Scots Greys Lieut. Finlay and two men wounded. General Babington, further to the west, had fifty-three officers and men of the Imperial Light Horse killed and wounded.

Gallant conduct of Privates Stanley and Westray. During the morning's fighting Lieut. Terrott, Inniskillings, advanced his troop some distance to take advantage of a small piece of cover to his front; on reaching this two of his men, Privates M. Stanley and F. Westray,

MR. WOOD, REGIMENTAL SERGEANT-MAJOR OF THE
INNISKILLING DRAGOONS.

rushed straight on down a perfectly bare glacis for a
distance of over two hundred yards, in face of a very
heavy fire, and threw themselves down behind a small
heap of rocks, where they lay for the space of three
hours, firing on a group of at least six Boers who
had good cover further down the hill. Afterwards
it was proved that these Boers were only 167 yards
distant from them. During this time the enemy's
fire from all parts of the hill was so heavy that the
men even much higher up were unable to change
their positions. By this gallant conduct Privates
Stanley and Westray did much to prevent the Boers
enfilading us, and for their plucky action were
mentioned by Lord Kitchener in despatches (July 28,
1901).

The next few days were spent reconnoitring the
Magaliesberg, the Inniskillings generally acting
detached, with two guns. On the 8th a
convoy from Krugersdorp was attacked by
1,500 Boers and six guns, the Boers being repulsed
with loss.

Jan. 8.

The Inniskillings, 14th Hussars, two guns, and a
pom-pom, all under Major Allenby, reconnoitred towards Breedt's Nek and got into
signal communication with General Clements.

Jan. 9.

Moving north of Krugersdorp, the force proceeded
to Kaalfontein. Here it was discovered that the
Boers under Beyers had gone east after their attack
and repulse at this place, so Gordon's force returned
to Johannesburg. The Inniskillings were detached
with one squadron Scots Greys, two companies Scots
Guards, four guns, and two pom-poms, under Major
Allenby, to clear farms to the north and north-west of
Johannesburg. Bivouacking at Rietfontein, near the

Q

Jokeskie River, they accomplished their mission with a little sniping only, and reached Johannesburg, after a thirty-five mile march, on January 16. Here the regiment was joined by B squadron, under Major Dauncey.

Jan. 16.

To return to the doings of this squadron during the past month. Having left Johannesburg on December 13 as part of a provisional regiment, it marched on to Lindequee and joined the 21st, General Bruce Hamilton's, Brigade. It was here increased by 300 Cape Mounted Rifles and two Cape Mounted Rifles field guns, the whole under command of Colonel Maxwell, R.E. These field guns were drawn by mules, driven by natives, and went at a great pace—an artilleryman sitting humbly beside the native driver.

B Squadron's march. Dec. 13.

Dec. 15.

Colonel Maxwell's force always worked on the right, several miles off the large convoy, Colonel Rimington, with his Guides (200), fifty Driscoll's Scouts, a gun and a pom-pom, working on the left. Three other field guns, a pom-pom, and 700 Cameronian Highlanders marched with the convoy.

Marching to Parys, two Inniskillings, who were rear points to the rear troop, were taken prisoners through stopping to eat plums.

Dec. 16.

At Vredefort Colonel Maxwell's force was detached, and proceeded eleven miles south-west to Klein Bloemfontein to look for reported buried guns. The informant and guide was a Boer prisoner under capital sentence for murdering Kaffirs. A short time previously he conducted a force to find buried treasure at Losberg, which he could not show. He now conducted another wild-

Dec. 17.

COOKING ARRANGEMENTS.

THE OVEN.

goose chase to dig on an open plain where, needless to say, there were no guns, so, after fruitless long marches, the force, after crossing the Rhenoster River at Winkel's Drift, rejoined General Bruce Hamilton at Witbank, near the junction of the Rhenoster and the Vaal.

Rounding up farms *en route*, the march was continued to Coal Mines Drift on the Vaal, which was held by the Northamptons, under General Bruce Hamilton's brother, Colonel Kekewich being in command at Klerksdorp. A good deal of sniping now took place as the column proceeded and cleared the farms.

On Christmas Day Colonel Maxwell made a daylight dart fourteen miles south-west to Rooiplaats, crossing the Vaal and pursuing a large party of the enemy, and captured eight wagons and 1,000 head of cattle. The men had a ration of rum to celebrate Christmas Day, and sang merrily to the accompaniment of an awful melodeon.

Dec. 25.

Continuing the march along the Vaal, many lovely farms were passed and much sniping continued. The heat was very severe, and the country extraordinarily dry and parched for the time of year.

About seventy Boers, retreating, wounded two of the Cape Mounted Rifles and killed one of Rimington's Guides on the left flank. Next day a drive was attempted, but only resulted in the capture of cattle, and on the 30th the column entered Hoopstad, which was garrisoned by 320 South Wales Borderers, seventy Berks Mounted Infantry, and two guns. They were rejoiced at our arrival, being on short rations and having been without tobacco for two months.

Dec. 28.
Dec. 30.
Hoopstad.

Q 2

A cricket match was played against the garrison, the latter winning by three runs.

The new year, however, was not to open peacefully, for Colonel Maxwell's force was again detached and started at 7.15 on a night march to clear the farms and country round Steenkamp's Kraal. Two hours before daylight, the Inniskillings and Scots Greys, in advance, encountered the Boers, who barred the way from behind stone buttresses and wire fences on each side of the road. The cavalry rushed the posts, but, owing to the darkness, most of the Boers escaped on foot into the trees on the river bank, and only one was captured. Six ponies and saddles were taken, and three ponies shot. Later in the day three wagon-loads of inhabitants, 300 cattle, and two old men were collected from the farms, and at 8.30 another night march was begun.

Next day the Boers, although sighted, everywhere declined to come in reach, and the chief incident was heavy firing on the left, which revealed the main column shelling some of Rimington's!

During the advance about seventy Boers tried to get into some kopjes in front in order to check us; but the Inniskillings and Scots Greys, racing for the position, forestalled and drove them off with loss. Two rich, splendid farms, with lovely orchards, Hartenbosch and Bissiepoort, were passed, and Bultfontein was occupied. Miss Richards, sister of the Civil Commissioner of Hoopstad, and others came along with the main column, under Rimington's charge.

From Bultfontein the Inniskilling Squadron, with Rimington's Guides, two guns, and two companies

Royal Irish Regiment, was detached from the main column to escort a convoy of women, refugees,

Jan. 6.
prisoners, cattle, and sheep to the railway at Vet River Station. This having been accomplished, the force headed for Kroonstad; but, at Nooitgedacht, the Inniskillings and Scots Greys Squadrons received orders from General Hunter to

Jan. 15.

Venters-

burg

Road.
proceed to Ventersburg Road Railway Station. Here, after entraining once and being detrained, they finally left by rail for Elandsfontein, and on January 16 reached Johannesburg and joined the remainder of the regiment, which marched in on the same day from its Magaliesberg trek.

CHAPTER XVIII

GENERAL FRENCH'S GREAT DRIVE THROUGH THE EASTERN TRANSVAAL

FROM January 16 to January 26 the Inniskilling

Jan. 16, &c. Gordon's force broken into two. Dragoons halted at Johannesburg, during which time preparations were made for General French's grand combined drive east towards Piet Retief.

For these operations Colonel Rimington, having handed over his Guides to Major Damant, took command of the Inniskilling Dragoons, Lieut.-Colonel Allenby being given a column of his own.

Starting from Johannesburg on January 26, 1901,

French's big combined drive through the Eastern Trans- vaal. the regiment marched *viâ* Bethel to Ermelo, then south-east to Piet Retief, on south to Paul Pietersburg and Vryheid, thence to the Natal Railway at Glencoe, where they arrived on April 3 ; they then entrained right away up to Belfast on the Delagoa Bay line.

The following columns took part in this great drive, viz. : Smith-Dorrien's, Campbell's, Knox's, Pulteney's, Allenby's, Dartnell's, and Colville's.

General French himself accompanied the centre (Pulteney's) column, and it is with this column we are principally concerned. It consisted of the Inniskilling Dragoons (Colonel Rimington), two Squadrons 14th Hussars (Major Brown, V.C.), T Bat-

GENERAL M. F. RIMINGTON, C.B.

A GROUP OF INNISKILLING OFFICERS.

tery R.H.A. (Major Lecky), one howitzer, one pom-pom, and 900 Scots Guards (Major Cuthbert), the whole under Colonel Pulteney.

Proceeding by Boksburg, Springs, and Droog-fontein to Nooitgedacht, Allenby's column, which was close on the right of Pulteney's, was engaged while nearing the latter place on the 28th, turning about 300 Boers off Boschmanskop. They had lost one man killed and about ten wounded (Scots Greys and Carabiniers), when the Inniskilling Dragoons from Pulteney's column galloped up to reinforce, but were ordered back to allow the guns to open fire. Lyddite shells were burst on the hill, and the Boers driven off. Following on, one dead and one wounded Boer were picked up, but, owing to one of the columns having hung back, most of the enemy managed to escape through the line.

Arriving at Nooitgedacht, the enemy put five shells into Pulteney's baggage column, killing a few oxen only. The Inniskilling Dragoons at once galloped for the ridge from which the Boers were shelling, but only to see about 400 in flight and pour volleys into them at 2,400 yards' range. Much damage might have been effected if our guns had only been galloped on after the charge. Later in the war, guns were kept further ahead, and 'pushed' with great effect.

Terrific storms and wet weather were now encountered, which rendered the black, boggy soil very difficult for transport. Two troops of the Inniskillings escorted the Engineers nine miles back to repair the telegraph line to Springs, which the enemy had destroyed, and safely accomplished their mission.

Jan. 28. Engagement at Nooitgedacht.

Jan. 31. Bad weather.

The enemy now took up a position, extending about six miles across the hills by Vaalbank and Zondagsfontein. Knox's, Pulteney's, and Allenby's columns attacked, driving them off. French's Scouts, riding to the top of one ridge without 'scouts out,' had one man killed and one wounded. B Squadron Inniskillings then charged it in open order, about 500 Boers flying in the direction of Bethel. Many were knocked over by our rifle fire at about 1,000 yards' range.

Bethel was reached on February 4, and Ermelo on the 7th. Here a few days' halt was made, during Feb. 4. Bethel. which fifty Inniskillings escorted a convoy to Standerton for supplies. Lieut. Wood got a despatch through to Standerton and back under very difficult conditions.

General Smith-Dorrien's column, on our extreme left, was at this time at Bothwell, near Lake Chrissie. The Boers, everywhere being driven before our huge line of columns, which covered nearly 100 miles of front, determined, under the leadership of Botha, to attack Smith-Dorrien, and so effect an escape to the north. Accordingly, in the dark and mist of Feb. 6. Smith-Dorrien's battle. February 6, they delivered a fierce night attack. The West Yorkshires bore the brunt of the onslaught, but coolly and bravely repulsed it. General Smith-Dorrien had taken every precaution with entrenchments, and the Boer night surprise had quite failed. Daylight found them repulsed everywhere, leaving twenty or thirty of their dead actually within the British lines. General Smith-Dorrien's casualties numbered nearly seventy, which showed how desperate the fighting had been.

The general advance now proceeded on Piet
Retief. Moving on Damascus, we picked up
a Kaffir despatch rider, evidently murdered
and shot through the head that morning at
an inch range.

Feb. 11.
Damas-
cus.

The Vaal was crossed at Camden about 6.30 A.M.,
when numbers of Boers were viewed retiring on the
ridge above Tobias Smuts's farm, named
Klipfontein, about seven miles south of the
drift over the Vaal. The column (Pulteney's)
moved on through Smuts's farm and over the ridge.
An immense number of Boers, with wagons, were
then seen three miles off, making away up the
Viljoen Spruit.

Feb. 12.
Charge of
Innis-
killings.

About mid-day the advanced guard, one squadron
14th Hussars, with a pom-pom, became engaged with
the enemy, and could advance no further. After
repeated gallant attempts to take the position, they
sent back for reinforcements. The Inniskillings, on
Colonel Rimington's urgent requests, were at last
sent on to clear the ridge, supported by artillery fire.
We moved in column of troops to the front, and,
when in dead ground in the valley, changed direction,
head half right. On reaching the top, well to the
right of the 14th Hussars, it was found that the
enemy had moved to the right.

A Squadron, under Major Mosley, extended, supported on its right rear by C Squadron, under Lieut.
D. Johnson, and B Squadron, under Major Dauncey.
Trotting on, the whole came immediately under rifle
fire from front and both flanks, and drew swords.
A Squadron, cutting a wire fence, kept on straight
towards this fire, until pulled up by a second wire
fence in front of a deep ravine which ran down the

far side of the ridge. Here they dismounted and
kept the enemy occupied with a good return
fire.

In the meantime C and B Squadrons had inclined
to the right, cut two wire fences, and were approaching a third. Here C Squadron was joined by one
troop of A Squadron. As soon as the last fence was
cut, the charge was sounded by the Commanding
Officer. C Squadron giving a cheer extended and
charged straight at the left flank of the Boers
who were opposing Major Mosley. The Boers
immediately fled and went down the hill as fast as
they could, C Squadron getting right in amongst
them. The Maxim at once opened fire and made
good practice. After crossing the valley below, this
squadron was recalled. The pom-pom soon after
came into action and threw 348 shells into the midst
of the Boers galloping up the hill opposite. The
Boer ambulance later made two visits to the neighbourhood of this place. The Boer losses, not counting
those inflicted by the pom-pom, were five killed,
fifteen wounded, and ten prisoners.

In this fine charge the Inniskillings lost only one
man, Private H. Love, killed, and two wounded,
Privates J. Leary and M. Clear. It was one of the
few instances of a successful cavalry charge during
the war, and only proves what can be done by cavalry
well handled and well led.

The pursuit was carried on, C Squadron being
again pushed forward and capturing over 1,000 head
Captures.   of cattle, fifteen wagons, twenty Cape carts,
and thirty to forty saddle horses. These had
all been abandoned by the Boers in their flight. Some
rich farms also were cleared. It was not, however,

till 10 P.M., and with great difficulty in the pitch darkness, that the column which had moved on east to Lyden was found and rejoined.

It had been a long day on the horses—from 5 A.M. to 10 P.M., saddled throughout.

Many of the captured wagons laden with farm produce, following on with a small escort, lost their way, were attacked at dawn, and recaptured. Two Inniskilling Dragoons of the small escort were wounded and taken prisoners.

The march was continued through hills and plains to the junction of the Thelo River and Taaibosch Feb. 13. Spruit at Lochiels. Many wagons (about Lochiels. twenty), laden with mealies and all sorts of goods, were discovered by the Inniskillings' advanced scouts, hidden in the hills ; but, owing to the combined movement and the column having bent to the left, they had to be abandoned, as there was not even time to destroy them. Boers now were daily to be seen miles away making off with their wagons. Sniping continued, and many of their wagons fell into our hands.

Piet Retief was reached at mid-day, February 16, several columns uniting there. At 2 P.M. a flying Feb. 16. column, consisting of the Inniskilling Dra- Piet goons, one squadron 14th Hussars, two guns Retief. and a pom-pom—all under Colonel Rimington—started off again south-west. Crossing the Assegai River, which was very deep, it proceeded eight miles to a German farm named Meyershoop, the centre of a regular German district. Here it remained three days, reconnoitring the country and effecting a junction with Allenby's column moving to Piet Retief.

On the 19th the flying column marched by night
to Marienthal, where General Dartnell's
column was encamped. The roads were
awful, and there was a fearfully difficult
climb in intense darkness and pouring rain.

Feb. 19.
Marien-
thal.

At 6 A.M. it was off again towards the Intombi
River, on a day of continuous rain and over terrible roads and drifts, in some of which the
water was over the horses' backs. After
getting over Chaka Spruit, Tambootiesbult
(seventeen miles) was reached after dark.
The Chaka rose too high at last, and several wagons
had to be left on the other side till next day. The
ambulance wagon, with two men on it, passed the
night in the midst of the torrent—the drowned mules
in their harness were bobbing about. At daylight
Captain E. C. Holland, Inniskilling Dragoons, found the flood still rising and the two
men on the top of the hood of the wagon in
imminent peril of being washed away, hood
and all. He pluckily swam out with a rope
and managed to get them off—a deed for
which he obtained the bronze medal of the Royal
Humane Society.

Feb. 20.
Terrible
rains.
Tamboo-
tiesbult,
17 miles.

Captain
E. C.
Holland
gains
Royal
Humane
Society
medal.

Rain continued all night; the men were in a
deplorable state of wet and misery, without tents,
and it was almost impossible to light a fire.

Next day the little column was quite cut off by
flooded rivers; but, reconnoitring south-west, met a
patrol of the Royals and, later, the advanced
wagons of the expected convoy from Utrecht,
escorted by General Burn-Murdoch's force.
Unable to cross the spruit, the day was spent in
improvising a sort of rope bridge on which rations

Feb. 21.
Burn-
Murdoch's
force met.

DESTROYING A CAPTURED WAGON TO PREVENT ITS AGAIN FALLING
INTO THE HANDS OF THE ENEMY.

DRIVING SHEEP ACROSS A RIVER.

were got across. It was again raining all day, and continued to pour incessantly all the following day, during which a raft was improvised to get stores from the advanced wagons over the drift. The troops and also the column at Piet Retief were on very short rations, the men living on mealies and meat only. The camps were a regular swamp.

Feb. 22.

Short rations.

By means of a wire-rope ferry, eighteen wagon-loads of stores were brought over, box by box, by hand. One squadron reconnoitred west to Potgieter's Farm (Schuilhoek), and located Burn-Murdoch's camp, under the Elandsberg. A great find was also made in the graveyard outside the farm by the drift: a newly dug grave, being opened, revealed an iron tank, covered with sheep-skins, full of flour, which was badly needed, and which provided all the men with over 1 lb. each.

Feb. 23.

Work at the drifts continued. Patrols being sniped from the hills to the east, the guns were turned on the snipers, but they only took cover when the guns went off, and, picking up a bit of our shell, caught the sun on its surface and flashed it like a helio in our faces to show their scorn.

Feb. 24.

Major Hamilton and his fifty Inniskillings, who were left at Ermelo to escort wagons to Standerton for supplies, now rejoined, having come along with General Burn-Murdoch's convoy column from Newcastle. The next three days were spent in escorting convoys to General Dartnell's column at Luneberg Mission Station and bringing refugees back, camping at Welbedacht, and finally at Pongola Spruit, between Welbedacht and

Feb. 25.

Escorting convoys.

Tambootiesbult.   The supply of candles having run out caused another inconvenience.

March opened with the usual downpour of rain, which continued nearly every, and often all, day for the next fortnight.   This period was spent in watching the country, protecting the passage of Burn-Murdoch's provision-wagons for the Piet Retief columns, and in repairing the drifts of our own small section of the country, six miles between Chaka Spruit and Luneberg Mission Station, from whence General Dartnell's column took it up to Marienthal.   Thus the convoys were passed on to Piet Retief, and the terribly deep, difficult, and frequent drifts kept bridged or in repair. They were so difficult owing to the amount of rain which was continually falling, and to the black, boggy soil.

March 1
to
March 16.
Protecting
convoys
and
repairing
drifts.

Rimington's force marched off to Knopaan (eight miles), driving the Boers off a high, rocky ridge; and next day the Inniskilling Dragoons, pursuing about 250 of the enemy, occupied Paul Pietersburg (eight miles).   As there was hardly any food left for the horses, it was a great disappointment to find only about twenty sacks of mealies in the town.

March 16.
Knopaan,
8 miles.
March 17.
Occupa-
tion of
Paul
Pieters-
burg,
8 miles.

Dartnell's column following on, Rimington's force pushed forward seven miles and occupied the rocky hills commanding Pivaan's River Bridge.   It was a long day, owing to a big deviation for reconnaissance, with fearful thunderstorms and enormous hailstones.

Men and horses were again very short of food, the men, except for the unlimited supply of meat, living entirely on crushed mealies ; these were secured

LIEUTENANT J. R. SIDDALL,
QUARTERMASTER, INNISKILLING DRAGOONS.

by scouring the country and getting the Kaffirs, who were all Zulus, to bring them in, for which they March 19. were paid on the spot. Our excellent Quar- Food scarce. termaster, Lieut. Siddall, was learning the Dealings with the Zulus. Kaffirs' language, and he could be heard arguing with them and exclaiming in despe- ration, 'Picaninny mealies, picaninny mâli' (= Little mealies, little money).

Some of the Zulus being discovered acting as spies, Colonel Rimington had a parade, and two of March 20. them were sjambokked. The nature of the offence was explained to the natives, and they kept applauding the interpreter's oration by raising their right arms and chorusing the word 'Inkos' ('chief' or 'my lord and master'). Great applause ('Inkos') was raised when the interpreter announced that one of the prisoners, on account of his age, should receive only six instead of twelve strokes of the sjambok.

Dinizulu, the Zulu chief, son of the late Cetewayo, sent a runner into camp with information that the March 21. Boers meant to attack that night. This Dinizulu. proved later to be correct, but the attack was frustrated by Colonel Rimington's tactics. General Dartnell threw some of his mounted troops towards Engage- ment with Potgieter. the junction of the Pivaan and Pongola, whilst Major Dauncey, with one and a half squadron Inniskillings and a pom-pom, was despatched eight miles east to the Zand Spruit Drift to make a demonstration against the Boers. They were found in force, strongly holding the opposite side of the drift. Much sniping and a pom-pom duel took place, in which the Boer gun was silenced. Later information was received that the enemy

numbered 600, under Potgieter. At nightfall fires were
lit in pretence of bivouacking; then, in the pitch
dark and a terrible storm of rain, the troops marched
off with Zulu guides and united with General
Dartnell's mounted troops at Pivaan River Bridge.
It was not reached till the middle of the night—every
man soaked to the skin, and the blankets also soaked
and the ground a swamp. The men had to walk
about till daylight, when the intended attack by the
Boers was not put into execution.

The day was spent in crossing the Pivaan River
bridge. General Dartnell's column with its convoy
March 23. marched over first, followed later by Riming-
Across the ton's. All then joined Pulteney's, which had
Pivaan
River. already crossed, and bivouacked on the south
side of the river.

On this day, far off in the Western Transvaal, a
splendid victory was gained by the New Zealanders
Raleigh and Bushmen, under Colonel Raleigh Grey,
Grey's
victory in late Inniskilling Dragoons. This force was
Western forming an advance guard to General Babing-
Trans-
vaal. ton, who was engaged in the Magaliesberg
district against General De la Rey. Emerging from
a pass, near Haartbeestfontein, they beheld the Boer
army moving across a plain below. Lieut.-Colonel
Grey at once gave the order to charge. With wild
cheers the New Zealanders and Bushmen raced down
on their foes. The Boers attempted to unlimber and
bring their guns into action, but were overwhelmed,
and the whole force fled terrified before the furious
charge. Over fifty Boers were picked up after the
charge, killed or wounded; 140 were taken prisoners;
also two field guns, one pom-pom, six Maxims, and
fifty-six wagons.

The united columns now marched to Vryheid (eleven miles), where a day's halt was made. A March 24, combined drive was then arranged towards 25 and 26. Vryheid. the Zululand border—Pulteney's to be the Combined southernmost column, and lead on the Ngomi drive to Zululand Forest ; Dartnell's next, on the north, on border. Kolfontein ; Allenby's next, on the north, on Zuikerkan ; another column, still further north, on Langdraai on the Pongola. Thus the right rested on the Umvolosi and the left on the Pongola River covering a longitude of about forty miles. General French accompanied, directing.

Pulteney's column proceeded by Welgevonden (27th), Vaalkrantz (28th), and Blumendal to Banke-March 27. roet, where a halt was made, and the column March 29. returned to Blumendal the same day. In this sweeping operation many good mules, a lot of grain, and several carbines were secured—amongst them a Westley-Richards, W. and R. Blakemore, and Swinburne patent with a Henry barrel. Seven Sur- good fighting Boers also surrendered. They renders. said that their laagers were always guarded at night, to prevent their own men deserting to surrender, and that for five weeks they had been watching their own chance to escape.

More bad Terrible lightning and rain heralded more weather. wet weather.

March 31. Accompanied by General French, Pul-Vryheid. teney's column reoccupied Vryheid, and then April 1. marched, on April 1, to the Blood River (six-Blood River, teen miles), which, although very deep owing 16 miles. to the rains, was successfully crossed.

Next day, on to De Jaeger's Drift on the Buffalo River (fourteen miles), where another crossing was

R

April 2.
De
Jaeger's
Drift,
14 miles.

just accomplished, and, next day, on to Dundee and Glencoe station, twenty miles ; a dreadful march, in continuous rain.

April 3.
Glencoe,
20 miles.

The same night Colonel Pulteney's column entrained for the north.

This ended General French's great and successful sweeping movement across the Eastern Transvaal.

Success-
ful end of
General
French's
eastern
drive.

During it some 300 Boers had been killed or wounded, and over 1,000 taken prisoners or surrendered ; six guns, about 1,000 rifles, and 4,000 horses had been captured.   Towards the end of the operations the Inniskilling

Innis-
killings
entrain
north to
Belfast.

Dragoons were almost all mounted on captured Boer ponies.   In addition some thousand wagons were taken or destroyed, and the country greatly denuded of supplies. Vast quantities of stock cattle and sheep were also taken, many of which found their way back into the hands of the enemy, as they could not all be driven off, and as yet our troops did not shoot them down.

Undoubtedly far greater captures would have been effected but for the terrible rains which rendered the country a quagmire ; in these circumstances rapid pursuit in such a country of mountains and rivers was an impossibility.   The Boer forces were, however, utterly demoralised, crippled, and broken up, and this part of the country never recovered from the blow struck.

PONTOON BRIDGE OVER THE INTOMBI RIVER.

PONTOON BRIDGE OVER THE PONGOLA RIVER.

CHAPTER XIX

OPERATIONS UNDER SIR BINDON BLOOD

April 3.
Railway
journey. AFTER five weary nights and days in the train, Colonel Pulteney's column reached Belfast on the Delagoa Bay Railway, on April 8.

April 8.
Belfast.

Royals
join
column. The Royal Dragoons, under Major Carr-Ellison, now joined the column, and the two squadrons of the 14th Hussars left it to rejoin their regiment.

This same day Plumer, after a magnificent dash north, had seized Pietersburg. Viljoen and numbers Plumer
takes
Pieters-
burg. of Boers were known to be in the Roos Senekal district, to the north of the Delagoa Bay line. Accordingly Plumer was directed to block their escape to the north, whilst seven columns, under the direction of General Bindon Opera-
tions
under
Bindon
Blood. Blood, lately arrived from India, made a sweeping and encircling movement to hem in these Boers. Plumer meantime advanced east from Pietersburg, through the Chunies Pass, and took up positions along the Olifant River, so as to block the passages north. The encircling columns then advanced: Beatson's and Benson's, from Middelburg, to close the west; Pulteney's and Douglas's from Belfast in the south, to advance on Dullstroom and Roos Senekal in the centre; whilst

R 2

General Kitchener, with three columns, came from Lydenburg to close the east.

On April 16 Pulteney's column marched north

April 16.
Zwart-
koppies.
from Belfast to Zwartkoppies, driving back a few Boer snipers, who only wounded one man of the Royals.

Next day the column, under more sniping,

April 17.
Dull-
stroom,
8 miles.
marched into Dullstroom (eight miles), and there met Colonel Douglas's column of the 18th and 19th Hussars, &c.

The cavalry, under Colonel Rimington, made a twelve-mile reconnaissance east, driving off about

April 18.
seventy Boers. The Scots Guards rejoined Pulteney's column, escorted by C Squadron Inniskilling Dragoons, which had been left behind at Belfast for that purpose.

Pulteney's column, complete, advanced over steep hills and through a bad drift to Windhoek (eight

April 19.
Wind-
hoek,
8 miles.
Good
work of
Scots
Guards.
miles). The Scots Guards, as usual, did splendid work, lifting wagons out of drifts, and, on reaching camp, made the most sensible, businesslike, invisible trenches, even insisting on digging these trenches for the cavalry. They were men of fine physique and on excellent terms with their officers, who worked hard with them in their shirt-sleeves.

On reaching Windhoek the tail of a Boer convoy could be seen making off north, about ten miles

April 20.
Captures
by Benson.
distant, over the opposite mountains, and Benson's column, eight miles south-west, making north from Middelburg. Many Boers were surrendering to him, and his captures this day included 130 prisoners, fifty-five wagons, 1,400 cattle, and 8,000 sheep.

The columns were now converging. Marching on to Klipbankspruit, the Inniskilling Dragoons, with April 21. Pulteney's column, had some fighting, knocking over four Boers, and Lieut. Terrott, Inniskillings, with a small patrol, captured four more; twenty others surrendered, whilst our losses included only two wounded.

April 21.
Klipbank-
spruit
captures.

Advancing through a regular defile of bad kopjes, with frequent long halts to drive snipers off the different hills, Roos Senekal was occupied. Forty-eight Z.A.R.P.'s (Transvaal Police), under Commandant Kriel, surrendered, their horses having all died of horse-sickness; as well as about twenty other Boers. Information was also received that about 250 dismounted Boers were in the surrounding hills; but that Viljoen and Botha had broken back across the line into the Carolina district.

April 22.
Roos
Senekal
occupied.
Surrender
of
Z.A.R.P.'s
under
Kriel.

Commandant Kriel and most of his men were Germans. Dining with us that night he was very quiet and guarded, drinking nothing until about to leave, when, filling himself about half a tumbler of crème-de-menthe, he tossed it off at a gulp! He said those guns of ours could never have been captured at Colenso had we guarded them with rifle fire; that they had to swim the river to get at them, then drag them by hand to and across the flooded river by means of long ropes, the guns being entirely submerged as they were dragged across.

Guns at
Colenso.

On this day (April 22) Captain E. S. Jackson, Inniskilling Dragoons, was very severely wounded. He was Provost Marshal on the Staff of Colonel Allenby, whose column was working on our left. A Boer having surrendered the

Captain
E. S.
Jackson
wounded.

previous evening, Captain Jackson, with a small
escort of Carabiniers, left the column as it moved off,
with orders to bring in the family of the Boer. Whilst
so doing, the Boers in the neighbouring hills attacked
the escort, wounding one of the Carabiniers, whose
horse galloped away riderless. Captain Jackson, who
was at the house with one man effecting the removal,
caught the horse and went to the man's rescue. A
stiff fight ensued between Captain Jackson, with only
three men, and the opposing Boers. Matters were
critical, when the guns from the rear of the column,
which was moving away, opened on the enemy,
enabling the plucky little band to effect a retirement, not, however, before Captain Jackson had had
his arm badly shattered by an explosive bullet.

It is a strange coincidence that twice during the
war Captain Jackson should have been reported
killed. On the first occasion his name was mistaken
for that of Captain Jackson, 7th Dragoon Guards,
who was killed whilst attached to the Inniskillings ;
now an error was made in the casualty report.

The Inniskilling Dragoons reconnoitred north,
April 24. blowing up a mill which the Boers were
Recon-
nais- using for grinding mealies to make flour, and
sances. clearing farms—reconnaissances that were
attended with a good deal of sniping.

Colonel Rimington left for Middelburg to take
April 25. over command of a column, Lieut. and Ad-
Riming-
ton takes jutant G. K. Ansell accompanying to act as
a column. his Staff officer. In his absence, Major
Dauncey
com- Dauncey assumed command of the Innis-
mands
regiment. killing Dragoons.

April 26.   The cavalry, ' Royals ' and ' Inniskillings,'
were employed reconnoitring and escorting convoys

COLONEL THURSBY H. E. DAUNCEY,
INNISKILLING DRAGOONS.

of prisoners to Middelburg and taking provisions back.

Lieut. Wood, with his troop of Inniskillings, went into the hills to the north under the guidance of the Landdrost of Roos Senekal, unearthed and brought into camp a large chest containing many important papers, correspondence of the Boer Government, and 50,000*l.* in unsigned notes. After flight from Pietersburg the Boer Government had made Roos Senekal their headquarters. They were now once more a wandering community.

Lieut. Wood secures important documents.

Captures and surrenders continued. Four wagon-loads of women and children came in from the Mapoch's Hill direction, accompanied by fourteen burghers, who were their husbands or relations. Colonel Kitchener's column, operating west of Sekokoeni's country, secured over 100 prisoners, totalling about 500 for Pulteney's, Benson's, and Kitchener's columns.

April 27.

During a farm-clearing reconnaissance we also discovered one of our destroyed field guns ; it was one of the 66th Battery that had been lost at Colenso.

April 28.

In the morning the Roos Senekal Court-house was blown up. As usual on destroying buildings or farmhouses, ammunition proved to be concealed under the corrugated iron roof. In exploding it sounded like continued musketry fire.

Destruction of Court-house.

Pulteney's column then left Roos Senekal and marched south by west to Blinkwater (fourteen miles), *en route* to Middelburg. Horse-sickness was at this season prevalent, about two

April 29.

horses per regiment dying each day from the disease,
for which experts have for so many years
failed to find any cure.

General Sir Bindon Blood was encamped here,
and escorts were passing, conveying Boer families,
prisoners, and cattle from General Kitchener's column
to Middelburg.

At 10.30 on a bright moonlight night, Pulteney's
column commenced a return march (fourteen
miles) to surprise Roos Senekal, rightly
judging that the Boers lurking in the hills
would again be in occupation of it.

At daylight the Royals and Inniskillings surrounded and rushed the town. In the fighting that
ensued four Boers were killed and ten wounded ;
one had both his legs blown off by a pom-pom
shell. The column then marched back six miles to
De Jaeger's Drift, where a destroyed Boer pom-pom
was found ; thence to Klipspruit (fifteen
miles), and thence to Elandslaagte and Brakfontein, five miles from Middelburg.

Lieut. Raymond Johnson and Second Lieuts.
Dixon and Holland joined at Brakfontein
with a draft, but Lieut. Raymond Johnson
left next day to go upon Colonel Rimington's
staff as galloper to his column, which was
forming at Standerton.

This draft, with the regimental band, under
Captain Anstice, Second Lieuts. Dixon,
Holland, and Oates, had landed at Cape
Town on January 10, 1901. The band be-
ing left there under Mr. Prosser, the band-
master, the draft entrained at Salt River
Junction, where it was joined by Second Lieut. Close,

who had just been gazetted to the regiment. It then proceeded to Piquetberg Road, took over fifty-four horses, and, instead of going on to the regiment, was employed reconnoitring, owing to rumours that the Boers were advancing from Calvinia. It remained Jan. 23. here on this duty till January 23, and, before leaving to hold Groenfontein, was complimented by General Settle ' on its behaviour, and the excellent example it had set the Irregular troops during its stay.'

After occupying Groenfontein till February 10, Captain Anstice, with Second Lieuts. Dixon, Oates, Feb. 10. and fifty men, entrained to Prince Albert's Road and joined Colonel Sir C. Parsons' column. The remainder of the draft, with Second Lieuts. Holland and Close, was left at Karroo Poort.

After a good deal of marching about, and a few scraps with the Boers, the beginning of March found the draft at Willowmore. On proceeding to Aberdeen Road on March 5, as the advance force March 5. of Colonel Sir C. Parsons' column, a telegram was received that Aberdeen was invested, and ordering a demonstration in that direction.

Leaving fifty Imperial Yeomanry (Scottish Sharpshooters) to guard the transport, Captain Anstice at once marched with the Inniskillings and remainder of the troops under his command on Aberdeen, which was successfully occupied, the Boers retiring. The enemy had, however, only moved into the hills. Next morning Colonel Sir C. Parsons, having arrived, sent out three strong patrols, consisting of a subaltern and fifteen men each. About 8 A.M. orderlies came in with reports from each of these patrols that they were engaged. There were one Inniskilling and two

Imperial Yeomanry patrols. Captain Anstice, with the few men that could be immediately collected, was ordered to the support of Lieut. Clarke's Imperial Yeomanry patrol. The latter was soon perceived effecting a retirement, pursued by the enemy. To cover it Captain Anstice, with a troop of Imperial Yeomanry, supported by Second Lieut. Dixon with the Inniskillings, galloped for a low range of hills about 2,000 yards to the west of the camp.

When within 500 yards of the ridge they came under heavy fire from the Boers, who had previously occupied it. Galloping on, they dismounted under the lee of the ridge, which they stormed on foot. The Boers were in strength, and a fierce fight ensued, during which Captain Anstice himself was wounded in four places, Lieut. Edlmann (Imperial Yeomanry) also wounded, and two men Imperial Yeomanry (Scottish Sharpshooters) killed. The ridge was taken, and, our guns coming into action, the Boers retired.

Captain Anstice wounded.

Lieut. H. Dixon, with the Inniskillings, was now ordered to gallop back to the other side of the town, and repulsed an attack there, capturing one of the townsmen who was treacherously signalling to the enemy.

Meantime the other Imperial Yeomanry patrol had been captured, whilst Lieut. Oates, with the Inniskilling patrol, was making a splendid fight in a river-bed about six miles out. Taking advantage of all cover, he directed each man, as he finished his ammunition, to creep back to the town with his rifle ; several were seriously wounded, but managed to crawl away. In the end, after four hours' fighting, only

Gallant fight of Lieut. Oates with Inniskilling patrol.

Oates himself remained; with one of the last shots fired by the enemy he was shot through the thigh, the bone being broken. Twice during the engagement, Scheepers, who was in command of the Boers, had sent a white flag demanding surrender, but on both occasions got the same reply—viz. 'that they were there to fight, not surrender.' At one time the Boers got up to within twenty yards of the small party, but finally gave up the attempt to capture it, and did not secure a single rifle. It was not till 6.30 P.M. that Lieut. Oates was picked up by the ambulance under Captain White, which had been searching many hours for him, for he had lain wounded in the hot sun since 10 A.M. He was taken to Mr. Harvey's house in Aberdeen, where Captain Anstice had been conveyed earlier in the day. That night the enemy, doubtless hearing of the approach of Colonel Grenfell's column, withdrew.

Next morning the Inniskilling draft, now numbering only thirty-five men out of the original fifty, March 7. marched to Murraysburg (twenty-five miles), Expedition under Colonel Scobell. where Colonel Parsons lent it to Colonel Scobell for two days. Colonel Scobell had arranged for all the outlets to the big hills overhanging Graaf Reinet to be stopped, and sent the Inniskillings that night, with a squadron of the Cape Mounted Rifles and a pom-pom, into the centre of the hills to drive the Boers out. After marching all night through the mountains in pitch March 8. darkness and rain, the Boers were found at 2 A.M., but they refused to fight, and escaped by climbing up the sheer faces of the mountains, which ran up both sides of the road. The net result

of the expedition was that one Boer had his head
blown off by a pom-pom shell.

After a week at Murraysburg, Colonel Parsons
handed over his column to Major Warden (now
Major Colonel Warden, D.S.O.).   Before doing so,
Warden. he thanked the Inniskilling draft on parade
for their good work.   Under Major Warden they
trekked to Graaf Reinet, Pearston, Craddock, and
back by Aberdeen Road to Graaf Reinet.   Colonel
Scobell's and Colonel Grenfell's columns were here ;
with the latter were Second Lieut. S. L. Holland and
forty of the Inniskilling draft that had previously
been left at Karroo Poort ; they had taken part in a
big engagement outside Jansenville, when about forty
Boers were killed and wounded.

At Colonel Scobell's request both portions of the
Inniskilling draft were now transferred to his column,
and formed a squadron sixty strong under their
officers, Second Lieuts. Dixon, Holland, and Close.
For the next two months Colonel Scobell was continually hunting Scheepers' commando about the
Karroo, several times being engaged with him, and
twice very nearly bringing off the *coup*, which he
eventually succeeded in doing.   In this dry country
the water was often bad, and the hardships great, but
the men were always cheerful and willing, and, when
eventually the Inniskilling draft was ordered up
country to join its regiment, Colonel Scobell said he
was very sorry to lose them.   Shortly afterwards this
dashing leader captured, killed, or wounded Scheepers
himself with his entire commando.   Now at last this
draft reached the regiment.

These experiences and doings of a young draft
under young officers (Captain Anstice having been

wounded), joining their regiment for the first time, are unique and worthy of all praise.

May 7 to 11. Further operations under Bindon Blood. During the few days' halt at Brakfontein, near Middelburg, another combined movement of six columns under Sir Bindon Blood was arranged. Once more the Eastern Transvaal, to which the Boers had broken back, was to be swept.

On this movement, which occupied from May 12 to July 4, Pulteney's, which was one of the columns, marched south-east to Lake Chrissie, thence east by north to Steynsdorp, and on to the Komati River; then back south *via* Amsterdam; then north-west up past Lake Chrissie again to Carolina; and thence west to Middelburg once more. The column still consisted of the Inniskillings, Royals, and Scots Guards, with four field guns, one howitzer, and a pom-pom.

Starting on May 12 by Rockdale, about 200 Boers were encountered at Driehoek. They captured one

May 12. Driehoek. man of the advanced guard, Private Clark, of the Inniskillings, but, having taken his rifle and bandolier, released him and fled. An hour later this man's bandolier was found complete in one of their wagons which we captured.

Whilst moving on by De Monsen's Store to De Witte's Krans a good deal of sniping took place.

May 15. De Witte's Krans. Successful pursuit by Inniskillings. The Inniskillings, who were in advance, received permission to pursue a large party of the enemy and succeeded in capturing nine Boers, four wagons, two Cape carts, two spider carts, also many horses and cattle.

With constant sniping and flight of the snipers, Haartebeeste Spruit, Klipstapel—the highest point in the Transvaal—Botha's Rust and Simonsdale were passed.   At Simonsdale General Bindon Blood was

May 16 to 18.   in signal communication from Carolina, and Bullock from Ermelo.   The plan was for General F. W. Kitchener's and Pulteney's columns to block the roads between Steynsdorp and Amsterdam.   In very hilly country and bitterly cold weather,

May 19 to 23.   with intense frost at night, daily advances were made to Bothwell (Lake Chrissie); Lillieburn, on the Umpilusi River; Vlakfontein, where S. S. Davidson, an Inniskilling Dragoon scout, was mortally wounded; Holnek, where a post was left, and Zonstraal.   Two days were spent here getting a convoy of provisions from Carolina.

May 25.   During reconnaissances three Boers and two wagons were captured.

Leaving a post of Scots Guards at Zonstraal, an advance was made to Tygerkloof (ten miles).   The

May 26. Destruction of telegraph offices.   Inniskillings reconnoitred on five miles to Oshoek, on the Swaziland border, destroying a telegraph office there in full working order;

Captures.   and another one, *en route*, on the Haartebeestefontein Farm.   Nine Boers were also captured by C Squadron.   That evening a company of the Scots Guards were having their kits searched, as something had been reported stolen.   ' What are you looking for?' facetiously asked one of our 66th Battery *en passant*.   ' Looking for the guns you lost at Colenso,' replied one of the Scots Guards.

Leaving the rest of the infantry at Tygerkloof, the mounted troops descended into the valley, a deep drop into a milder temperature that was delightful, and halted by Steynsdorp.   Next day an advance was made to Kranskop on the Komati River, the

Inniskillings reconnoitring far east, but only capturing large herds of cattle which numbered 700 head. The

May 27.
Steyns-
dorp.
May 28.
Kranskop.

Komati here was twenty yards broad, very rocky and deep, and fordable in very few places. We squeezed a big frog out of a snake, which was captured in the river and killed. The frog then hopped off quite happily.

On the march back to the Tygerkloof Hills news was received that some Boers were in hiding there,

May 30.
Captures
by Royals
and Innis-
killings.
Tyger-
kloof
Hills.

so A Squadron Inniskillings were sent up as 'stopgaps,' and the Royals drove the hills. The result was successful, as fifteen Boers were sandwiched, one of whom had an Innis-killing carbine in his possession. Our ambulance also brought in two Boers from the Sheba Queen Mine, who had been wounded in Swaziland by McCorquodale, of Steinacker's Horse.

During the return to Zonstraal trying weather was experienced : furious hurricanes and intense

Trying
weather.

frost. During reconnaissances many Boer families were found hidden in comfortable little camps in the steep kloofs and brought in ; Trichardt's big telescope was also found hidden in a kloof, and 300 dynamite cartridges. Operations continued in the neighbourhood of Zonstraal, with

June 9.

many long marches and reconnaissances, till June 9, when the column moved by Bonnie Braes, Avondale, Mayflower, and Maryvale to Amsterdam.

Amsterdam was found totally destroyed, and thence the column worked up the Compies River

June 10
to 15.
Amster-
dam.

and Zand Spruit, turning north to Lake Chrissie and Carolina. Daily marches, with constant sniping, surrenders, pursuits, and

captures, brought the column to Glen Eland, Bank-
Daily marches. plaats, Schimmelhoek, Driefontein, and
Lilliefontein; and Carolina was reached on
June 21.

All the Boers who surrendered seemed anxious to
betray their comrades: a curious trait of the Boer
Boer character. character! Many who surrendered took up
arms for us against their own fathers and
brothers, and we nearly always found them staunch
and true to our cause. 'Tame Burghers' we termed
them, and most proved right good fellows, thoroughly
to be trusted. What better proof of this than the
Corps of National Scouts, enlisted later?

June 20. At Driefontein one of the Royals' rear-
guard, who stayed behind to assist a sick
man, was shot dead by snipers.

Passing Lilliefontein by Tevreden, we saw the
graves of Lieut. Swanston and Private Gardner,
Tevreden. Inniskilling Dragoons; Sergeant Hunter,
Kitchener's Horse; Corporal Mullion, 10th
Hussars; Corporal Porter, Scots Greys; and others
who were killed in the fierce fight there the previous
October.

Colonel Hughes-Hallett was commanding at
Carolina, with the 5th Lancers and a half battalion
of the Seaforths.

Leaving there the next day, the column marched
west to Maudesbank, over a burnt, black country,
June 23. which on all sides and as far as the eye could
reach looked like a huge peat-bog. There
was no grazing for the horses, but old mealie patches
afforded some nutriment for the mules. Grobler's
Recht and Vaalbank were occupied until the column
united at Boschmanspan (Monsen's Store) on July 1.

Snipers were still active all round, and, when moving off at daylight in a thick mist, a corporal of the Inniskilling Dragoons' rear-guard post was shot dead at the building of Monsen's Store.

By Aaronsfontein and Rockdale, Middelburg was once more reached.

Viljoen, Jack Hinton, and about 800 Boers were supposed to be about ten miles north of Middelburg, and snipers were active on all sides. A few nights previously seventy-one horses had been driven off by the Boers from the remount kraals at Middelburg.

News was received that Colonel Rimington, Inniskilling Dragoons, whose column was operating in the Pongola district, had himself captured Field-Cornet Emmett, having ridden him down and held him up with his Mauser pistol.

CHAPTER XX

RIMINGTON'S COLUMN

COLONEL PULTENEY's column was now broken up, the Royals and Inniskillings, under command of Lieut.-Colonel Lord Basing (Royals), starting on July 8 *en route* to Pretoria and marching along the railway line. Halting at Olifant's River Station, Outspan, Balmoral, Bronkhorst Spruit, Eland's River Station, and Silverton, Pretoria was reached on the 14th.

Pulteney's column broken up.

July 8.
March from Middel-burg to Pretoria.

July 14.

Colonel Rimington having requested that his regiment might join his own column at Heilbron, the Inniskilling Dragoons entrained next day for Vredefort Road Station, marching thence twenty miles to Heilbron. A night march was then made by the regiment, in conjunction with the Heilbron garrison, in order to surround some Boers on ridges four miles south of the town, but daylight found the Boers 'not at home.'

July 15.
Vredefort Road.

July 17.
Heilbron, 20 miles.

July 19.

Rimington's column arrived at Heilbron, and the Inniskillings joined it and remained with it till the end of the campaign. No column did more towards finishing the war. The enormous work they did and their successes are universally acknowledged. It was Colonel Rimington who originated, planned, and caused to

July 21.
Innis-killings join Riming-ton's column.

GENERAL RIMINGTON AND HIS STAFF.

COMMANDING OFFICERS OF RIMINGTON'S COLUMN.

be executed that system of 'drives' which did more than anything to overcome the resistance. The Boers themselves acknowledge this.

The strength of this column was as follows :

	Officers.	Men.	Horses.
6th Inniskilling Dragoons . .	16	450	499
8th Hussars	7	173	204
J Battery R.H.A.	1	38	53
74th „ R.F.A.	2	58	48
Pom-pom	1	10	18
Maxims	3	—	—
Colts	2	—	—
2nd Queen's	8	289	12
3rd New South Wales M.R. . .	47	749	909
Canadians	3	47	60
40 Army Service Corps . . .	1	13	15
85 „ „ „ . . .	2	23	15
17th Royal Engineers . . .	1	12	9
4th Field Hospital . . .	2	22	7
Intelligence and M.M.P. . .	2	28	67
Headquarters	6	30	36
	104	1,942	1,952

Lieut. G. K. Ansell, Inniskilling Dragoons, was Staff Officer ; Major H. R. Gale, D.A.A.G.

The Inniskilling Dragoons were under the command of Major Dauncey ; the 8th Hussars under Major Wood ; the Queen's Regiment under Lieut.-Colonel Pink, D.S.O. ; the Artillery under Lieut.-Colonel Wing, R.H.A. ; the Canadian Scouts under Captain Williams ; and the New South Wales Mounted Rifles under Lieut.-Colonel Cox.

July 22.
Transport
under
Capt. E. C.
Holland.
The whole of the transport was reorganised and placed under the charge of Captain E. C. Holland, Inniskilling Dragoons, who had

s 2

hitherto so capably managed the regimental transport. The system of regimental transport was now abolished, only a sufficient amount to carry a minimum of baggage being allowed to units, and only one Cape cart to each officers' mess. The new plan was to form a column transport.

At 7 P.M. the force divided into two columns : A, consisting of four and a half squadrons 3rd New South July 23. Wales Mounted Rifles and a section Royal Night opera- tions. Field Artillery ; and B, three squadrons Inniskilling Dragoons and two squadrons 3rd New South Wales Mounted Rifles. A, under Lieut.-Colonel Wing, B, under Colonel M. F. Rimington, marched off approximately parallel to the Frankfort and Lindley roads till dawn, dropping detachments as they moved along.

At dawn the columns, having covered over twenty miles, wheeled inwards and drove back to Heilbron. The infantry, under Lieut.-Colonel Pink, C.M.G., D.S.O., with two troops and a pom-pom, had been left to hold the line of the Klip River. A good many farms were rounded up during the night, and July 24. next morning the Boers were completely surprised. They were not sleeping in laager, but were scattered about the country in twos and threes. Our casualties were only two men New South Wales Mounted Rifles wounded, through their horses falling. One Boer was killed, one wounded, and twenty-two taken prisoners, practically all being Captures. armed. Forty-five riding horses, two mules, about 1,800 cattle, twenty-two wagons, and seventeen Cape carts were also captured. All the prisoners belonged to Steenkamp's commando. It was a hard trek on horses, the night being very cold and the day hot, the distance covered being fifty-five to sixty miles.

A light column was now organised, carrying a minimum of baggage and eight days' supplies, the dismounted men and weak horses being formed into a depôt and left at Heilbron under charge of Major Burbage, 3rd New South Wales Mounted Rifles.

July 25.

In the afternoon Colonel Rimington's force marched to Holland Farm on the Frankfort road in two columns, one feinting to the north as if the whole force was moving towards Grobler's Drift, then, after dark, bearing again to the south and reaching Holland's Farm at 10 P.M.

July 26.

At this point the columns divided into two parties, half, including the Inniskillings, under Colonel Wing, marching east, half, under Colonel Rimington, south-east to Twee-fontein, throwing out a detached force of three squadrons New South Wales Mounted Rifles, under Lieut.-Colonel Cox, to the right; the object being to drive the triangle of country formed by the Krom Spruit, running from the south-west, and the Klip Spruit, from the south-east. The country was found to be full of mealies and supplies, such as poultry, sheep, and cattle.

July 27.
Combined drives.

Colonel Rimington's force was engaged with some thirty to forty Boers lodged in the rocks on the Tweefontein ridge, and drove them out. During the operations Trooper Morris, 3rd New South Wales Mounted Rifles, was dangerously wounded in the abdomen, and left in charge of Mrs. Faassen at Twee-fontein Farm, who undertook to look after him on receiving a protection order.

Colonel Wing's force, on reaching the Krom Spruit, sighted some Boers and wagons and gave chase. B Squadron of Inniskillings first came up with them, after a six-mile gallop, capturing four wagons. Private Prentice, Inniskillings, was killed, one man wounded, and another captured owing to his horse falling. The force rejoined Colonel Rimington at night, after a long day. The wagons captured (six) were burnt, and 300 head of cattle shot. It had become a stern necessity at this stage of the war to destroy all captured stock that could not be taken away ; otherwise it could only be left to fall again into the enemy's hands and so prolong the war. The shooting of fine cattle and valuable trek oxen and the bayoneting of sheep sounds terrible, but we had learnt that it must be done.

Innis-killings pursue.

Destruction of stock.

At daylight, in bitterly cold wind and driving sleet, the whole column marched to Jagersrust. At midnight it started on again across country to Elandskop by bright moonlight, with a hard white frost. Trammil Farm was rounded up on the way, and information received that a large number of wagons belonging to Steenkamp and De Wet had gone along the Bethlehem road the day before. Acting upon this information, the column turned south and marched fast until 4.30 A.M., when the moon set. The 2nd Queen's then surrounded Lamplaats Farm. Owing to too much talking and noise, this was not successfully done. About six Boers, sleeping in a kraal with their horses, were disturbed too soon. In the shooting that followed one of their horses was killed, but the men got away and warned the wagons that we were pursuing.

July 28.
Jagers-rust.
Cold night march.

DESTROYING BUILDINGS.

SLAUGHTERING CATTLE.

At dawn, after an hour's halt, Colonel Rimington, leaving the baggage, weakest horses, and 2nd Queen's to follow under Lieut.-Colonel Pink, C.M.G., D.S.O., himself pushed on at a great pace with the bulk of his force, and at last sighted the wagons rounding the hill at Groenvlei, north-east of Lindley. Here they broke into two lots. One which continued towards Lindley was pursued by the Inniskillings, and captured with slight opposition; the other turned to the right, and about half were caught by the 8th Hussars, who charged with drawn swords. Our casualties were only one man slightly wounded. The captures included two Boers killed, three taken prisoners, twenty-one wagons, seven Cape carts, and about 2,000 mixed cattle, 500 of which were trek oxen.

July 29.
Lindley.

Pursuit and captures.

The Inniskillings followed beyond Lindley and then returned to Groenvlei, where the whole force bivouacked, having covered thirty-eight miles since the previous midnight.

The baggage under Colonel Pink was continually sniped and the bivouac fired into at night, one horse being killed and another wounded.

July 30.

Colonel Rimington, with half his force, started at 2.30 A.M. in order to get well to the west of the baggage and the rest of the force which was marching back towards Heilbron. Marching off by night he kept off the roads, where the Boers generally placed their picquets, and so got right through them, and only just missed making a big capture owing to a wire fence. Both forces were engaged, eight Boers being killed, including two brothers Mentz (Field Cornets), and young Christian

July 31.

De Wet, a boy of fourteen.   Most of these Boers were found to have been killed by shell fire, which shows that a lot of damage may be done by guns without knowing it.   The captures comprised five wagons, three carts, four horses, two mules, and about three hundred head of cattle.

The force bivouacked at Inloop, having covered twenty miles, and then marched on to Riet-fontein (sixteen miles) and Heilbron.

Aug. 1, 2.

The Inniskillings, one hundred of the 8th Hussars, the Canadian Scouts, and a section R.H.A., under Major Wood, 8th Hussars, reconnoitred before daybreak to Elandskop on the chance of catching any Boers attempting to escape from General Spens, who was operating on the Wilge River and advancing to Heilbron.   A few Boer snipers only were encountered ; these Lieut. Clarke, command-ing the two guns of J Battery, R.H.A., soon silenced.   Lieut. Clarke was a most perfect judge of distance, and had, on more than one occasion of late, proved this by killing, first shot, with shrapnel, at 3,000 yards range, one out of a pair of Boers as they were riding away.

Aug. 3.

Lieut. Clarke, R.H.A.

Colonel Wing, who commanded the Artillery of the column, was a great horseman and horse-master.   The Artillery horses were always in splendid condition and thought nothing of accompanying the Cavalry on a six-mile gallop after Boers at the end of a long night march.

Colonel Wing, R.H.A.

The way in which Colonel Rimington used his artillery was a revelation to us, and showed what they could do.   Previously, on many occasions, we had seen whole batteries held up by one

Use of artillery.

long-range Krupp of the enemy's, just because our
guns were not allowed to gallop to within their own
range of the Krupp, although six to one, and escorted
by a great number of excellent cavalry only too
eager to be unleashed. Now matters were different,
and we meditated on what might have been done
with our artillery on many occasions—notably after
Paardeberg.

Two Boers came in and surrendered with their
cattle, followed by Goff's Mounted Infantry with
General Spens's captures on the Wilge River,
Aug. 4, 5. and next day General Spens himself arrived.
In accordance with orders received from the Commander-in-Chief, Colonel Rimington then arranged
with him a plan of operations to the south and south-
east of Heilbron.

General Spens himself, taking all the more cum-
bersome part of Rimington's force, consisting of sick
Opera- horses, surplus wagons, &c., was with the in-
tions with fantry to sweep the country towards Kroon-
General
Spens. stad. Rimington's column, starting thirty-six
hours previously, was to sweep the country on a wide
front to General Spens's left, swinging round on the
second day towards him. Accordingly, Rimington's
column marched off that night—a pitch-dark night—to
Vetchkop, and concealed itself in the orchards of the
low-lying farm lands, which lent themselves to the purpose, no fires or smoking being allowed. Before dawn
strong posts were hidden in the bushes on the Kop.
So well was the camp concealed that a Boer rode up
during the day, and watered his horse at the dam
before perceiving the camp. He managed to escape,
and later we found out that he was V. C. Boshoff of
Mentz's commando. At midnight the force again

marched (twelve miles) to Winterhoek.   It was then divided into three columns, A, B, and C.

(A) under Lieut.-Col. Wing, R.H.A., consisted of the 8th Hussars, 3rd N.S.W.M.R., 2 squadrons, a section R.H.A., and a Maxim gun.

(B) under Col. Rimington, C.B., of the Inniskilling Dragoons, the 3rd N.S.W.M.R., 1 squadron, the Canadian Scouts, and a section R.H.A.

(C) under Lieut.-Col. Cox, 3rd N.S.W.M.R., of the 3rd N.S.W.M.R., 4 squadrons, a pom-pom, and a Maxim gun.

The columns marched together south until nearly dawn, crossing the Rhenoster at Rivier Plaats, by which time they had reached Rietfontein. C column. Here (C) halted to give the others time to get out wider ; (B) on Waaehoek, (A) on Doorn- A and B kloof.   The whole movement was to end up columns. at Blydschap, but detached forces were to pursue and capture any Boers met with.   A Boer post at Rietfontein fired in the dark on the advanced Boer post guard, killing one horse.   They were galloped surprised. at and had to bolt, leaving their blankets, cooking materials, and saddles on the ground.   After daylight all three forces turned west and pushed on fast.   (A) soon got into touch with a Boer convoy, galloped them for several miles and captured some prisoners.   Each of these forces caught wagons, carts, and cattle, which were scattered all over the country.   The turn west had evidently surprised the Boers.

The captures for the day were ten Boers (one Captures. wounded), thirty-one wagons, fourteen Cape carts, fifty riding horses, and about 2,500 head of cattle.   Andries Wessels, late Peace Dele-

PART OF A CAPTURED CONVOY.

BOUND FOR A REFUGEE CAMP.

gate, was also found on one of the wagons. Colonel Wing had his horse shot dead, which was our only casualty. Having covered about thirty miles, the forces bivouacked at Blydschap, failing to get communication with General Spens.

A letter was found from Steyn, dated June 22, from Villiers, ordering August 8 to be held

Aug. 8.
Steyn's
letter.

as a day of thanksgiving, and August 9 as a day of prayer.

Marching off towards Kroonstad, an ambush of thirty men, under Lieuts. Terrott and Wood, Inniskillings, was left at the farm Blydschap.

Ambush.

After the column had moved off, four Boers came down and were fired on by the ambush ; but, owing to bad shooting, only one man was wounded. Lieut. Terrott galloped after another, and, after a chase of a mile, shot him dead with his Mauser pistol. At this period the Boers were very careless of the way in which they came to the bivouacs directly the troops had left, in order to pick up ammunition, and in many places it was found possible to plant effective ambushes. The best position for this purpose was an isolated house on open ground, where the men forming the ambush could hide behind walls, and the house could be used to put horses in. Mounted men were required to ensure the capture of wounded Boers, and a detached force, hidden within a couple of miles, to pull out the ambush party if necessary. It was of the greatest importance that the ambush party should be in position and hidden before the camp packed up to move.

August
8 to 14.

The next few days were spent in camps at Welgeluk and Helvetia, within six miles of Kroonstad.

Aug. 9.   The 8th Hussars, being required in Natal,
8th Hussars leave left the column.
column.

On two nights, feint night marches were
made just before sunset; the squadrons returned to
bivouac after dark, having seen the Boer picquets
gallop off.   These feints caused much needless work
to the Boers; their scouts would go galloping back
to warn the laagers and outlying Boers of the
column's march, and get them all on the move, only
to find next morning that the whole thing was a false
alarm.   They also caused them to lose faith in their
scouts.

The Inniskillings played the Kroonstad garrison
Aug. 10.   at polo.   Colonel Rimington and General
Polo.   Knox played for their respective sides, and
the regiment won.

General Spens with his own force, Rimington's
Aug. 12.   Infantry, and details, arrived at Kroonstad.
Kroon-   A small depôt was established there under
stad.
Aug. 13.   Major Mosley, of the Inniskillings.

All the intelligence gained during the foregoing
operations pointed to De Wet's making use of
Rounding   Trammil (about twenty-nine miles south-east
up Tram- of Heilbron) as a centre at which to stop
mil.
himself and feed up his horses.   Accordingly, Colonel Rimington decided to round up this
place one night in conjunction with General Spens,
who was to hold a line which was to be driven on to.
The night of August 22–23 was settled on, each
column being ordered to get in position during this
night by a long march of not less than twenty miles;
the country near Trammil was to be carefully left
untouched until after this raid.   Although De Wet
was not there himself, a big capture would have been

made had General Spens kept the appointment ; but, having heard the day before of 120 Boers on the Valsch River, he went for these instead. As it was, during these operations, Colonel Rimington accounted for four Boers killed, two wounded, seventeen captured, also 1,195 cattle, 2,000 sheep, eighteen wagons, fourteen carts, and thirteen mules. His own casualties were two men wounded.

Long night marches were made to Blydschap, then on to Paardefontein, Rivier Plaats, and Marksfontein. Daily sniping, long pursuits, and captures continued.

August 15 to 18.

On the 17th the Inniskillings covered over twenty miles, during which Private Hutchings was killed. Next day two more Inniskillings were wounded in the fighting. The right flank was engaged with 150 to 200 Boers under Hättinge and Mentz. Colonel Rimington, taking the mounted troops, galloped these Boers for about eight miles past Palmietfontein : they were well shelled with 12-pounders and pom-pom for several miles, but only Lieut.-Colonel Cox, who pursued with a few Australians, got into them, killing several and capturing one. He himself, in advance, had a duel with Commandant Hättinge (Chief Commandant of the Heilbron district). Cox had his revolver only, Hättinge a rifle. After firing two shots, Cox found he had only one cartridge left ; so he managed to slip behind some rocks and get back to his men.

Innis-killing losses.

Cox's duel with Hättinge.

Jan Mentz was found buried on his farm, Uitkyk. After marching to Rietfontein, the column moved camp on the morning of the 22nd to Leeuwfontein, so as, by going in the opposite

August 20 to 22.

direction, to make any Boers at Trammil more comfortable.   An ambush of the 2nd Queen's (100) was
Ambush. left behind the garden fences, with twelve
Canadian Scouts in a house.   Two Boers were
wounded by it, one mortally.   Unfortunately a
Canadian Scout, when pursuing one of the wounded
Boers, was mortally wounded by being fired on in
error.

Leaving the Infantry and weak horses in charge
of the camp at Rietfontein, the column, viz. Inniskillings, New South Wales Mounted Rifles, section
R.H.A., section R.F.A., and pom-pom, moved off
after dark straight across the veldt on the Trammil
raid, of which much was expected.

At Steilfontein it was heard that Mentz and all
his men had gone to Trammil.   Marching fast and
Aug. 23, continuously till 2 A.M., the column halted
36 miles. within five miles of Elandskop.   Major
Bennett, with three squadrons New South Wales
Mounted Rifles, then went on to round up Trammil,
and Lieut.-Col. Cox, with three squadrons New
South Wales Mounted Rifles, to round up Rooidraai,
Barend Wessels' place.   The former got eight
prisoners and the latter four, one of them being
Barend Wessels himself; others, on horseback, broke
through the circle of bayonets in the dark.

Forming three columns, Colonel Rimington now
swept the country with a front of about ten miles,
travelling fast towards the line arranged to be held
by General Spens.   About sixty Boers, wagons, carts,
and cattle were sighted in front.   Disappointment was
great to see them all escape across the river, General
Spens's force not being there to block them as was
expected.   Thirty-six miles had been covered since

the previous evening, so the column had to turn back,
the Boers driven across the river returning to snipe
the rear-guard.   Three of our police, who pursued
some Boers, were entrapped and captured by twenty-
eight men of the Mentz and Haasbruck commandos,
who stripped them and sent them off on foot.

The column marched back to Rietfontein (twenty-
two miles) by Steilfontein, where a quantity of
Aug. 24, mealies and furniture were found hidden.
Riet-
fontein, On the way back one of the Inniskillings was
22 miles. wounded, also four artillery horses.   It was
unfortunately found necessary to destroy 400 head of
captured cattle that could not keep up.

The force, after this, proceeded to Kroonstad by
Paardekraal and Bloemhof, passing many comfortable
Aug. 26 to farms, which were rendered less so.   A good
28.   deal of flour and 2,000 rounds of small ammunition also were discovered and dug up.

CHAPTER XXI

COMBINED OPERATIONS—PURSUITS AND CAPTURES

OPERATIONS were now arranged with General Spens and Lieut.-Colonel Wilson to move against the Boers south-east of Kroonstad. Colonel Wilson had already met them near Jaskraal, about 300 in number, under De Vos. Not having guns or men sufficient to engage them, he had retired on Kroonstad. Roughly, the plan was for the three columns to march south-east with an interval of twelve hours between them : Colonel Rimington first, then Colonel Wilson, and General Spens in rear. All were to turn off south suddenly and try to close round the Boers.

Colonel Rimington's column accordingly made a night march to Mierkatfontein, continuing next morning past Modderfontein and close to Maquanstad, and back to Modderfontein. Boers, with cattle and wagons, were seen in small lots all round, and pursued ; the result for the day being two Boers killed, eight wagons, four carts, and 150 head of cattle captured. Our only disaster consisted in the capture of Captain Hilliam with two of his Canadian Scouts and two Australians, who pursued too far over the Vaalsch River and were cut off by the enemy,

2ND QUEEN'S CROSSING THE VAALSCH RIVER.

and two of whom were wounded. They were afterwards released. When covering these big distances in pursuit, there was always the danger of small parties pursuing too far and getting out of touch of support.

Marching to Maquanstad, heliograph communication was obtained with both General Spens and Colonel Wilson.

Sept. 1.

Next day, after marching about twelve miles, a large Boer convoy was seen from a high ridge moving south. The Boers themselves first drew attention to this convoy, which was many miles in length, by lighting almost simultaneously, shortly after we had shown on the ridge, a line of grass fires between us and their wagons. Colonel Rimington at once pursued the convoy for eleven miles, killing two Boers and capturing eighteen prisoners, fifty-two wagons, twenty-two carts, twenty-three riding horses (100 unfit horses, shot), and 1,200 head of mixed cattle. A large number of women were in the captured wagons. These, instead of being brought in, were left at a farm. By not taking in women, a great encumbrance was put on the Boer leaders, who had to find food for them, which, at this stage of the war, was a great consideration. The burghers preferred the women to be left out, but their leaders hated it.

Sept. 2.

Captures.

Treatment of Boer women.

Having no baggage or rations, the column started back again at 10 P.M., when the moon rose, and finally by firing off guns found their convoy, at 2.30 A.M. near (Bester's Farm) Kaffirfontein. It had been a hard day, over forty miles having been traversed since the previous morning!

Sept. 3, long march, 40 miles.

T

A small force, sent out reconnoitring for mealies, discovered a flour mill belonging to Kemp, and destroyed the engines; they also brought in twenty horses and 150 head of cattle. Ten thousand sheep, brought in the previous day, were destroyed with bayonets to prevent their falling into the hands of the enemy again.

The column marched to Blaaubank on the Jasspruit (ten miles), securing two prisoners, five carts, three mules, three horses, and 120 head of cattle, and next day on to Meriba (fifteen miles), sending wagons to Kroonstad for supplies, which returned next day.

Sept. 4.
Blaau-
bank,
10 miles.
Captures.
Sept. 5.
Meriba,
15 miles.

Information was received from a Boer prisoner that De Wet and Steyn had both been staying at Brakoog, near Tweefontein, since August 21; so Colonel Rimington decided to round up this place, after a long night march from the other side of Heilbron. Later, information was received from the G.O.C., Kroonstad, that Nagel, with some thirty Boers, who practised some sort of drill, were near Uitkyk, south-east of Rhenoster, and that he would co-operate with a small force of Mounted Infantry if Colonel Rimington would endeavour to carry out a surprise. This was accordingly arranged for dawn on September 9.

Sept. 6.

Crossing the Vaalsch River by a very bad drift, where all heavy wagons had to be double-spanned, a halt was made at Omega (eight miles) and Uitenhage (fourteen miles).

Sept. 7.

A good many horses were lost at this time owing to the prevalence of the young tulp grass, the poisonous nature of which I have before alluded to. No fewer than forty-eight horses

Tulp
grass.

LENDING A HAND.

TEAMS DOUBLE-SPANNED.

of the 3rd New South Wales Mounted Rifles were poisoned by grazing on it this day, and died the following day.

At 2.30 A.M. the night march to surprise Nagel's commando, reported at Uitkyk, twelve miles north-east, was commenced. At daylight communication was established with the Mounted Infantry from the railway line ; but the Boers had escaped, and were only visible in the far distance, travelling rapidly with galloping Cape carts. The surprise column accordingly rejoined their main body at China, having covered twenty-one miles, but having collected some thirty horses from the surrounding country, which, though unbroken, were useful as remounts.

Sept. 9. China, 21 miles. Nagel's escape.

At Leeuwfontein information was received that small Boer commandos, under Bucknel and Bester, about eighty in number, were in the habit of sleeping in a small laager near Middenin, so it was decided to include this place in the night march on Brakoog, where De Wet was reported to be.

Sept. 10.

At 7 P.M. the surprise force, consisting as usual of the Inniskillings, New South Wales Mounted Rifles, Canadians, and section R.H.A., under Colonel Rimington himself, started on the night march. After crossing the Klip River near Parys, about 2 A.M., the column was obliged to halt on account of the intense darkness. The moon had gone down and heavy rain set in. The troops lay by their horses in bitter cold and rain until dawn, and then pushed on fast and rounded up Brakoog. Ten Boers escaped. Pushing on to Anderkant and towards Sodas, a few Boers were

Sept. 14. Surprise force.

46 miles.

caught, and our convoy was rejoined in the valley below Kat Kop.

The night had been against the enterprise. About forty-six miles had been covered, and De Wet had not been taken. But the capture included six Boers, six rifles, 300 rounds of small-arm ammunition, six wagons, nine Cape carts, 350 cattle, eleven mules, and six riding-horses.

Captures.

Camp was moved a few miles on to Brakoog in pouring rain. When the troops moved off an ambush was left hidden in a spruit. Eight Boers came down together, but before they got nearer than 400 yards a native warned them, so only one was wounded and one horse shot.

Sept. 16.
Ambush.

Holland (eight miles) was occupied next day, a reconnoitring party bringing in four wagon-loads of mealies, 200 sheep, and 220 rounds of small-arm ammunition.

Sept. 17.

A halt was made here whilst a convoy was sent to Heilbron for supplies and to take sick men there. Mealies, too, were collected from the surrounding country.

Sept. 18
to 20.

Captain Burgoyne, 3rd Dragoon Guards, joined and took over the duties of signalling officer to the column.

Burgoyne
joins.

Colonel Rimington met General Bruce Hamilton half-way to Heilbron, in order to arrange future movements.

Rimington
meets
Bruce
Hamilton.

The supply wagons having returned from Heilbron at 6 P.M., the horses were given a good feed of hay all round. Colonel Rimington then marched at 8 P.M. with his force divided into three columns, under himself, Colonel Wing, and Colonel Pink. His own was to move down the

Sept. 22.
Night
march.

LIEUT. R. B. JOHNSON WITH HIS CORPS OF SCOUTS, COMPOSED OF
INNISKILLINGS AND NEW SOUTH WALES BUSHMEN.
These Scouts captured 42 Boers in one month.

GENERAL RIMINGTON, CAPTAIN ANSELL, AND COLONEL WING
AFTER A NIGHT MARCH.

Klip River, cross the Wilge at Leeuwbank, then open out between the two rivers and sweep fast down towards their junction. The others were to move together all night to Cyfergat, from which place one column was to move on sharp into the high ground overlooking the Wilge River.

It was a cold night and a hot day's march, but the plan was well carried out and successful. The

Sept. 23. Captures by Lieut. R. B. Johnson.

Boers were completely surprised and many small parties captured. Lieut. R. B. Johnson, Inniskillings (Provost Marshal), with his police, came across a small laager of seventeen Boers, who were taken with all their wagons; two were killed and one wounded. It was a smart performance. For their gallant and dashing conduct Lieut. R. B. Johnson and Lieut. F. W. Moffitt, who was serving under him, were mentioned by Lord Kitchener in despatches (October 8, 1901). Another party took four in a farm just before daylight. Altogether two Boers were killed, two mortally wounded, and thirty prisoners, seventeen wagons, nineteen carts, forty horses, twenty-two mules, and 1,180 mixed cattle were captured.

In the afternoon the columns returned and rejoined their convoy at Leeuwbank, a distance of

48 miles.

forty-eight miles having been covered since the previous evening. One of the prisoners reported that De Wet was ill with inflammation of the lungs in some farm near Uitenhage. This was confirmed to a certain extent by information received from women, so Colonel Rimington decided to move back sharp and round-up the Uitenhage district, on the chance of the report being true.

Starting at 7 A.M., the whole force moved to

camp, two miles north of Heilbron (sixteen miles),
where Colonel Rimington himself took on 300 men
on selected horses, consisting of 100 Inniskillings, with a Maxim, and 200 3rd New South
Wales Mounted Rifles, with a Maxim. Marching
through Heilbron just as it got dark, they
went fast all night, and straight across
country to Uitenhage. Arriving just before
dawn, he surrounded it with 150 of the New South
Wales Mounted Rifles, dismounted, with fixed
bayonets. Five good fighting Boers were captured
asleep in the garden, with their horses, but no De
Wet! All the neighbouring farms were rounded up
at a gallop, but, alas! the information was false, and
De Wet was not in the vicinity.

Sept. 24.

Surprise night march.

Returning to Heilbron, Major Dauncey was met
with the remainder of the Inniskillings and New
South Wales Mounted Rifles, with supplies. They
had been given some trouble by Mentz's men coming
through Paardekraal, and had one man hit.

Despite the very hot days, Colonel Rimington,
with his 300 men, had covered sixty miles in
thirty hours, with a loss of only seven horses.
This shows the distance that fit horses can move.

Fine marching.

Regarding the rounding-up of houses by night,
the system adopted was to use a large number of
men (100 to 150, according to the size of
the grounds) armed with rifles and fixed
bayonets. These left their horses at least
three-quarters of a mile away, and advanced
quietly on foot. They were formed into two bodies,
and, when near the house, enclosed it by moving
round each side in single file, the men gradually
dividing the distance all round, each lying down in

Rounding-up of houses by night. Plan adopted.

turn and waiting for the circle to close, the leaders of
the two parties in the end meeting on the opposite
side of the house. The whole then advanced till the
circle was somewhat narrowed a bit; they then lay
down and waited whilst a separate party advanced
and searched the house. No firing was allowed, and
care was taken that all the gardens and cattle kraals
should be enclosed.

During the day, whilst firing at the enemy, two
rifles burst. It was afterwards shown by a Court of
Dynamite Inquiry that this was due to dynamite car-
cartridges. tridges having got amongst the ammunition,
and that these rounds had been taken from Boers
captured the previous day. It is interesting to note
that neither man was in the least hurt by the
accident, but the rifles were destroyed, the breeches
being irreparably damaged.

Sept. 27. Orders were received from headquarters
Departure for the Canadian Scouts to return to Pre-
of the
Canadian toria. They had rendered excellent service,
Scouts. and all were sorry to lose them.

Colonel Rimington's column now marched from
Heilbron to Standerton (seventy-four miles), in con-
Sept. 29. junction with Colonel Rawlinson's column,
Opera-
tions in which was operating in the Transvaal, the
con-
junction object being to capture any Boers whom he
with might put across the river from the Trans-
Raw-
linson. vaal. Rimington's plan was to make consecutive night marches, lying quiet in the day;
thereby deceiving the Boers as to the presence of his
column and counting on their not expecting more
than one night march at a time.

Night Moving by Wolverfontein, the column
march. proceeded at 2 A.M. to Onlangs; next night

through Broederstroom Drift, on the Wilge River, which, owing to its rocky nature, took three hours to cross, to Wingfield. Two Boer scouts of Ross's commando were galloped down and captured here, with their rifles; also four horses, a wagon, and two carts. At midnight the column started on their third consecutive night march. Moving fast, with the infantry in wagons, Braspruit (seventeen miles) was reached at dawn. Leaving the remainder of the troops with the convoy, Colonel Rimington took two squadrons Inniskillings, four squadrons New South Wales Mounted Rifles, a section Royal Field Artillery, and a pom-pom, and pushed on fast to Grootvlei, where a small Boer laager was spied. Sending two squadrons of the Australians round on the right, the Inniskilling Dragoons galloped straight at it, and pursued the flying Boers, killing two with swords. The guns also shelled the Boers in retreat from 1,500 yards range upwards.

In the pursuit Captain Ansell, Inniskilling Dragoons (Staff Officer to the column), had a single-handed combat with a very lusty Boer, both mounted. During the chase Captain Ansell overtook the Boer, who twisted suddenly round, firing his rifle at one yard range. Ansell, who was only armed with an infantry bayonet in his hand, closed and tried to stick him, but the bayonet hit his bandolier. The Boer again fired his rifle, scorching the sleeve and side of Ansell's coat. The latter then got his bayonet about two inches into the Boer's back, and, clutching hold of him, they both rolled off their horses on to the ground. There Ansell got

Marginal notes:

Sept. 30. Night march.

Oct. 2. Night march. Braspruit, 17 miles.

Boer laager surprised. Charge of Inniskillings.

Captain Ansell's combat.

him by the throat and gained the upper hand. This Boer had a splendid 'Steyr' rifle, quite new, in a waterproof case. In this rifle the magazine loads at the side; it is beautifully sighted, but is said to have been refused by General Joubert for the Transvaal Government in favour of the Mauser.

The Boer laager with all their wagons was captured. Four Boers were killed, and the captures Captures. included twenty prisoners, fourteen wagons, twenty carts, 2,000 cattle, four mules, eighteen horses, all of Buys's commando.

The column moved on to Springbok Laagte, Marny Botha's farm, where Lieut. Gibson, Inniskilling Dragoons, found his sword which was taken from him when he was captured in July last year, near Rhenoster Kop, west of the railway. On that occasion, Lieut. Gibson was returning to the regiment on recovery from his severe wounds, previously narrated. *En route* he was called on by a General Officer to undertake, with a small party, a risky reconnaissance after De Wet, during which he was captured.

After the continuous night marches, during the last of which over twenty miles had been covered, Oct. 3. the troops welcomed a night's rest; but they Goed-gevonden, moved on next day twenty-five miles to Goed-25 miles. gevonden, within six miles of Standerton. In the morning, an Australian was hit and an Inniskilling horse killed by H. Botha's snipers. It was learnt afterwards that H. Botha himself was slightly wounded in the arm by our reply shell-fire.

The Boers took the Medical Officer's horse and his orderly's, as they found an empty bandolier in the ambulance which he had taken out for the purpose of picking up our wounded Australian. The ambulance and team they left untouched, the doctor craftily telling them he had been carrying measles patients in it.

After three days' halt, Rimington's column started off again south of Standerton to Bothasberg and back Fresh   by Leeuwkop and Tafelkop—about 173 miles, operation. with the intention of acting against Bothasberg from the north, while General Elliot was to send two columns, General Broadwood's and Colonel De Lisle's, from the east and south—the columns to be there on the morning of the 11th. The latter part of the programme was not carried out, as General Elliot's columns were unable to be there. Van Zoulecum, the O.C. Burgher Corps of Standerton, requested permission to bring his corps with Rimington's column in order to scout and pick up straggling cattle. This was sanctioned, on condition that all horses they captured were handed over to the column.

Crossing the Vaal River by the bridge at Standerton the column marched to Delange's Drift, crossing Oct. 8.   through it and chasing Boers, but only Delange's capturing about 300 head of cattle and a Drift, 20 miles. few horses. The distance covered was over twenty miles.

Continuing towards Vrede, the column turned off to the north corner of Leeuwpoort. One man of Oct. 9. the Inniskilling advanced guard was wounded by snipers; one Boer also was wounded, and one was killed by the Burgher Scouts. After a very wet night, an advance was made to the Slang River.

Taking two squadrons of the Inniskillings, four squadrons of the New South Wales Mounted Rifles, a section R.H.A., and a pom-pom, Colonel Rimington started at 4 A.M., marching rapidly to Bothas-

TRANSPORT IN BED OF THE RIVER VAALSCH.

berg. Disappointed at not finding General Elliot's columns there, he proceeded, on native informa-

Oct. 10.
Woodside,
32 miles.
tion, to Leeuwkop and Rooderand, where Boer convoys were seen moving in several directions. It was late in the day, and very wet, when, the troops having covered thirty-two miles and captured four wagons, two Cape carts, 400 head of cattle and six riding-horses, Colonel Rimington gave the order to return to Draake's Store, Woodside. Hither the remainder of the force, with the convoy, had previously moved by signal communication.

In passing the eastern spurs of Leeuwkop a New South Wales Mounted Rifle sergeant-major was

Oct. 13.
Oct. 14.
mortally wounded and two horses of the Inniskillings killed by snipers. The sergeant-major was buried next day under the Sugarloaf Kopje on the march to Langspruit (fifteen miles).

Returning towards Standerton, the spoor of wagons was struck; the Inniskillings pursued, cap-

Innis-
killing
pursuits
and cap-
tures.
turing one prisoner, fourteen wagons, thirteen Cape carts, eight riding-horses, and 800 head of cattle. Including the chase five miles out and back, the regiment covered twenty-seven miles this day.

Hearing guns (Rawlinson's) at 6.30 next morning, Colonel Rimington at once took out 400 men in the

Oct. 15.
direction of the sound and came across the Boers of Strydam's and Buys's commandos, who had crossed the Vaal from the Transvaal at Villiersdorp and were being pursued by Colonel Rawlinson. It was too late to head them, but the Inniskillings gave chase, capturing twelve Boers, thirteen rifles, three mule wagons with mules

complete, one wagon, one spider and one Cape cart. At Perth the retreating Boers abandoned all their 36 miles. transport and got away, the column getting a further seven wagons, three carts, four horses, and 1,200 head of cattle. Camp was again reached after a very hard day of about thirty-six miles.

The following day the column returned (twenty-one miles) to Goedgevonden, a few miles south-west Van Zoule-cum's scouts. of Standerton. Van Zoulecum was given 600 head of cattle, as he had been useful with his corps scouting and driving in stray lots. His men were very useful as cattle-drivers, but all their scouting was done with the main object of finding cattle, not Boers.

Intelligence, with instructions, having been received from the Commander-in-Chief, that General Louis Botha had crossed the Piet Retief line and was in the neighbourhood of Amsterdam with his Rimington and Raw-linson's dash to capture Botha. Government and about 100 tired horses, Colonel Rimington, in conjunction with Colonel Rawlinson, arranged a combined dash to effect, if possible, his capture. This was within an ace of being accomplished by the Inniskillings ; Botha's hat, Mauser pistol, psalm-book, hymn-book, note-book, and private papers being taken, but Botha himself escaping when in view.

Starting from Standerton on October 19, the column marched south-east down the Natal Railway Oct. 19 to 22. line to Plaatrand and Paardekop stations. Here sixteen days' rations were supplied by rail from Standerton, and the columns struck north-east to Scholspruit, just south of Amersfoort. Proceeding via Knelpoort and Goedehoop, the Mambusa Spruit was reached.

Robinson's Farm, Rolfontein, said to be the best in the Transvaal, was passed this day. It contained Robinson's Farm and Observatory. a fine grand piano with case destroyed, and many fine books lying about; there was an observatory, too, with many astronomical books and instruments. Whilst halting there, a guard was placed over the property to prevent any further destruction. Later, a Staff Officer, catching up the column, passed some Kaffirs with coils of piano wire round their heads, and ivory piano keys behind their ears. This shows the wanton destruction done by natives, which was often put down to our soldiers.

We then passed De Emigratie, where a Boer hospital was found with one doctor and three assist- Boer hospital at De Emigratie. ants; also some nurses and hospital comforts that had been supplied from Pretoria. All the occupants were Hollanders, who would give no information.

Crossing the Mambusa Spruit, both columns— Oct. 23. Rimington's and Rawlinson's—bivouacked at Klipfontein, Tobias Smuts's farm.

At midnight Colonel Rimington's force marched to Weltevreden, rounding up Mrs. Cloete's farm, Oct. 24. where Tobias Smuts was said to stay frequently. Here a despatch rider, Biddulph, was caught carrying a letter from Louis Botha to Chris Botha, addressed from Schimmelhoek the Capture of Boer scout Biddulph. previous day, saying that the Government was still there, unable to move in any direction, owing to their ignorance of the British plans. This man was in a great state of fright when caught, and agreed to guide us to the heights overlooking Schimmelhoek, so as to avoid the Boer laager which he said was at Onverwacht. Colonel

Rimington sent full particulars of this information to Colonel Rawlinson, suggesting his co-operation, and, well guided by Biddulph along a circuitous rout, the column advanced to Schimmelhoek.

Day dawned, but a thick mist favoured us until within a mile of the place. About 7 A.M. it suddenly cleared, revealing the column to about one hundred Boers, who immediately opened fire at fairly close range. Luckily there was low ground close at hand, which gave cover, and the guns soon silenced the Boers. They were across a nasty, stony kloof, from which they were driven out with fire of all sorts. Colonel Rawlinson's column, coming up later on their other flank, was just too late to capture them.

This firing, which started when Rimington's column was only half a mile from the top of the hill overlooking Schimmelhoek, gave the alarm to General Louis Botha. Directly the firing commenced, Major

Narrow escape of General Louis Botha.

Dauncey was ordered to collect what Inniskillings were at hand and charge down upon the farm. A party of four men with pack-horses and another man, who was General Botha himself, were observed from the top of the hill, making off from the farm below. Owing to the rocky descent it was impossible to go fast until reaching the bottom of the slope, by which time the party had got a start of nearly a mile.

Gaining the bottom, Major Dauncey galloped his men in pursuit for nearly three miles, when only four men were left with him, the rest not being able to keep up. Botha was still going as strong as ever, now 1,200 yards in front. It was useless to pursue further into trappy country with no men; so, dismounting, Major Dauncey endeavoured to bring down the fugitives with long-range rifle fire. Alas! it failed, and so General Botha escaped.

The Inniskilling losses from the firing earlier in the day were remarkably small; two horses were killed, several men had their clothing pierced by bullets, and two sword scabbards were struck. The Australians had one man and five horses wounded, and the Artillery had one horse killed.

Our captures were four Boers, three riding-horses, and 150 cattle. The property of Botha previously mentioned was found in the farm. With the exception of the papers, all was returned to him later by order of Lord Kitchener.

Having covered twenty-eight miles, the column
Oct. 25. bivouacked at Blaauwkop, starting back again to Klipfontein (sixteen miles) at 2 A.M.

Continuing to Goedehoop, the Mambusa was re-crossed by night, and the column proceeded to
Oct. 27, 28. Kalkoenkrants. Snipers were persistent; so,
Sniping. sending the convoy on, the columns separated to the flanks, and, by marching back fast, endeavoured to encircle the snipers, but without success.

Halting at Elandspoort, Sand River Station was
Oct. 29 reached, whence, by daily marches to Paarde-
to 31. kop and Platrand, Standerton was once more
Nov. 1, 2. made the base for further movements.

The 2nd Queen's (West Surrey Regiment),
Nov. 3. Colonel Pink, were replaced by the 2nd
2nd Black Watch, under Lieut.-Colonel Car-
Queen's
replaced thew-Yorstoun, C.B. The loss of the
by 2nd Queen's was much regretted; they were
Black
Watch. good men, in hard, fit condition.

Alias, a native scout, also one of the men in the Standerton Burgher Corps, gave evidence that Nov. 4. Biddulph, who was captured on the night Biddulph. of October 23–24, had murdered a wounded soldier and cut off the finger of a wounded officer for the sake of his ring, near Ermelo. They stated that his real name was Wolhuter. The case was placed in the hands of the A.P.M., Standerton.

AUSTRALIANS CROSSING THE VAAL.

CHAPTER XXII

A BIG CIRCULAR DRIVE—FIGHT WITH DE WET

A COMBINED drive on a large scale, in which about twelve columns co-operated, was now arranged from Headquarters. In this case, instead of driv-

Combined circular drive round Asvogelkrans.

ing against a line of blockhouses, all the columns were to be on the circumference of a circle round Asvogelkrans at dawn on the seventh day of operations, the preceding six days being occupied in manœuvring so as to attain this object.

The result was that the Boers lost most of their cattle, but nearly all managed to get out themselves between columns, as no attempt at joining up outposts during the operations was possible until the last night. The height of the Wilge River and Liebenberg's Vlei made difficulties.

On the first day of operations Rimington's column marched to and crossed the Vaal River at

Nov. 6.

Roberts's Drift, which was flooded ; the water also was very muddy and bad to drink. The Black Watch found the marching very hard, several having to fall out sick ; but this was only to be

Nov. 7.

expected on their first day. Continuing to Kopjes Alleen, across the Venters Spruit, Strydam, with about eighty men, was driven across

U

Hartebeestfontein, in the direction of another of our columns, one prisoner, two horses, and a mule being captured.

Marching in terrible rain and hailstorms, Tafelkop was reached next day. Enormous hailstones fell, and one storm it was physically impossible to face. Eight riding-horses, seventy mixed cattle, one Cape cart, and 800 sheep were collected. At 8 P.M. Colonel Rimington rounded up Wilde Dagga Kraal with four squadrons New South Wales Mounted Rifles. Although only two miles and a half distant, it was 2 A.M. before they regained the bivouac, owing to the darkness of the night and awkward riding. No Boers were taken, but useful information was gained from Mrs. Pretorius.

Nov. 8. Terrible weather.

Nov. 9.

Signal communication with Standerton and with General Spens was obtained from the top of Tafelkop.

Major Dauncey, with the Inniskillings, made a demonstration towards the Wilge River, returning after dark, and having lit camp-fires in order to make the Boers believe they were remaining there. Four wagons, five carts, two horses, and 600 sheep were taken.

A Dutch scout attached to the Inniskillings, who came in to report at night as the officers were drinking ' The King ' (it being His Majesty's birthday), was invited to join in the toast.

The Wilge River being too high, Colonel Rimington decided to cross by the bridge at Frankfort. Leaving a dummy signalling station on the top of Tafelkop—which, it was learnt later, kept the Boers off for forty-eight hours—

Nov. 10. Rivers flooded.

the column went to Groenplats, capturing *en route* one wagon, nine horses, and 200 sheep.

Having previously despatched, at 3 A.M., a force of three squadrons New South Wales Mounted Rifles

Nov. 11.
Sloot-
fontein.

under Lieut.-Colonel Cox, with orders to conceal themselves and hold the drifts at Roodewal, Colonel Rimington continued to Frankfort. Leaving dismounted men and sick horses here, the column, with light baggage and three days' supplies, crossed the Vaal by the bridge and pushed on fast to Liebenberg's Vlei, intending to cross and drive Bollingstroom to Colonel Cox's force. Unfortunately the drift was too high to cross; so, signalling to Colonel Cox to come round by the Frankfort bridge, the column moved to bivouac at Slootfontein, three prisoners and three horses having been captured. Damant's column was now communicated with on our right, and De Lisle's column on the left.

This being the day of concentration on the circle, the column started in the dark of the early morning

Nov. 12.
Concen-
tration on
Asvogel-
krans.

(3.30 A.M.) to march on Asvogelkrans, and found the country full of columns, but few Boers. Major Dauncey, with two squadrons Inniskillings, just managed to cross the swollen Conveniente Drift, the horses being nearly carried off their legs by the strong current. He then searched the right bank of the Liebenberg's Vlei, the column searching the left. Four prisoners, twelve wagons, twenty carts, 200 cattle, and 1,500

Captures.

sheep were captured. Private O'Hara, Inniskillings, a fine big man, who was an old servant of mine, captured two Boers single-handed. They were hiding on a small island in the river, and he held them up with his rifle. They were both armed.

Returning by Zorgvleit to Frankfort, the column took two prisoners, thirty-three horses, eight wagons, and two carts.

Nov. 13, 14.

The distance covered since leaving Standerton had been about 109 miles, without any casualties to the men.

After a two days' halt, Colonel Rimington arranged with Colonel Damant a plan to round up Van Reenen's Kop, Weening Hoop, and then drive on to the river, where the South African Constabulary and Railway Pioneer Regiment had arranged to hold the drifts.

Nov. 15.

Starting at 6.30 P.M., Rimington's column continued marching through the night north to the Vaal River as far as Bankplats, where the men lay by their horses' heads from 1 A.M. to 3.30 A.M. Then, spreading out wide, the column moved very fast, straight towards Van Reenen's Kop, covering about four miles of front, with the right resting on the Vaal and the left thrown well forward. Colonel Damant was already on the kop, covering the ground from it to the river. Many Boers were put up and sighted, but escaped over the river, as the Railway Pioneer Regiment (Major Fisher) was not strong enough to hold the drifts. So the drive was wasted. One Boer, mortally wounded, who died three days later, one wagon, sixteen horses, and ten mules were captured. The column returned in the direction of Frankfort to Bendigo, having covered twenty-six miles.

Nov. 17.

Nov. 18. Bendigo, 26 miles.

On November 20 two squadrons Inniskillings, two squadrons New South Wales Mounted Rifles, and two guns crossed the Vaal at Villiers-

Nov. 20.

REGIMENTAL SERGEANT-MAJOR WOOD, INNISKILLING DRAGOONS, AND BOER PRISONERS.

MEDICAL OFFICER DRESSING THE WOUNDED LEG OF COMMANDANT BUYS.

dorp, and, working west, found parties of Boers, about 200 in number, going in the direction of the Hex River mine. The Inniskillings pursued, coming

up with about fifty of the Pioneer Regiment, whom the Boers were in the act of taking away prisoners ; they were mostly stripped of their coats and boots, and some were almost naked. They said that they had just met with a disaster, their

commanding officer, Major Fisher, and five men having been killed, and three officers and ten men wounded. The Boers were chased for two hours into the Roodewal Hills, the Inniskilling horses dropping back, through being unable to keep up any longer. Hidden under a rocky kopje a Cape cart was discovered, containing the commandant

of the Boer commando which had just fled, by name Buys, with a German doctor in attendance. Buys was badly wounded in the shin-bone. His capture was a most important one, as he held great influence over the Boers, and was determined in his views as to the continuance of the war.

Directly the disaster to the Royal Pioneer Regiment was discovered, our doctor, C. S. Maxwell, galloped off to the scene, as there was no other doctor there, and was in time to save the lives of some of the wounded. The arrival of Rimington's force had only just been in time to save the small permanent post of the Royal Pioneer Regiment, as the Boers were about to attack it. Thirty (!) mounted men, sent all the way from Greylingstad to their relief, would also have suffered the same fate.

Rimington's force then returned to Villiersdorp, having captured one Boer wounded (Buys), two wagons, five carts, seventeen horses, and 600 sheep.

One Inniskilling was wounded. The distance covered was about thirty-four miles.

Next day Colonel Rimington moved the column to Rietfontein, near the South African Constabulary post, north of where the disaster occurred. This he did as they were weak, and in order to rearrange their line of posts.

Nov. 21.
Riet-
fontein.

At 2 A.M. Lieut.-Colonel Cox took three squadrons New South Wales Mounted Rifles and hid in a spruit below Barnard's Kop, the remainder of the column moving later, at daylight, in extended order, on Barnard's Kop. No Boers were seen by our column, but Colonel Cox caught seven Boers and eleven horses. The Hex River hospital was visited, from which one unwounded and three wounded Boers were brought away. This Boer hospital was in a very bad state. The doctor, a German, had practically no drugs left, and the wounded under him were much neglected.

Nov. 22.

Next day a combined movement was carried out with Colonel Damant. After a night march, Rimington's column extended east from Villiersdorp, holding the north bank of the Vaal for seven miles. Damant's column, marching during the night from Frankfort, drove on to this line. He caught seventeen Boers and killed one. In addition to the Vaal being much swollen by the heavy rain, Rimington's column effectually blocked the line. Two hundred cattle and seven horses were secured.

Nov. 23.

Heavy rain continued to fall. The drift at Villiersdorp was found too high to cross, so a whole night and day were spent passing the force over by pontoons. One wagon complete and about fifteen horses, or about forty horses

Nov. 25.
Villiers-
dorp.

INNISKILLING DRAGOONS CROSSING THE LIEBENBERG VLEI,
ORANGE RIVER COLONY.

ARTILLERY CROSSING THE LIEBENBERG VLEI.

only, constituted a load for a single trip. Commencing
at 9 P.M., the whole force was not across until
6 P.M. the following day. It then marched
to Bankplats at 2 A.M., and continued that
morning past Frankfort to Kromspruit
(twenty-four miles), where it arrived at 1 A.M.

The next few days were spent, in conjunction with
Colonel Wilson's column, in moving down to
Lindley, on the occasion of the Boer Krijgsraad (Council of War meeting) at Spytfontein.

Colonel Rimington's intelligence that this Krijgsraad and concentration were taking place was undoubtedly correct, and it was unfortunate that more
troops could not be sent to operate immediately.
Colonel Rimington heard on the morning of the
28th that this large Boer concentration was to last
four days, till December 1. Having telegraphed
the information to the Commander-in-Chief, and to
Colonel Damant, asking him to be ready to act if
necessary, he arranged with Colonel Wilson, who was
at Spion Krans, to join him before dawn next day at
Jagersrust.

Starting at 7 P.M. with a force consisting of 400
all ranks of the Inniskilling Dragoons, with 500
horses and two Maxims, 650 all ranks of the 3rd New
South Wales Mounted Rifles, with 750 horses, one
Colt gun, and two Maxims, a section Royal Horse
Artillery, a section Royal Field Artillery, with one
pom-pom, 100 all ranks of the 2nd Black Watch, and
mule supply wagons, and marching continuously all
night, Jagersrust (nineteen miles) was reached at
dawn. Colonel Wilson's column was found already
there, engaged with some snipers. Not hearing from

Headquarters during the day (Colonel Damant was waiting at Kromspruit to bring an answer from the Commander-in-Chief in reply to Colonel Rimington's telegram, if one should arrive), the united columns decided to go on together at night towards Spytfontein, and continued marching till daybreak.   It was intended to leave the convoys of both columns behind, but, not finding a strong enough position to do so safely, they were directed to follow on with an escort of 100 mounted men of Wilson's column, 150 mounted men of Rimington's column, 100 men 2nd Black Watch, 200 men 2nd Royal West Kent, and one gun Royal Field Artillery, under Major Bennett, 3rd New South Wales Mounted Rifles.   The fighting force then pushed on to the east of Spytfontein and pursued forty to fifty Boers over Korte and Groenvlei.   Luckily three squadrons were dropped back to keep touch with the convoy, which was now seven miles behind, for a messenger came through from Major Bennett to report that the convoy was being attacked from the right, left, and rear, and that, if it could be spared, he would like some assistance.   Colonel Rimington at once galloped back all the troops he had, and sweeping to the south, drove off the Boers.

It appeared that practically the whole Boer force in the neighbourhood, under De Wet, had attacked the convoy.   Three men of the West Kent of Wilson's column, with the rear party, had been wounded.   Two troops of the Inniskillings were on the left flank.   One, under Second Lieut. Oliver, the last joined subaltern, gallantly charged a hill of which the Boers had got possession and from which they were shooting into the

Nov. 29.
Jagersrust,
19 miles.

Attack by De Wet.

Charge of Inniskillings.

OX WAGON CROSSING THE LIEBENBERG VLEI

OXEN WASHED DOWN BY FORCE OF CURRENT CROSSING A SPRUIT
ANKLE-DEEP IN DRY WEATHER.

flank guard. They galloped straight at the ridge, whilst the other troop, under Lieut. Wilkins, went round the right.

Lieut. Oliver topped the ridge twenty yards in advance of his men, and was immediately pierced by four bullets (he was hit nine times) ; another of the troop, Private Tremayne, was killed, and another wounded. Two men, Privates Bates and Claffey, Inniskillings, whose horses fell, hid in some long grass close to the Boers and shot two of them. On the retirement of the troop, Private Bates became separated from his horse, which ran away after the troop. Private Claffey's horse stumbled, leaving him some way behind. Instead of remounting and galloping after the troop, he lay down by Bates, and the pair began firing on the Boers, some forty yards distant, and over fifty in number. One Boer ran out to catch Lieut. Oliver's horse, and they both shot him. They then agreed that Claffey should go off and find Bates's horse ; accordingly he mounted and galloped away under a heavy fire. Ere long he met Private Rodd returning with the horse. Meantime Bates lay still in a little hollow of the ground, where he had good cover, and continued to fire at the Boers who could not see him in the long grass, and killed another of them. Soon one of our shells burst just in front of him ; jumping up under cover of the smoke he ran down the hill, and met his comrades returning with his horse, all then getting away safely. Lieut. Wilkins's troop, although under very severe fire, got through scot-free.

Death of Lieut. Oliver.

The Boers, although about 100 in number, fled when they saw the troop coming, but were rallied by their leader, and drove it back.

Repulse of the Boers.

Our guns then opened fire, and the New South Wales Mounted Rifles charged the hill in flank, driving the Boers off.

Heavy storms now set in. After dispersing the Boers in the immediate neighbourhood, the whole force moved on to Victoria Spruit. Here Lieut. Oliver and Private Tremayne, Inniskilling Dragoons, were buried on a ridge, Captain Stevenson-Hamilton reading the burial service. Another fearful storm came on during the funeral, the whole ground becoming a swamp two inches deep in water which would not run off. The enemy were persistently sniping, and the intelligence pointed to the probability of their attacking next day, 1,600 strong ; so, as it was a bad position, and the gun ammunition short, Colonel Rimington decided to move to a better one after dark.

Storm.

In the evening Wilson's men caught a Boer on picquet close to his laager at Groenvlei. He gave information that De Wet had been commanding in person that day ; his force consisting of the Winburg, Ventersburg, Kroonstad, Senekal, and Bethlehem commandos ; and that the Heilbron, Vrede, and Harrismith commandos were expected that night or early in the morning. The result of the day was : two Boers killed (one of them V. C. Klopper of Kroonstad), one mortally wounded, and four others wounded ; one wagon, three Cape carts, three horses, 115 trek oxen taken. On the other hand, we had to deplore the loss of Lieut. Oliver and Private Tremayne, killed, and two men wounded.

Boer losses.

About thirty-three miles had been covered since leaving Jagersrust, but at 11 P.M. the columns started marching all night long in a down-

Dec. 1.
33 miles.

pour of rain to the Heilbron road. The ground was boggy and in a sodden condition; three wagons from each column broke down and had to be abandoned, the contents being brought in or destroyed as

Capture of far as possible. An advance party of one
Boers. squadron Inniskillings and two squadrons New South Wales Mounted Rifles, under Lieut.-Colonel Cox, going on to cross the Spruit just south of Bissel Put and occupy high ground facing south, captured two lots of prisoners, including Field Cornet Piet Theron, member of the Commission, De Wet, an uncle of C. R. De Wet, and three of Mentz's best scouts. After covering eighteen miles, the column bivouacked at Rustfontein, having captured twelve prisoners, twelve horses, one wagon, two carts, two mules, and 281 mixed cattle.

About 11 P.M. a party of twenty to thirty Boers—to judge from their shooting—fired into the bivouac; they stampeded some horses, which were recovered next day, and slightly wounded one man and killed three horses. The firing only lasted about five minutes. The Australians gave a cheer in derision of the sniping; perhaps it was this cheer which made the snipers decamp, as a Boer is suspicious of anything which he does not understand.

Next day we had a peaceful march to Heilbron, with no Boers to be seen.

Dec. 2.
Heilbron, It is clear from the foregoing that, when
13 miles. he gained his accurate information of the Krijgsraad on the morning of November 28, Colonel Rimington acted with great promptitude, dash, and boldness. Not a moment was to be lost. Recognising the opportunity of striking a heavy blow to the Boer cause by surrounding this large concentration,

and the probability of capturing De Wet himself, he
started lightly equipped with the only column (Wilson's) at his immediate command ; at the same time
he telegraphed the Commander-in-Chief for further
columns and prepared the nearest (Damant's) to be
ready to act on orders.   As events proved, it was
truly unfortunate that the columns which were hoped
for could not have been spared.

It is interesting to read General De Wet's own
account of these few days ('Three Years
War,' pp. 330–332), which is as follows :

De Wet's
account.

When November was drawing to a close, I had
an engagement with the English to the south of
Lindley.   I had with me at that time General
Hattingh, General Wessel Wessels, and General
Michal Prinsloo.

An English force had encamped two days previously on the farm of Jagersrust, which lies some
ten miles to the south-east of Heilbron, and about
the same distance from Blijdschap.   I had wished to
make an attack on them the night they arrived, but
they were too near to Heilbron for me to venture
on it.

The previous week three columns which came
from Winburg and Kroonstad had been operating
near the Liebenbergs Vlei, and driving a laager of
women before them towards the north-east of the
Liebenbergs Vlei.   But they had now left the laager
alone and returned to Kroonstad.   The women had
arrived at Blijdschap at noon on November 28, on
their way back to Lindley.

The morning following, two hours after sunrise,
I received a report from General Hattingh, who,
with Commandant Celliers and a hundred men, was
stationed close to Blijdschap.   The general reported
that the English from Jagersrust were hotly pursuing the women's laager.   And it soon appeared

that the women were being driven to the west of Blijdschap.

When General Hattingh heard that the English were hard by, he was some twenty minutes' ride from Blijdschap, but he mounted his horse at once and rode there as quickly as he could. On his arrival he immediately gave orders to up-saddle, and, having sent me a second report, he started in pursuit of the enemy.

As soon as I had received General Hattingh's reports, I followed him with General Wessels and a force of only a hundred men. I was at least five miles from General Hattingh, and the English were twelve miles ahead.

General Michal Prinsloo was unfortunately a considerable distance away; and thus it was that I could not get together my whole force of six hundred burghers.

But General Michal Prinsloo had spent the time in attacking the English force on their left front. Shortly after he had engaged the enemy I came up behind them and delivered an attack on their right. But the veldt was very uneven, and high hills and intervening hollows made any co-operation between us impossible, for one force could not tell where the other force was.

Meanwhile, General Hattingh had attacked the enemy in the rear, and thus compelled them to withdraw their vanguard, which was then not far from the women's laager, and had nearly succeeded in capturing it. But now that the whole force of the enemy was opposed to General Hattingh, he was forced to give way and leave his position. We lost two killed and three wounded. Among the dead was the valiant F. C. Klopper, of Kroonstad.

When I, with General Wessels and Commandant Hermanus Botha, hurried up, Commandant Hattingh was just on the point of retreating.

The English I saw numbered about a thousand

mounted men, and they had three guns with them.
I determined to make a flank attack, and accordingly
marched round to their right, at the same time sending orders to General Prinsloo to get in the rear, or,
if he preferred, in front of the enemy, so that we
might make a united attack upon them as they
marched in the direction of Lindley.

It now began to rain, and a little later a very
heavy thunderstorm burst on our heads. This
forced the English to halt on the farm of Victorie-
spruit.

The rain continued to fall in torrents and
hindered General Prinsloo carrying out my orders.

And now the sun went down.

As our horses were quite exhausted by the hot
pursuit after the English, and the burghers wet
through to the skin, I decided to postpone the attack
to the following day. I was also influenced in my
decision by the consideration that, as the English
were so far from any point from which reinforcements
could come, it was quite safe to let them alone until
the morning. Nobody could have foreseen that they
would escape that night.

We slept about five miles from them to the
north-east, whilst General Prinsloo and his men were
not very far away to the south-east.

That night we placed the ordinary outposts, but
no 'brandwachten.' [1]

When on the next morning I sent my scouts out
to discover the movements of the enemy, what was
my surprise when they reported that they had fled!
They had gone, my scouts informed me, towards
Heilbron, which was about eighteen miles off, and
they had left behind them five laden wagons and one
cart; and where they had crossed Karoospruit they
had, very naturally, lightened their wagons, and flour,
seed, oats, tarpaulins, and tents marked the point

---

[1] 'Brandwachten'—watch-fire men—the furthest outposts, whose duty
it was to signal by fires.

where they had crossed the spruit. The enemy were already so far ahead when I received this report that it was quite out of the question to catch them before they reached Heilbron; so all idea of pursuing them had to be abandoned.

So far as I was able to find out, this column was under the command of Colonel Rimington.

As regards the 'women's laager' which General De Wet mentions, it was well known that Colonel Rimington preferred the women to be left out for the Boers to look after; but comment is needless.

Colonel Rimington now met the Commander-in-Chief at Wolvehoek on his way from the south to Pretoria, and laid before him plans for a combined drive in conjunction with General Elliot. This was approved, Colonels Damant's and Wilson's columns being placed under Rimington's orders for the drive in question, which was to be from east to west on to the Kroonstad-Wolvehoek line, with General Elliot between the two block-house lines, Kroonstad to Lindley (completed only as far as Kalfontein Bridge), and Wolvehoek, Heilbron, and Frankfort.

Arrangements having been completed, and 100 bad remounts received from Germiston, Rimington's and Wilson's columns marched to Brakvlei (fourteen miles) and on to Vaalbank (nineteen miles), two miles west of Frankfort. Passing Kromspruit, Lieut.-Colonel Carthew-Yorstoun, C.B., 2nd Black Watch, was left with all spare wagons. It was reported that the Boer leader, Ross, had been annoying the block-house construction party, wounding six men of the East Lancashire Regiment the previous day. These

(margin notes: Dec. 4. / Dec. 8. Brakvlei, 14 miles. / Dec. 9. Vaalbank, 19 miles.)

blockhouses had now been completed for a distance of ten miles on the road to Tafelkop.

Taking only one day's supplies, one waterproof sheet and one blanket per man, Rimington's column marched south to Bordeaux (sixteen miles), Damant's column in touch on his left, marching to Zorgvleit, Wilson's on the right to Slootfontein.   General Elliot's three columns were on the left again of Damant's.   Late in the afternoon all Rimington's columns sent parties across the Liebenberg's Vlei River, so as to give the impression that they were going to drive east.   At 4.30 A.M. the drive west commenced.   About 8 A.M. some 100 Boers were sighted on Anderkant, and communication was established with Colonel De Lisle (General Elliot's right column).   At Klipfontein about 200 were also sighted by Damant's column.

Dec. 10.
Bordeaux,
16 miles.

Dec. 11.
Klip
River,
24 miles.

Whilst moving on across Tweefontein more Boers were seen.   Pushing squadrons to the high ground two miles beyond the Klip River to light fires, and so deceive the Boers, Colonel Rimington then fell back to take up the line of the Klip River for the night. Twenty-four miles had been covered since the morning, and several thousand sheep and 250 cattle taken, and passed to the railway line.   This night every man was on picquet, in posts of six men and a non-commissioned officer at every hundred yards. The guns were kept in the centre with one and a half squadrons Inniskillings as escort.   Not a dog could have passed through the line of outposts without being seen ; but about 200 Boers broke back through the columns to the left.   No fires were allowed, so there was no tea or coffee—only water to drink.

Next day the drive continued west. The columns crossed the Rhenoster at Slangfontein, and then turned north-west, ending up at Waterval on the Rhenoster, six miles east of Kopjes Station. Many Boers were observed in the morning, and during the last five miles about fifty were pursued, who eventually got away in the bush under cover of darkness, only three being captured. Rimington's column had marched some twenty-five miles and captured twenty prisoners, about a hundred horses, immense quantities of cattle, and all the Boer commando's wagons, which latter were destroyed. The troops bivouacked as they stood, without cloaks, blankets, or food.

Dec. 12. Waterval, 25 miles.

Starting very starved at daylight, Rimington's columns united at Schoongezicht (nine miles), obtaining much-needed food there from Wilson's column. Next day they marched to Leeuwfontein (twenty-two miles). During the march a herd of blesbok were sighted and one fine buck shot.

Dec. 13. Schoongezicht, 9 miles.

Dec. 14. Leeuwfontein, 22 miles.

Much had been learnt by this drive. The main features had shown the necessity of a thorough system of night outposts, and that adjoining columns must line up their outposts. Unless there were troops enough to do this, the whole drive was a waste of time as far as catching men went; for Boers, unhampered by cattle, could always get through a gap of half a mile. There were undoubtedly several hundred Boers in front on the 11th, and at least 300 on the 12th; but all their cattle and wagons were taken. A noticeable point was the large number of riding and pack horses which they left behind. Rimington's three columns picked

Lessons of the drive.

X

up over 300, all dead beat.   This showed that in a
drive like this the Boers worked their horses very
hard, going backwards and forwards in their efforts
to find a way out ; whilst our horses, if the drive was
well regulated, need only go the length of the advance
in a straight line.

CHAPTER XXIII

CO-OPERATING WITH GENERAL E. HAMILTON—
DISASTER TO A COLUMN

RIMINGTON's and Damant's columns now proceeded to Frankfort with a view to co-operating with the troops under General E. Hamilton, at that time engaged in pushing on the blockhouse line towards Tafelkop. This line had reached Dundas.

Leaving Leeuwfontein on December 17, and halting at Brakvlei (fourteen miles) and Deelfontein (sixteen miles), Ayr, three miles north-east of Frankfort, was reached on the morning of the 19th. Here Colonels Damant and Rimington planned a night march in order to attack any Boers near Tafelkop in the morning. The columns were to move to-gether along the left, and about three miles off the blockhouse line, pass Tafelkop, then swing round the west of the kop and sweep back south-east towards the Wilge River, the two columns to be in line, covering a fairly broad front. The convoys of both columns were to move together along the block-house line to Dundas Camp, under Lieut.-Colonel Carthew-Yorstoun, and there await orders. Here General E. Hamilton was encamped with a small force of Infantry and 33rd Yeomanry, much hindered

Dec. 17.
Brakvlei,
14 miles.
Dec. 18.
Deel-
fontein,
16 miles.
Dec. 19.
Ayr.

in his work of continuing the blockhouse line by a large force of Boers, supposed to be in Tafelkop itself, or the adjoining kopjes of Leeuwkop and Riet Spruit.

General E. Hamilton having been informed of the move, the column started at 7 P.M. Although fine at the start, the night turned out terribly stormy. One very severe storm, which lasted about an hour, the horses refused to face, so it was necessary to halt and turn about. Very close and dangerous lightning threatened during this storm, and it was a wonder that no one was struck. Deluges of rain fell. The men, marching 'light,' without cloaks, had a terrible night of it : they were drenched to the skin and bitterly cold. At times, also, it was too dark to move. The night was passed by moving east when possible, and halting when too dark to see.

Terrible night-march.

About 3.45 A.M., when the first streaks of dawn appeared, the columns were just north of Dansler's Kop (about one mile and a half north-west of Tafelkop), and, putting on the pace, swung round Tafelkop. Just before daylight our scouts on the left flank (N.) surprised some Boers in a farm, killed one, and captured three, one of them being Commandant Keyter. Damant's column now made straight for Tafelkop at a great pace ; drew it blank, then turned sharp to their right, and went off to draw the Riet Spruit kopjes, where the Riet Spruit runs into the Wilge River. Rimington went off fast south, towards Leeuwkop. Seeing Boers getting away across the front there, he detailed two squadrons to act in that direction, and was working back fast to the kopjes on the Wilge, to which Damant's column had gone. This was about 8 A.M. While still five

Dec. 20. Damant's disaster.

miles from these kopjes, and when the view was quite impeded by undulations of the ground, a very smart burst of firing commenced from Damant's direction and continued for about ten minutes; then it as suddenly ceased. We expected that Damant had surprised and captured a laager! Colonel Rimington pushed on as fast as possible, hoping to get round to the back of any Boers in front of Damant, but no fugitives could be seen as he approached near the scene of firing, and, as yet, he could get no view of the kopjes.

At last about 150 Boers were seen riding off south some 3,500 yards away, and shrapnel was put into them; at the same time about forty, each leading more than one horse, were seen about the same distance away, going fast north-west, down the Wilge. Then Lieut. Maturin, R.A., arrived from the Riet Spruit kopjes, which were still a mile distant, saying that Damant had suffered a disaster, that the Boers had attacked his guns, wounded Damant himself in four places, killed thirty-one of his men, and wounded forty-two! Lieut. Maturin himself had been wounded, but had managed to escape and get away with the gun limbers, thus preventing the Boers from moving the guns. The pom-pom also they had been unable to take away and had rolled down the hill.

Hurrying to the scene, the doctors had all their work cut out for several hours. Ambulances were sent for to General E. Hamilton's camp at Dundas, five miles north-west.

It appeared that Damant had been pursuing Boers in front of him to the south, with his forces much extended, he himself being in the centre with two guns and a pom-pom and only a small escort of about forty Imperial Yeomanry ; his other squadrons were wide away left and right.   Damant himself, with a black scout, was first on this kopje, and, seeing, as he thought, ' all clear,' signalled for the guns to come up. That side of the kopje was not too steep for the guns, but the far face—the kopjes overlooking the Wilge Valley—was.   These ' kopjes ' were really *one* very long (perhaps one mile and a half), irregular kopje, steep on the Wilge side ; the top was about forty yards broad, and covered with loose, flat stones, piled up here and there along the hill into low Kaffir kraals (old, broken-down, and uninhabited), which considerably impeded the view.

The long kopje was sinuous in its length, forming bays on the steep river-side.   As soon as the guns were on the top, sniping commenced from a ridge in front (W.), evidently to distract Damant's attention from the right, whence the real attack was coming. This sniping had the desired effect, and Damant was busy with his guns turned on the snipers.   At the same time he saw a lot of men hurriedly crossing, towards him, one of the ' bays ' on the river-side of his kopje on the right.   He remarked to some one near him that they must be some of his own men, and thought no more about them, as they were hidden, almost as soon as seen, under the steep face of the kopje.   As they were dressed in khaki, they were thought to be some of General Hamilton's mounted troops.

He continued, therefore, shelling the snipers to his front, who were getting rather lively, when, all of a sudden, Boers poked their heads up over the edge of the kopje front and right, opening a murderous fire on him at thirty to sixty yards range, simply mowing him and his men down. In a very few minutes all were killed or wounded, but Damant's force accounted for fourteen Boers before they suc-

Gunners' fine performance. cumbed. The limber gunners behaved most gallantly ; luckily, the limbers were not on the top of the hill, but they were severely fired at, at close range, as they were making off from the foot. One wounded driver got his limber safely into General Hamilton's camp, a distance of five miles ; two gunners, both of whom were wounded, got the other to camp, one falling off just before they reached the camp.

Captain Scott, with the remainder of the Imperial Yeomanry, charged the hill after he knew what had happened ; this, coupled with Rimington's approach, caused the Boers to clear off fast. Rimington pursued them until he was certain that all had crossed the Wilge River, broken up, and gone off in different directions.

It appeared that about 800 Boers, under Louis Botha, of Vrede (brother of H. Botha), Ross, and De Koch, the whole under W. J. Wessels, Asst. Hoof. Commandant, had collected from all round to attack General Hamilton's camp at Dundas. Damant had suddenly come on these without any idea of the proximity of such a large force.

During the two hours and a half in which the doctors were collecting the dead and dressing the

Awful storm. wounded, a frightful storm, which lasted half an hour, came on. During it several of the wounded died. The ground was two inches deep in water, which would not run off. When the doctors had finished and were starting off with the ambulances to Hamilton's camp another bad storm came on. Private Kemp, of the rear-guard, C Squadron Inniskillings, and his horse were killed by lightning, and Second Lieut. O'Callaghan, who had joined only three weeks previously, was severely injured. When they had nearly reached Hamilton's camp another bad storm came on, and *this same squadron* was again struck by lightning, another man (Private Stanley) and two horses being killed, and two other men and horses struck down and injured.

Disasters to C Squadron.

Altogether this was a day which will never be forgotten by those who experienced it. We were without cloaks, and were drenched to the skin twice during the night and three times during the day. The sight of the wounded dying in the storm and of the dead in rows, sodden with rain, was terrible, and the 'last straw' was reached when the regiment was twice struck by lightning while escorting the dead and wounded into camp!

The distance covered since the previous evening was about forty-three miles.

43 miles.

Next morning Lieut.-Colonel Cox, with 200 New South Wales Mounted Rifles and 100 Inniskilling Dragoons, went out to cover the construction of, and learn how to build, blockhouses. In camp the funerals took place between 8 and 10 A.M.

Dec. 21

The whole force, including Damant's and Hamilton's, moved camp to Tafelkop without opposition. Four blockhouses were built this day by Rimington's column.

Dec. 22. Building blockhouses.

The next three days were spent in assisting General Hamilton to prepare this position for defence. A 15-pounder gun was pulled up to the top, and blockhouses were built on all

Dec. 23-25.

TYPE OF BLOCKHOUSE.

TYPE OF BLOCKHOUSE.

important ridges round, practically no Boers being seen.

Dec. 26.   Leaving General Hamilton's force secure,
Frankfort.   Rimington's column marched back to Frankfort.

The change of tactics adopted by the Boers, dating from the Krijgsraad at Spytfontein, previously mentioned, was noticeable. De Wet then said that there was too much wastage of Boer forces in small captures by our columns, and that he meant to stop this by concentrating his men, and, if he got the chance, by dealing blows at weak columns or badly protected convoys. There is little doubt that he had this in view in the case of the brush with Rimington's convoy on November 30, and the projected attack on his camp at Victoria Spruit the following day. He was now operating with this intention from the neighbourhood of Reitz, with 1,000 to 2,000 men at his disposal. This change of Boer tactics necessitated a similar change on our part, as a column of even 2,000 was useless as long as it remained with its convoy, and, the moment the convoy was left, half the fighting strength of the column had to be left with it. Further, the Boers had three horses to each man and no convoy, and could disperse at any moment all over the country.

In the successful Boer attack on Damant's guns on December 20 the escort of the guns was too small to make any counter-attack. Escorts to guns should be strong enough to have part of the men mounted, who can make a counter-attack in the form of a charge, and thus give the guns a chance to gallop away.

The next few days were occupied with long

reconnaissances from Frankfort, during which a few captures were made. On the last day of the year

Captain Herbert and Lieut. Oates, who had previously been invalided home, rejoined the Inniskillings, with a draft of sixty men, an escort having been sent out the previous day to Kromspruit to meet them. They brought 160 remounts, chiefly Walers, for the force.

Since December 10, 1899, the Inniskilling Dragoons had marched 4,083 miles, and during the past five months with Colonel Rimington (July 24 to December 1, 1901) they had covered 1,574 miles. These distances are reckoned as the crow flies, and reconnaissances of less than eight miles are not included.

After a twenty-five mile march on December 31, owing to the Heilbron-Frankfort blockhouse line

being threatened, the New Year opened with Rimington's column on another night march to Villiersdorp, which was reported occupied by Alberts with a large commando. The town was

surrounded at dawn. Women gave information that Alberts had been there the previous day with 472 men, but only stray parties could be seen in the distance escaping. These were pursued but got away, abandoning their cattle (about 180, mostly milch cows), and the column returned to Frankfort, having covered thirty-nine miles.

Rimington's command was now increased to about 3,400 men, by the addition of the Canadian

Scouts under Major Ross (17 officers, 315 men, 361 horses); Colonel Damant's column; and the Royal Artillery Mounted Rifles, under Lieut.-Colonel Sir John Jervis-White-Jervis (32 officers, 758 men, 921 horses).

THE RUINED TOWN OF FRANKFORT, ORANGE RIVER COLONY.
Alternately occupied by British and Boers throughout the war.

CAPTAIN BEGBIE, COLONEL SIR J. H. JERVIS-WHITE-JERVIS,
GENERAL RIMINGTON. AND COLONEL ROSS.

At this period of the war there was little use for guns, mounted men to hunt down the scattered Boer commandos being more essential. In consequence, many of our artillery batteries were made up into mounted rifles (their guns being discarded), and, as such, rendered great service, always performing magnificently.

A point to be noticed is, how much columns increased their horses in proportion to their men. This was found essential for mobility; the Boers themselves, when possible, always had two or three horses for a man.

In accordance with orders received from the Commander-in-Chief to act against a reported concentration of the Boers near Leeuwkop, Rimington's command, increased by the above-mentioned forces, moved by independent columns along the blockhouse line to Tafelkop (fifteen miles), advancing next morning to Leeuwkop. A few Boers and wagons only were observed moving south. The force encamped at Woodside (twenty-four and a half miles), where it was joined by Damant's column, consisting of Damant's Horse, 700; Imperial Yeomanry, 300; Royal Field Artillery, 49; all under command of Major Campbell, 9th Lancers, in place of Colonel Damant, who had been so seriously wounded.

Jan. 7.
Tafelkop, 15 miles.
Woodside, 24½ miles.

Rimington divided his troops into two divisions:

(A) Under himself, consisting of his old column with the Canadian Scouts.

(B) Under Lieut.-Colonel Sir John Jervis-White-Jervis, consisting of Royal Artillery Mounted Rifles and Damant's column.

The Inniskillings, under Major Dauncey, marched

at 2 A.M. to Strydport, thence up the Wilge River to
Jan. 8.   Holspruit whither the main force advanced
Holspruit. direct.   A few Boers only were seen, and
two Canadian Scouts were wounded.

The force now turned west, moving through the
hills north of Holspruit to Bezuidenhouts Drift on
Jan. 9.   the Wilge River, where it outspanned from
8 A.M. to 3 P.M. to allow for crossing.   It was a bad
drift, with a steep bank on the west side.

A considerable number of Boers attacked the rear-
guard under Major Dauncey, consisting of the Inniskillings with two guns.   The regiment repulsed the
attack with one man, Private McLeary, killed, and
one, Private Dales, wounded.   Whilst the force was
crossing the drift, Major Ross with his Canadian
Scouts went in pursuit of some Cape carts which were
seen leaving De Jaeger's Farm along the Reitz road.
They rode into a large party of Boers and lost one
man killed and five wounded, and had to fall back
Canadian   on the main body.   During their chase an
Scouts'   unfortunate incident occurred.   A woman,
losses. Un-
fortunate one of the nurses at a Boer Hospital at
incident. Jaeger's Farm, was wounded.   The Red
Cross flag on the house used as a hospital was not
apparent, and a bullet went through one of the
windows of the house, which was between the opposing parties, wounding the nurse.

The troops halted at Tweedecamp, Spitzkop,
moving on to Liebenberg's Vlei, Bordeaux, and
Jan. 10-11. Koppiesdam, then by the left of Kleinkop to
Treurkop.   About seventy Boers were found in the
neighbourhood, and news was received that De Wet,
Jan. 12.   with 400 Boers, had moved south on the
previous day towards Lindley.   After a long day's

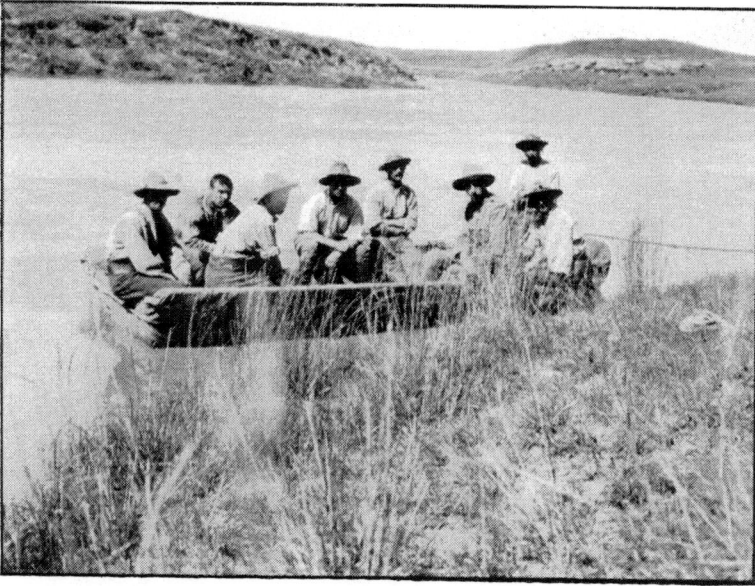

A "FLYING BRIDGE" ACROSS THE WILGE RIVER.

Boat formed from English pattern wagon, made water-tight by placing tarpaulins underneath.

THE BRIGADIER REVIEWS HIS TROOPS AS THEY CROSS.

march of thirty miles the force then moved back to Welvaand. The captures during the last few days consisted only of two prisoners, four rifles, eight wagons, sixty-eight trek oxen, and 291 mixed cattle.

Moving to Blaauwkrans, Damant's Horse, in advance, captured a Boer near Brakoog and pursued

Jan. 15.
Blaauw-
krans. a Boer convoy, being attacked by some 300 Boers from the direction of Trommel whilst so doing. They also caught a native with a letter from Carl Mentz to General Louis Botha asking for advice as to his movements. Colonel Rimington, coming up with the remainder of the force, drove the Boers away and captured and burnt the convoy of seven wagons which belonged to Mentz.

Jan. 16.
Night
march,
20½ miles. When advancing by Omdraai to Noble's Mill, information was received pointing to De Wet having doubled back, so Colonel Rimington decided also to double back in two columns by a night march and surround Elandskop (Sterkfontein). He started at 9 P.M., but rain and intense darkness made it impossible to continue ; so, after having covered twenty and a half miles, a halt had to be made till dawn.

At 4.30 A.M. the forces marched on to Middelpunt, dividing round the Elandskop, but only in

Jan. 17. time to shell some 200 Boers who were making off. De Wet was reported afterwards by natives to have been in one of two Cape carts that

Jan. 18.
Mooihoek. were pursued. The spoor of these carts was followed to Geelplaats, where owing to the heavy rain it was lost, and the force camped at Mooihoek.

Doubling back again by a night march on Elandskop, the force at dawn moved quickly past the kop,

towards the Lindley-Heilbron road. Three Boers—
Piet Bezuidenhout, Landdrost, Frikkie Mentz, the
commandant's brother, and Scheeders, the
Boer signaller, with his heliograph—were
caught on Elandskop; also a lot of sheep.
During the subsequent advance snipers were
persistent.   About fifty Royal Artillery
Mounted Rifles, who were doing rear-guard,
stopped some who were following by a charge, during
which the Royal Artillery Mounted Rifles lost one
man killed and one wounded.   An ambulance (Cape
cart), which was sent to bring in the dead body, fell
into the hands of the Boers, who stripped and sjambokked the black boy in charge of the cart and sent
the medical orderly back without his coat, keeping
the Cape cart.   The force camped at Rietfontein
(thirty-one and a half miles), having taken three
prisoners, four rifles, 256 rounds of small-arm
ammunition, nine horses, four wagons, one cart,
eighty trek oxen, 386 cattle, and 3,000 sheep.

Proceeding to Braakvlei, on the blockhouse line, Damant's column left the force.

Margin notes:
Jan. 19, Elands-kop.
Jan. 20, Riet-fontein, 31½ miles. Captures.
Jan. 21. Braakvlei.

CHAPTER XXIV

RIMINGTON'S DRIVES

COLONEL RIMINGTON went to Johannesburg and had a long interview with the Commander-in-Chief on Jan. 22. the subject of adopting drives, submitting a scheme for a drive west from Liebenberg's Vlei, on the Kroonstad-Wolvehoek Railway. Riming- Jan. 23 to 25. ton being instructed to proceed to Reitz with this object in view, the force spent the next Jan. 26. few days marching there and clearing the Jan. 28. surrounding country. The driving move- ment west was, however, changed for a drive east, towards Harrismith, in conjunction with General Elliot on the right, Rawlinson and Byng on the left. Jan. 29. Accordingly, Rimington's column, which had advanced to Plat Kopje preparatory to form- ing up for the drive west, extended to get into touch with General Elliot's left (Colonel De Lisle), and marched to Morgenzohn.

When advancing to Goothoop (twenty-six miles), for the night outposts, a message was received from Jan. 30. General Elliot that he would not be able to Goothoop, advance his line so far that day. Learning 26 miles. from a native woman that a Boer convoy was moving across the front, Colonel Rimington judged that they would head back in the night; so,

taking his mounted troops, he executed a night
Jan. 31. march back, and captured the whole Boer
Surprise of Alberts's convoy as it was crossing the Morgenzohn
commando drift in the rear.   Twenty-three prisoners,
and captures. sixteen wagons, five carts, all of Alberts's
commando, were taken, and the force was back at
Goothoop by 9 A.M.   The drive then con-
Feb. 1 tinued by Majoor's Drift to Harrismith.

Riding in ahead of the troops with a small escort
of Inniskillings, Major Dauncey had a narrow escape
of being shot by the Harrismith blockhouse men,
who mistook the party for Boers.   Luckily the
bullets just missed their mark.

These miscellaneous moves during the past month
had shown the impossibility of catching the Orange
River Colony Boers in any numbers, now that they
were without wagons and had adopted the plan of
remaining at night in small parties on the
Harrismith. veldt with their horses ready saddled, so as
to move off immediately they were alarmed.

Colonel Rimington for a long time had urged
that, given a sufficient number of troops, the only
effectual way in which to catch these Boers was to
drive, keeping one continuous line both by day and
at night.   Thus, once in the area driven, they could
not break back through our columns, but, like fish
in a net, would dash about, endeavouring to find a
way of escape, so wearying their horses, whilst our
horses, on the other hand, would only have to
advance in one line.   Then, finally, they would be
compelled to surrender or fight.

The result of Colonel Rimington's interview with
the Commander-in-Chief on January 22 was the
adoption of his plan, which proved so successful, and,

as the Boers themselves afterwards acknowledged, had such a powerful effect in bringing hostilities to an end. At last they were going to find themselves fairly cornered.

The operation now to be recorded was a three days' drive from Liebenberg's Vlei on to the Kroonstad-Wolvehoek railway. About 9,000 men formed the driving line, which advanced from the river with its flanks resting on the blockhouse lines. In addition to the regular garrison of the railway and these two blockhouse lines, two regiments of infantry and five armoured trains were employed on the former, while two small columns acted on each flank of the latter.

Drive.

The actual drive lasted three nights and three days, and brought in a total of 283 Boers killed, wounded, and captured, besides a very large number of cattle and wagons.

This, compared with previous work in this area, was successful, but it would have been much more so had the southern blockhouse line been more thoroughly reinforced.

On the third and last day of the drive General Elliot and Colonel Rimington's left had almost too great a distance to cover, as this flank had to wheel round to the north, and, as all the driving line started at the same hour (6 A.M.), the right got much too far forward. It was also found that three nights running of outposts made the work too hard on the men, if they were formed in posts of six with a double sentry.

On February 2 orders were received for the following columns from right to left—Rawlinson's, Byng's, Rimington's, Elliot's—to be in position on Liebenberg's Vlei by the night of the 5th,

Feb. 2.

Y

extending from the north to the southern blockhouse line. The drive west was to commence next day.

Crossing the Wilge River Ridge, Rimington's column, with the Inniskillings in advance, moved by Schoongezicht and Mooidam to Reitz, from which it took up its position in the evening on Liebenberg's Vlei, from Slabbert's Wag to Vrischgewaag. In executing this move a distance of over seventy miles had been covered.

Feb. 2 to 5.

Rimington's force was divided into five small columns and took up a line along the west bank of Liebenberg's Vlei, the flank columns getting into touch with Byng's on the right and De Lisle's on the left. Colonel Rimington himself was with the centre column of Inniskillings. It was an awkward line to hold and very long, the river having a multitude of small bridle drifts. Information was received from natives that De Wet, with from 700 to 1,100 men, was in front of the line.

The drive now commenced. Passing Elandskop, signal communication was established with columns on the right and left, who confirmed the previous information that De Wet, with 1,200 Boers, was in front. A good many Boers also were seen from the kop. Moving on in the afternoon, a night outpost line was taken up from Morgenster to Palmietfontein. This was greatly strengthened by a wire fence which ran along nearly the whole front. Distance covered, seventeen miles.

Feb. 6.

The line drove on again at 6 A.M., and took up an outpost line for the night along the Heilbron-Kroonstad road from China to Rosepan, which was again strengthened by a wire fence. During the day fifteen Boers were captured

Feb. 7.

THE WILGE RIVER.

GUNS CAPTURED FROM THE ENEMY.

hiding in a kloof, and numbers of sheep were destroyed. During the night the Boers made several attempts to break the line by bringing a very heavy fire to bear on different parts, but they did not attempt to rush it. Major Bennett, 3rd New South Wales Mounted Rifles, had one man killed and one wounded. Everyone remained on the alert throughout the night, as the Boers kept visiting and trying one point after another, but always retired again in front of the very heavy fire and ironical cheers which we gave them.

Marching again at 6 A.M., the country was carefully worked to Doorndraai, on the Rhenoster River. A good many Boers were found hidden away in the reeds, and one or two were actually under water except their mouths.

Feb. 8.
Doorn-
draai.

Field Cornets Prinsloo and Odendaal, of Kroonstad, surrendered unconditionally with fifty-one men, and we learnt from them that De Wet had crossed the southern blockhouse line near Doornkloof the previous night with about 700 men.

The drive was now over, and Rimington's force concentrated at Schoongezicht, the captures being one killed, one wounded, eighty-nine prisoners, sixty-seven rifles, 1,800 rounds of small-arm ammunition, 105 horses, thirteen wagons, ten carts, and the carriage and fittings of a Maxim-Nordenfelt (pom-pom).

Captures.

Moving to Waterval, Colonel Rimington himself proceeded to Pretoria and the column marched to Heilbron. Squadron Sergeant - Major Crewe, Inniskillings, died this day of enteric fever after only eight days' illness. He was a great loss to the regiment.

Feb. 9.
Waterval.
Feb. 10.
Heibron.

Y 2

Orders were now received for the next operation, which comprised, briefly, a drive east between the northern blockhouse line and the Elandsfontein-Natal Railway.   When the right reached Tafelkop the driving line was to right wheel; then, crossing the northern blockhouse line, to drive south on to the southern line between Harrismith and Bethlehem, the right moving along the Wilge River, which was to be held by Elliot's Division, and the left along the Natal frontier. Rimington's force was to form the right-hand column in the drive east, with Byng on the left.   After wheeling, Keir was to come into position on its right for the drive south.

Feb. 11.

Colonel Rimington and Major Gale rejoined their force, which proceeded to Rietspruit, three miles south-east of Gottenberg, which was to be their right on the first night of the drive. The force was again divided into five small columns.

Feb. 14 to 19.

The next few days were spent in long day marches and night outpost lines, which comprised the first part of the drive, during which few Boers were seen. All information pointed to a large force of Boers being in front.   A good deal of danger and unnecessary alarm were often caused by men firing wildly at night.   In consequence, Colonel Rimington issued an order that if any single man insisted on firing at nothing, he was to be sent out to attack single-handed with his sword or bayonet the thing which was annoying him, whether ant-heap or dead horse. This effectually put a stop to it.

On this night Rimington's line extended from Driespruit to the junction of the Paardekop and Kalkoenkrans farms, the right resting on the blockhouse line. His scouts, on getting to the block-house line, found that a large number of Boers had effected a crossing in several places on the nights of the 19th and 20th. Large numbers of horses, some with pack-saddles, and of cattle were shot in doing so; also several rifles were picked up. The roofs of the blockhouses were perforated with bullets and five men wounded. The Boers probably conveyed their dead and most of their wounded away, as they had wagons with them.

Feb. 21.
Escape of
Boers.

Crossing the blockhouse line, Rimington's forces took up a very long night line from Roadside (south of Leeuwkop) to Bothasberg, fifteen miles in a straight line. In the morning a large number of Boers (about 800) were seen retiring across the open country between Leeuwkop and Bothasberg. An attempt was made by H. Botha's men to rush Lieut.-Colonel Cox's column of New South Wales Mounted Rifles, which was one of Rimington's five small columns; they succeeded in capturing four of his advanced guard, the latter mistaking the Boers for men of another column. They were stripped and sent back later in the day, and reported that the Boers had two men severely wounded in the engage-ment. The night passed quietly and the forces moved on, taking up the night outpost line along the Holspruit and remaining there next day.

Feb. 22.

Feb. 23-24.

During the night, between 12 and 1 A.M., the Boers attacked the right of Byng's line. They took several picquets in flank, and a certain number—probably 300 to 400—got through, several women being among them. Thirteen hundred were said to have made the attack. The pom-pom jammed after firing seventy rounds, and the gallant officer in

charge, Captain Begbie, R.A., was killed, shot
through the heart. He was a great loss,
having served bravely and with great dash
throughout the campaign.

Death of Captain Begbie.

The Boers came on amongst a lot of loose horses
and cattle, shouting in English, ' Don't shoot your
friends ; ' and they succeeded in overpowering one of
the New Zealand picquets, which had exhausted its
ammunition ; then, turning to their left, they rushed
down the line, taking each picquet in turn until they
came to Lieut.-Colonel Cox's New South Wales
Mounted Rifles, who were the left of Rimington's
line. Here they were stopped, as Lieut.-
Colonel Cox, realising what had happened,
had thrown back his left-hand picquets and
opposed their further advance by a very hot
fire. They then turned back and widened

Lieut.- Colonel Cox repulses Boer attack.

the gap a little more by rushing some more of the
New Zealand picquets on their right, after which
their main body commenced to stream through under
a heavy fire from each side. After about an hour
they were stopped passing, the line being re-formed
and not broken again.

In addition to Captain Begbie, Lieut.-Colonel
Cox had three men wounded, one Highlander and
two pom-pom gunners ; and the New Zealanders had
twenty-three killed and forty odd wounded.

Continuing the drive, a line was taken up along
the Cornelis River ; a good many horses, wagons, and
carts, left behind by the Boers, fell into our hands.
Whilst moving to Springfield Bridge after a
night of drenching rain, more captures were
made, and several horses were found in the
river, saddled up and ridden out. The river here

Feb. 26.

Springfield Bridge.

required a good deal of searching, and it is believed that a good many Boers were left behind in the reeds when the columns changed from their course to cross the river.

Next day the forces marched from Cornelis River to Nels Farm (map 'Mooihoek'), about four miles

Feb. 27. north of Harrismith. The captures by
Near
Harri-
smith. Rimington's force on this drive included twelve Boers killed, two wounded, twenty-one prisoners, 775 horses, seven mules, 7,308 cattle,

Captures. five wagons, and three carts. Our own losses comprised one officer killed, four men wounded, and sixty-three horses. The total results—about 900 killed and prisoners—must be considered satisfactory.

It would have been better if the drive had been divided into two portions, the first to terminate on the northern blockhouse line, after wheeling south. Instead of this we went straight on through, and as this line was not strongly reinforced, as it might have been, all the Boers were able to break through in front of us, so that in the latter part of the drive the force of the enemy was too strong for our thin line to deal with properly. The result was, that the majority of the best fighting Boers broke back through the driving line on the night of the 23rd–24th. Also, by dividing the operations, the troops forming the driving line could have rested on the northern block-house line. As it was, they were on outpost for eleven consecutive nights. On the previous drive the force was divided for outpost work into posts of six with a double sentry. This was found too hard on the men for even three consecutive nights; accordingly, on the present occasion it was divided up

into posts of eight men furnishing a single sentry.
Further, the line was so extended that it was impossible to keep a reserve in hand without leaving
gaps.

On the 24th, it is noted that 300 to 400 Boers
broke through ; it was found out afterwards that,
in reality, about double that number got through,
including De Wet, Wessels, Marny Botha, and other
important leaders. Marny Botha was reported as
having been killed or wounded on this occasion ; but
this was not the case.

Captain Mortimer, Remount Department, was
attached to the force as a collector of horses during
Collecting this drive. He had thirty Kaffirs to help him,
horses.   and got together between 500 and 700 horses,
wild and exhausted ones left by the Boers. He carried
a portable kraal of wire fencing, and kept his horses
in this every night. It was impossible for the columns,
which were marching twenty miles a day, to catch
or destroy these wild horses ; as every month passed
they became more wild, owing to their being so
constantly driven about.

The Commander-in-Chief, Lord Kitchener, in-
Feb. 28.   spected the force on their return from this
Inspection
by Lord   drive, and a few days later the following
Kitchener. telegram was received from him :

' 2nd March.   Please convey to all columns engaged in recent operations, that the Secretary of
Telegram   State has telegraphed his congratulations at
from
Secretary the very satisfactory result of their recent
of State. labours.   The casualties totalled fifty killed,
ten wounded and 759 unwounded prisoners.

' KITCHENER.'

Plans were now made for a big driving movement Plans for big drive. from the southern blockhouse line (Harrismith to Bethlehem) to the northern, the centre of the drive striking the latter about Frankfort.

The driving line comprised 10,000 troops, covering fifty miles of front, the columns engaged being, from the left, Elliot, Barker, Lawley, Rimington, and Keir.

The object was to clear a belt of country fifty miles wide, probably occupied by some of the Boers who broke through the last drive.

The line of advance of Rimington's force was, roughly, to be down the valley of the Wilge River, striking Tafelkop on March 6.

For these operations Rimington divided his force into four columns from right to left—namely, Lieut.-Colonel Cox with the New South Wales Mounted Rifles; himself with the Inniskillings, 1st Battalion Black Watch (which had just relieved the 2nd), a section R.F.A., and a pom-pom; Lieut.-Colonel Sir John Jervis-White-Jervis with the Royal Artillery Mounted Rifles; and Major Ross with the Canadians.

Standards and wire were distributed to troops in the force, with which to make portable wire obstacles for use in front of posts by night.

Marching to the Elands River Bridge, the river March 4 to 6. Natal, 28 miles. Bamboes Spruit, 25 miles. Kalk Spruit, 17 miles. was crossed, and the columns advanced across the Klip River and another bad drift to Natal (twenty-eight miles); then on by Holspruit to Bamboes Spruit (twenty-five miles), and next day on to the northern blockhouse line. They camped on Kalk Spruit, four miles south of Tafelkop (seventeen miles), thus completing the drive there.

The captures made by Rimington's force were considerable. Ross got 4,000 head of cattle, two wagons, two Cape carts, about 50,000 bundles Captures. of wheat, and found a large cave containing twelve wagonloads of ammunition, including 300,000 rounds of Martini ammunition, 10,000 Lee-Metford, several hundred Krupp and 15-pounder shells, several thousand fuses, some 600 Nordenfelt and pom-pom shells, 200 lbs. black powder, one Maxim gun complete, two helios, one field telegraph instrument, and one telephone ; also a large mill, and a quantity of clothing, harness, &c. This cave was on the farm Leeuwspruit. For some months there had been rumours of the existence of this great store of hidden ammunition, and Mr. Howard, an intelligence agent to the column, finally succeeded in finding a native who pointed out the cave.

About 300 men of the Canadian Scouts and Royal Artillery Mounted Rifles were kept working for six hours clearing the material away. Lieut.-Colonel Jervis also destroyed one bakery, one large mill complete, and a quantity of clothing, harness, wagons, and carts. He also brought in seventeen wounded prisoners from a Boer hospital. Colonel Cox took seven prisoners who were hiding ; eight wagons and three carts also were destroyed.

The force now marched to Bonplaats, on the west bank of the Wilge River. During this march March 8. two Canadian Scouts were wounded. Next Bonplaats. March 9. day they marched to Liebenberg's Vlei, taking Lieben- berg'sVlei. up a night line for new driving operations March 10. west. Whilst proceeding to Spitzkop, a Spitzkop, 30 miles. long march of about thirty miles, the rear and flank guards were engaged. The night line

AUSTRALIANS ON THE MARCH.

was taken up in the dark, a flying column of 4,000
New South Wales Mounted Rifles and 250 Canadian
Scouts, all under Lieut.-Colonel Cox, being sent
forward at midnight to act independently.

March 11.

At dawn he caught seven Boers of Franz
Mentz's commando. Following up the trail of the
remainder to the railway line three miles south-east
of Gottenberg, he found that Franz Mentz, with
400 Boers, had broken through the posts of
the infantry regiment which was reinforcing
the line, with only one man and a few
horses killed. The railway line here was weakly
fenced ; the Boers boldly charged it, breaking
down about sixty yards of it in their charge, and
apparently took the infantry guarding it by surprise. Lieut.-Colonel Cox was in pursuit, only one
hour behind !

Escape of
Mentz's
com-
mando.

Rimington's force, having covered another
thirty miles in the last two days, now camped
by Gottenberg.

March 12.
Gotten-
berg.

Three years of incessant work and strain were
now telling on even Rimington's iron constitution.
Previous to the war he had been engaged on arduous
and dangerous intelligence work in South Africa.
Since that time he had continually been leading
hazardous enterprises. The incessant roughing brought
on dysentery, which necessitated his proceeding to
Elandsfontein Hospital, when the command
of his force was temporarily taken over by
Lieut.-Colonel Baldock, R.A.

March 13.

The force marched to Modderfontein, three miles
north-east of Heilbron, where Christmas dinners were
issued to the men ! Constant operations and absence

from bases of supplies had allowed no opportunity of celebrating this feast before.

After a week's welcome and much-needed rest, orders were received for the next operations, which

March 14 to 20. A halt. Fresh drives. comprised a drive east, between the two blockhouse lines, right up to the Natal border, with halts of two and three days on the Liebenberg's Vlei and Wilge River respectively, in order to clear the country thoroughly. One column was to be loose in front of the driving line.

I will not weary my readers with a detailed account of these operations, but note briefly that, starting on March 21, the column completed the drive and collected at Muller's Pass, on the Natal border, on April 5.

March 21 to April 5.

In the earlier parts of the drive great difficulty was experienced on account of the two rivers, Wilge and Liebenberg's Vlei, being in flood and impassable. In consequence the scheme had to be much modified. When Rimington's force advanced, after at last crossing the Wilge River, instead of being forty-eight hours in front of the driving line, as was originally intended, it was under twenty-four hours ahead, and consequently could do little or no good; and, in attempting to carry out orders, had to keep making forced marches. This force of 2,000 men, being taken out of the driving line, left the latter weaker than was desirable, and H. Botha, with nearly 1,000 men, succeeded in breaking through it on the night of April 2.

During the latter part of the drives the marches were too long. For instance, on March 31, April 1, 2, 3, and 4, the marches were respectively twenty-seven,

twenty-six, thirty-six, twenty-eight, and twenty miles. On several occasions this made it impossible

Long marches. to select a good night line before darkness came on ; amongst them was the night of April 2, when the main lot of Boers broke through, and also April 3, when about eighty broke through Lieut.-Colonel Jervis's column. On this latter occasion the line ran across the bare veldt, and, although shelter trenches had been made and the men stood perfectly, the Boers got through. They galloped straight over two of the picquets, who picked up in the morning one killed, two wounded, and two unwounded Boers ; also one native killed, two wounded, and two unwounded. Several of them had fallen right into the trenches. Thirty horses were found dead and a lot more wounded. The Canadian Scouts also took thirteen prisoners in the morning.

This was the first drive in which Boers, after breaking through the line, turned and attacked our men. On the 4th Veldt-Cornet Mentjes attacked the rear of Colonel Nixon's convoy, who had to get back his troops from the driving line to clear them off.

The country running up to the Drakensberg Mountains, where the drive ended, is very rough, full of kloofs and dongas, and consequently a bad one in which to finish up the drive, as, with the long marches, it was impossible to search it thoroughly. On the whole, these last operations were not a great success, but a good many Boers and stock were accounted for, with trifling loss.

The next move was a rapid drive on a narrow

Another drive. front from the Natal border to the railway between Heidelberg and Standerton. Only three groups of columns, covering about thirty miles

of front, formed the driving line—Nixon in the centre, with Garratt on the right and Rimington's columns on the left.   Both flanks were left open, the centre travelling first of all along the blockhouse line to within twenty miles of Tafelkop, then turning north-west to the railway at Greylingstad. Troops were to be in position for the drive on the night of the 10th.

Whilst at Muller's Pass, six hundred of the Inniskillings and Royal Artillery Mounted Rifles went out, under Major King, R.F.A., to search the head of the Klip River Valley. They found a lot of clothing hidden in caves, and captured about 300 head of cattle and some sheep.

April 7.

Marching to Rooi Kopjes, Rimington's columns (Ross and Cox) cleared the Mollen Valley, where they found large quantities of grain and hidden stores, and then proceeded to Brewer's Hoek (fifteen miles). Starting on in the morning, a road was followed round the base of the Wittekopjes, which natives reported in good condition. It was found to be impassable, so a détour into the Priehoek Valley had to be made. Meantime the troops thoroughly searched the Wittekopjes, finding a few head of cattle and hidden wagons and carts. Six Canadians, who remained behind the troops, were, however, captured by the enemy. About 100 Boers sniped the rear and left as the force moved on to camp on the south end of Hartebeest Vlaken (twenty-two miles). Another twenty-five miles was covered next day, past Tweekopjes to Rishton.

April 8.
Rooi Kopjes.

April 9.
Brewer's Hoek,
15 miles.

April 10.
Haartebeest Vlaken,
22 miles.

April 11.
Rishton,
25 miles.

The last few nights' hard work was telling on the

artillery horses.   The captures since the 7th included one wounded, two unwounded prisoners, three rifles, twelve riding-horses, sixteen wagons, six Cape carts (destroyed), 140 trek oxen, and 699 mixed cattle.

April 12.
Nie-
meyers-
rust,
19 miles.

April 13.
Villiers-
dorp,
13 miles.

April 14.
Riet-
fontein.

April 15.
Major
Paynter.

Marching on by Niemeyersrust (nineteen miles) and Villiersdorp (thirteen miles), Rietfontein, three miles south-east of Vlakfontein Station, was once more reached.   Here Colonel Rimington rejoined his forces from sick leave.   Major Gale, Intelligence Officer, proceeded on a fortnight's leave, Major Paynter, late Inniskillings, acting for him.

Major C. H. Paynter during the earlier stages of the war rendered splendid service with the home depôt of the regiment at the Curragh, the doctors having refused to pass him fit for active service.   Keen to get to the front, he retired, joined the Monmouth Royal Engineer Militia, and proceeded with a draft to their Volunteer Company in South Africa.   After service with them he was appointed to act in his new capacity on Colonel Rimington's staff, and so was once more with the regiment.

This last operation was not a proper drive, as the flanks were left open.   The left of the line (Rimington's four columns) had to move very fast, and during the first three days could only superficially search the country.   Transport animals were very much done up, but the horses of the regiment were in splendid condition.   After an inspection, the General remarked that no other corps in South Africa could compare with them for fitness.

CHAPTER XXV

THE CLOSING SCENES

Two drives under General Bruce Hamilton were now arranged. (1) From the Germiston-Greylingstad Railway into the angle between the South African Constabulary posts and Olifant's River and Komati Poort. (2) Back again.

April 16.
Drives under Gen. Bruce Hamilton.

The drive, which commenced on the morning of the 18th, comprised, briefly, three marches north from the line, Springs-Heidelberg-Greylingstad, into the angle formed by the Komati Poort Railway and the line of South African Constabulary posts from Heidelberg to Olifant's River.

About seven columns formed the driving line. Lieut.-Colonel Lawley was on the left, with Colonel Rimington between him and Colonel Nixon; the right flank resting along these South African Constabulary posts, which were strengthened by Colonel Wing's column. All the columns were under the command of one man, General Bruce Hamilton; hitherto each column had worked on its own account, under orders issued from Army headquarters.

Lieut.-Colonel Sir J. H. Jervis-White-Jervis handed over the command of the Royal Artillery Mounted Rifles to Lieut.-Colonel F. S. Baldock, and proceeded on three months' leave of absence to

England. The section of ' J ' Battery Royal Horse
Artillery, under Lieut. Clark, also left for Elandsfontein, for conversion into Royal Artillery Mounted
Rifles. This section was a great loss, having for a
year rendered consistent good service with Rimington's column.

The first drive started on the 17th and was accomplished by the 20th, with disappointing results.
April 17   Alberts, with 500 Boers, had been in the net,
to 20.   but had got out by marching round the left
flank of the driving line. It was another example of
the quickness with which the Boers invariably discovered a weak point in our schemes. On the last
day Lieut.-Colonel Baldock's column took from a
farm five sick and wounded Boers and two hospital
assistants ; also a Boer ambulance. The two assistants
were sent back with the ambulance, although it was
drawn by our Government mules ; a small quantity
of provisions and medical comforts were also given
them.

Before the drive back commenced, Rimington's,
April 22   Lawley's, and Nixon's columns spent a few
to 24.   days clearing the angle between the railway
at Germiston.

Then the drive back (forty-seven miles) was
accomplished in two days, the result being only one
April 26.   Boer killed. It was thought that Alberts's
commando might still be in the net, but it appears
that, after getting behind on the previous drive, it
broke right away across the Heidelberg Railway.

This corner of the Transvaal was now absolutely
cleared of all stock and natives, except those with the
Boer commandos. The only mealies to be found
were the remains of old crops that had been standing

z

on the ground for the last two years.   These, though very hard, were in good condition, and we learnt from prisoners that the Boers were using them for food.   The absence of natives made it impossible to get local intelligence as to Boer movements.

The beginning of the weary end was gradually
April 28.   approaching, but still there was much hard work to be done.

The 3rd New South Wales Mounted Rifles, under Lieut.-Colonel Cox, entrained this day for Cape
Departure Town for embarkation back to Australia.
of New
South They had put in a most valuable year's
Wales service with Colonel Rimington's column.
Mounted
Rifles. Lieut.-Colonel Cox himself and many of the men had rendered conspicuous service in the earlier stages of the war with the New South Wales Lancers, when they were attached to and formed a squadron of the Inniskilling Dragoons.   The following extract from Force Orders by Colonel F. M. Rimington, C.B., was truly merited :

KRAAL, Monday, April 28, 1902.

The Brigadier, in saying good-bye to the officers, non-commissioned officers, and men of 3rd New South Wales Mounted Rifles, desires to thank all ranks for their good work during the year they have served under his command.

They have shown, by their dash in attack, steadiness in action, and alert behaviour on outpost duties, that they are thorough good soldiers, of whom the Empire may well be proud.

Their cheerful conduct under privations and exposure is above praise.

He wishes them God-speed and good luck wherever they go.

By order,

(Signed)   G. K. ANSELL, Major, C.S.O.

Rimington's Force.

Rimington's force now marched to Tamboekies-

OFFICERS, INNISKILLING DRAGOONS, AT KROONSTAD, 1902.

GENERAL RIMINGTON BIDDING GOOD-BYE TO COLONEL COX AND THE
3RD NEW SOUTH WALES MOUNTED RIFLES.

fontein and on to Klip River station, to act from there in conjunction with Lieut.-Colonel Lawley, west

April 29. Tamboekies-fontein.

April 30. Klip River station.

of the railway, against Boers who had been raiding cattle south of Johannesburg actually from within the area protected by South African Constabulary posts, which were too wide apart.

Proceeding to Hartebeestfontein, the Boers were sighted late in the afternoon on Klopper's Kraal,

May 1. Hartebeest-fontein.

about six miles south. Next day they were engaged and driven off, but as the force had orders to get back to Vereeniging without delay, pursuit was impossible. The Boers numbered 100 to 150, and during the engagement a small party of Canadian Scouts, who got cut off, lost one man killed and three wounded.

The force encamped south of the Vaal, on Marks' Farm, close to Viljoen's Drift station.

The next operation comprised a big drive in two stages : the first in two days' march from the Natal

May 3.

railway line on to the Heilbron-Frankfort blockhouse line. Colonel Rimington's and Lieut.-Colonel Lawley's columns were not used in this first move, but joined in for the second stage, when they prolonged the line from Heilbron to Kopjes station. The whole was then to drive south in one march on to the southern blockhouse line (Kroonstad-Lindley), the left of the line (Colonel Allenby's column) moving along the Liebenberg Vlei, which was held by Elliot's and McKenzie's columns.

Rimington's force formed the right of the whole line, covering about ten miles of front and moving between Lawley's column and the railway.

z 2

Three days were spent in executing this operation, during which Rimington's force marched

May 4.
18 miles.
May 5.
17 miles.
May 6.
31 miles.
Helvetia.

eighteen, seventeen, and thirty-one miles, driving right on the blockhouse line and camping at Helvetia.

General Bruce Hamilton reported the total captures of all the columns for these two stages

321 Boers
captured.

to be 321 Boers; which must be considered satisfactory, although, at the same time, 300 or 400 Boers broke out of the net in broad daylight by galloping through the left of the driving line, and also through some of the stops on the Liebenberg Vlei.

After getting into position, a long drive back on

May 9.
Kromel-
lenboog
Spruit
station,
36 miles.

to the line Wolvehoek-Heilbron-Frankfort was made in one day's march. Rimington's force marched thirty-six miles this day, and camped at Kromellenboog Spruit station, where the convoy rejoined it.

For these drives all wheeled transport, including guns, was left behind, supplies and one blanket per man only being carried on the horse.

The result of this last drive was the capture of twenty-eight Boers. The remainder had galloped back through the right centre of the driving line.

In each of the cases mentioned the Boers who escaped from the net did so by boldly charging either the driving line or the stops, our troops opposing them always having to cover rather a longer line than they could hold satisfactorily. The Boers, by their good scouting, always managed to pick weak places, and in no case had we any cavalry available to charge them. We met their rush each time by rifle fire, the result being that but little damage was done to the enemy.

Rimington's horses came wonderfully well through the two very long journeys on May 6 and 8, none falling out *en route*, and practically none being laid up afterwards—a proof of the splendid condition they

Mules poisoned. were in. Eighteen of the mules in Lieut.-Colonel Baldock's column died of poisoning from eating hay drawn at Kopjes Station. This was afterwards proved to have been obtained locally from Piet De Wet's farm, but how it had become poisoned was never cleared up.

The Boer resistance, to the overcoming of which these drives had done so much, was now

The end of the war. 'Vereeniging Conference.' getting worn out, and their leaders were treating for peace. Their negotiations during the last few weeks had culminated in the sanctioning of a general conference of the leaders at Vereeniging on May 15.

Meantime the orders to Rimington's force were to march to Heilbron, and from there to burn all

May 11. grass and clear the country of all stock and supplies round Trammil; other columns to do similar work over all this north-east corner of the Orange River Colony. At the same time no 'offensive' action was to be taken against any Boers met.

The force accordingly marched to Leeuwfontein, Rietfontein, and Nooitgedacht, carrying out the in-

May 12. structions. In order that the Boers should not mistake this action, it was explained by the Commander-in-Chief that the only agreement

May 14. made with the Boer leaders was that offensive action should not be taken against their

May 15. forces whilst they, the leaders, were away.

Next afternoon, however, on the march to Driefontein, the Commander-in-Chief telegraphed

that all columns were to cease burning and return to
Heilbron.   Later, a white flag came in from Commandant Celliers, asking what was the meaning of
the burning, as he understood that whilst the Boer
leaders were holding the meeting an armistice was to
be preserved.   Colonel Rimington replied that his
original orders were to destroy supplies, but not to
fire on Boers unless they fired first ; further, that,
as these orders had just been cancelled, he was returning to Heilbron.

Marching back to Rietfontein (eighteen miles),
two lots of Boers came in to talk to Colonel Rimington ; one from Veldt-Cornet Keeve's and the
other from Mentz's commando.   Both were
Mentz's brothers.   They were very anxious
to hear what terms were being offered ; how the Conference was getting on ; also what we were going to
do for the Boers who had turned round and were
helping us.   They were all 'biting' at surrendering,
and it was noticeable how keen for peace all the
Boers were who came in contact with us.   Colonel
Rimington met them with the rather offhand answer:
' Don't want you to surrender particularly ; and, in
any case, don't do so now whilst your commandants
are at the Conference.'

May 16.
Riet-
fontein,
18 miles.

Whilst proceeding to Leeuwfontein Farm, near
Heilbron, a telegram was received from the Commander-in-Chief to be ready to take the field
again at once.   It looked as if the peace
negotiations at Vereeniging were going to
prove a failure.

May 17.
Near
Heilbron.

As illustrating the work accomplished by Rimington's column during the past eleven months, it is
interesting to note that it had covered 3,424 miles ;

INNISKILLING DRAGOONS' BAND AT BLOEMFONTEIN,
AFTER THE DECLARATION OF PEACE.

RAILWAY SCOUTING CYCLE.

whilst the captures included forty-five Boers killed, eighteen wounded, 396 prisoners, 1,800 horses, 140 Work by mules, 30,021 cattle, 391 wagons, and 271 Riming- ton's carts. During this period its casualties only column. consisted of thirteen officers and men killed, forty-two wounded, and 1,617 horses. The average strength of the column was 2,500 mounted troops.

The force remained camped about Leeuwfontein till June 20, when it was broken up.

On June 1 a telegram was received from the Peace Commander-in-Chief that Peace had been signed May 31, signed on the previous night, May 31. This 1902. news was received by all our troops very quietly.

On the breaking up of the force, June 20, the Inniskillings marched to Bloemfontein. A small contingent, under Captain Raymond Johnson, proceeded to England early in June to represent the regiment at His Majesty's Coronation.

The band, under Mr. Prosser, which the regiment had not heard for nearly three years, rejoined at Bloemfontein early in July, having come out to the Cape from the home depôt the previous year.

A few months later the Inniskillings embarked for home, arriving once more at the Curragh, Ireland, on October 31, 1902. It received a hearty welcome, being met by a distinguished assembly, which included H.R.H. the Duke of Connaught, who made the following address :

Colonel Rimington, officers, non-commissioned officers, and men of the Inniskilling Dragoons,— I have come down here to-day specially to welcome you home from South Africa after a long and arduous period of active service. It affords me great pleasure

344   WITH THE INNISKILLING DRAGOONS

to greet you on your arrival home, particularly when
I see how well and fit the regiment looks, and the
splendid physique and appearance which the men
present.   As Colonel-in-Chief of the regiment, I
have followed its doings in South Africa with the
keenest interest, and I have often thought of the
trying times you must have had.   In the great trials
you have undergone, in the hard fighting by day and
by night in which you took part, and in the long
weary trekking which also fell to your lot, you have
always borne yourselves and carried out your duties
with the utmost credit, thus maintaining the proud
name and honourable traditions of the famous corps
to which you belong.   I have heard from the highest
authorities of the way in which the Inniskilling
Dragoons performed their work, and I am proud to
be here to-day in the uniform of such a distinguished
regiment, and to know that it had been placed in the
3rd Army Corps under my command.   I deeply
regret the losses the regiment has sustained in action
and from other causes, and I am sure that the names
of those who fell in South Africa will never be forgotten by all who appreciate devotion to their country
in times of danger.   I congratulate you, Colonel
Rimington, on your return at the head of so fine a
regiment, and I hope you may be long spared to
enjoy the many honours you have won.

Later, at a ceremonial parade, His Royal Highness
presented the well-earned war medals.

In conclusion, I must apologise to my readers for
the shortcomings of these notes, and further to those
concerned for imperfections and doubtless often
omissions in narrating their gallant deeds.[1]   My
object has been to give a brief regimental record of
one of our cavalry regiments during the war.

[1] The author would be obliged by notification of any errors or omissions for future correction.

From these pages a correct opinion may be formed of the hard and unremitting toil which fell to the lot of a regiment that was in the fighting line from start to finish without a rest. The 'go' with which hard work, continuous fighting, exposure to weather, and shortness of rations were invariably faced was due to the spirit and action of the officers. These, from the commencement, set an example to those below them of dash tempered with cunning, of indifference to danger where results might justify their action, of resolute acceptance of the odds without grumbling, and, last but not least, that care of the horses without which cavalry is useless. To this spirit, which most certainly permeated all ranks, must be added the previous experience of many of the non-commissioned officers and men, who joined from the Reserve, of rough work and trekking in South Africa from 1881 to 1890. The strong infusion of Irishmen, who love fighting for its own sake, was another incentive.

Happy the man who, at the head of such officers and such men, rides at the enemy with the knowledge that the fight is already half won, since the weight of *moral* is on his side. Fortunate he who in the retreat has but one fear, and that—that his men may 'hold on' too long.

The late war has shown us that, instead of the days of cavalry being past, this arm is still just as essential to the success of an army as ever. A successful termination to a campaign is not brought about by the exertions of one arm alone ; it is only by the skilful combination of the three that victory is to be attained. South Africa has shown nothing to alter this principle of war ; but it has proved that much of the former training of the cavalry in peacetime was useless, and that it is an arm which requires the very highest training and initiative, combined with ability and dash, distinct from rashness. Further, that these qualities are wasted unless a man is physically fit and hard as nails, and, above all, unless he has—and keeps—his horse in the same condition.

Finally, I should like to testify to the bravery, skill, and endurance of our late enemy. Bearing in mind the ignorance of their masses, and that 'slimness' or cunning was looked on as smartness, their general behaviour in victory and defeat was exemplary. Already, in Somaliland, a few of our late foes have been fighting side by side with us. May it ever be so. They have taught us much. We can teach them more; and powerful indeed would be an army of Britons and Boers.

LIEUT.-COLONEL J. W. YARDLEY.

APPENDIX

LIST OF KILLED AND WOUNDED

6TH (INNISKILLING) DRAGOONS

Roll of officers, non-commissioned officers, and men ' killed' and ' died of wounds' in South Africa, 1899–1902 :—

OFFICERS KILLED.

Captain C. G. Jackson, 7th Dragoon Guards (attached) 16.12.99
Second Lieut. F. N. Dent (drowned) 15.3.00
    ,,   A. J. Grant Meek 6.6.00
Lieut. J. Lawlor 30.8.00
Second Lieut. A. W. Swanston 16.10.00
    ,,   Oliver 30.11.01

5049	Pvte.	Lawrence, J.	1.1.00	5060	Pvte.	Dalziel, R. .	10.5.00
3171	,,	Barnes, J. D.	4.1.00	5081	,,	Day, C. .	10.5.00
3471	,,	Gardner, R. .	4.1.00	3446	,,	Flynn, M. .	10.5.00
3775	,,	Jones, H. .	4.1.00	5094	,,	Jeffries, F. A	10.5.00
3079	L.-Cp.	Paterson,		5099	,,	McClintock,	
		R. D. .	4.1.00			J. . .	10.5.00
3006	L.-Sgt.	Sales, W. D.	4.1.00	3772	,,	Mobbs, E. .	10.5.00
3639	Pvte.	Ward, J. .	4.1.00	5129	,,	Quinlan, T. .	10.5.00
3522	,,	Clark, F. G.	6.2.00	3722	,,	Webster,	
5056	Corpl.	Karl, H. .	10.2.00			W. E. J. .	10.5.00
3703	,,	Coleman,		3878	,,	Dow, J. .	16.10.00
		W. H. .	12.2.00	3586	,,	Gardiner,	
3585	Pvte.	Kirkpatrick,				E. J. . .	16.10.00
		S. . .	22.2.00	3282	Sergt.	Blevin, T. .	17.10.00
3990	,,	Ventham,		5033	Pvte.	Garlick, J. .	17.10.00
		E. F. .	22.2.00	5097	,,	Love, H. .	12.2.01

3594	Pvte.	Davidson, J.	25.5.01	3654	Pvte.	Stanley, W. .	20.12.01
5030	Corpl.	Grattage, C.	2.7.01	3604	,,	McLeary, J.	9.1.02
4302	Pvte.	Prentice, J. .	27.7.01	5092	,,	Hamill, J. .	23.3.02
3770	,,	Hutchins,		* Corpl. Fenton (1st Royals)			3.8.00
		C. W.	17.8.01	* ,, Mullion (10th Hus-			
4102	,,	Tremain,				sars) .	16.10.00
		W. G.	30.11.01	* Sergt. Hunter (Kitch-			
4121	,,	Kemp, F.	20.12.01			ener's Scouts) .	16.10.00

*Roll of officers, non-commissioned officers, and men 'wounded'
in South Africa, 1899–1902 :—*

OFFICERS WOUNDED.

Captain A. R. Mosley .	13.12.99
Lieut. T. G. Gibson .	4.1.00
,, C. F. D. Johnson	13.2.00
,, E. C. S. Jervis .	24.2.00
,, N. W. Haig	9.5.00
,, J. Harris .	16.10.00
,, E. S. Paterson .	16.10.00
Captain J. W. Yardley, late Inniskilling Dragoons (attached)	16.10.00
,, J. C. A. Anstice	6.3.01
Lieut. L. E. G. Oates .	6.3.01
Captain E. S. Jackson	22.4.01
Second Lieut. O'Callaghan (lightning)	20.12.01

3571	Pvte.	Gardner, A. .	1.1.00	3778	Pvte.	Murray, A. G.	7.2.00
2982	,,	Rainey, W. .	1.1.00	2877	L.-Cp.	Coltman, R. .	10.2.00
3286	Sergt.	McNaghten, J.	4.1.00	3256	Pvte.	Winston, R. .	10.2.00
3130	Sd. Cp.	Jones, J.	4.1.00	3528	Corpl.	Foreman,	
3592	L.-Cp.	Tobin, T.	4.1.00			J. T. .	12.2.00
3680	Pvte.	George, W. .	4.1.00	3912	Pvte.	Crowe, T.	17.2.00
2908	,,	Nicks, H.	4.1.00	3540	,,	Walker, W. .	17.2.00
4003	,,	Wardroper,		2740	Sergt.	Hanwell, A. .	22.2.00
		C. E.	4.1.00	3495	Corpl.	Hamilton, H.	24.2.00
3271	,,	Yacamini, R.	4.1.00	3466	Sergt.	Wall, J. W. .	10.5.00
3955	,,	Cowderry, W.	7.2.00	3378	Corpl.	Marshall, L. .	10.5.00
4007	,,	Whanstall,		3161	Pvte.	Wilson, H. .	10.5.00
		E. C.	7.2.00	2303	,,	Price, J.	10.5.00

* Serving with Inniskilling Dragoons.

3052	Pvte.	Griffin, S. .	10.5.00
3822	,,	Lawrence,	
		W. H. .	10.5.00
3813	,,	Burnes, J. .	10.5.00
3160	Corpl.	Cole, A. J. .	10.5.00
3809	Pvte.	Burford,	
		H. G. .	10.5.00
3932	,,	Myzoule,	
		A. C. .	10.5.00
3633	,,	Davies, J. .	10.5.00
3900	,,	Paul, F. S. .	10.5.00
5131	,,	Paisley, T. .	10.5.00
5069	,,	Beardwood,	
		H. . .	10.5.00
5070	,,	Manning, J.	10.5.00
3380	,,	Smith, W. .	10.5.00
5122	,,	Watkins,	
		F. M. .	19.5.00
2919	,,	Robinson,	
		E. G. .	27.5.00
3761	,,	Hughes,	
		W. A. .	27.5.00
3277	Sergt.	Turnbull, J.	28.5.00
3671	Pvte.	Vaughan, A.	30.5.00
3341	,,	Dolan, J. .	11.6.00
3092	,,	Butter, W. R.	16.7.00
3928	,,	Smith, H. .	16.7.00
3005	Sergt.	McCubbin,	
		J. . .	2.8.00
5146	Pvte.	Whittle, M.	3.8.00
5095	,,	Jeater, E. .	24.8.00
3274	Sergt.	Curly, J. .	4.9.00
3920	Pvte.	Sellwood,	
		J. H. .	14.9.00
3033	,,	Gledhill, W.	15.10.00

5114	Pvte.	White,	
		J. L. W. .	15.10.00
3492	Corpl.	Fagan, F. .	16.10.00
3310	Pvte.	Marshall, H.	16.10.00
4064	,,	Harris, W. E.	16.10.00
3151	,,	Bissett, F. .	16.10.00
3946	,,	Brooks, J. .	16.10.00
5139	,,'	Stinchcombe,	
		T. G. .	16.10.00
3952	,,	Gold, H. .	16.10.00
4014	,,	Banks, A. .	16.10.00
3401	,,	Steele, R. C.	16.10.00
3078	,,	Divall, J. .	19.10.00
5088	,,	Fortune, J. .	19.10.00
5051	,,	Leedham, B.	1.1.01
2984	,,	Leary, J. .	12.2.01
4087	,,	Clear, M. .	12.2.01
3807	,,	Hunt, T. .	13.2.01
4247	,,	Bratt,	
		J. W. R. .	6.3.01
3895	Corpl.	Brodie, F. C.	6.3.01
4187	Pvte.	Allcock, A. .	6.3.01
4160	,,	Anderson,	
		R. B. .	6.3.01
5083	Corpl.	Ellison, E. .	16.3.01
3910	L.-Cp.	Taylor, E. H.	15.5.01
4536	Pvte.	Warren, F. .	27.7.01
5135	,,	Slavin, W. .	15.8.01
4197	,,	King, E. S. .	15.8.01
3820	,,	Hammersly,	
		H. W. .	1.9.01
2594	,,	McLean, A. .	9.10.01
4459	,,	Dales, H. .	9.1.02
4045	,,	Johnson, H.	20.1.02
4054	,,	Hendry, J. .	23.3.02

Roll of non-commissioned officers and men ' died of disease '
in South Africa, 1900–1902 :—

3021	Corpl.	Mead, F. .	27.1.00		3196	Pvte.	Jackson, E. .	2.5.00
3152	Pvte.	Salter, E. .	31.1.00		3280	,,	Palmer, W. .	10.5.00
3954	,,	Reading,			3394	,,	McGeoghan,	
		A. H. .	15.3.00				W. . .	12.5.00

3590	Pvte.	Hilston, H. .	18.5.00	3867	Pvte.	Burke, E.	.	21.11.01
3163	S.S.M.	Harewood,		4171	,,	Barrett,		
		H. C.	. 23.5.00			A. T.	.	9.1.02
3229	Pvte.	Larkin, J. M.	25.5.00	4016	,,	Bedwell,		
553	Ar.Sgt.	Fisher .	. 25.5.00			W. G.	.	13.1.02
3888	Pvte.	Geraghty, P.	28.5.00	4419	,,	Hopkins, H.		14.1.02
3461	,,	Powley, A. .	29.5.00	4180	,,	Postins, H	.	14.1.02
3805	,,	Hancox, A. .	9.6.00	3217	,,	Stafford, A. .		18.1.02
3334	Corpl.	Keel, G.	. 20.6.00	4485	,,	O'Brien, P. .		2.2.02
4012	Pvte.	Seton, A. H.	29.6.00	3048	S.S.M.	Crew, F. W.		8.2.02
5015	,,	Dixon, T. .	2.7.00	3681	Sergt.	Woods,		
3846	,,	Douglas, H.	9.7.00			W. H.	.	23.2.02
5057	,,	Kaberry, L. .	23.10.00	3788	Pvte.	Lane, P.	.	14.3.02
3787	,,	Smith, B. G.	4.1.01	4389	,,	Blakeman,		
4279	,,	Dabbs, G. H.	4.3.01			F. J.	.	29.3.02
4073	,,	McConnell,		4541	,,	Fearn, G.	.	30.3.02
		H. S.	. 10.4.01	4124	,.	Darby, R. J.		2.4.02
3458	Sergt.	Senley, H. .	21.4.01	4533	,,	Ormston	.	
3533	Pvte.	Burnett, J. .	30.5.01	3361	,,	Burge, R. .		
3995	,,	Durrant,		2740	Sergt.	Hanwell, A.		
		G. V.	. 3.6.01	3003	,.	F. Kirby	.	
4010	,,	James, J.	. 23.7.01					

INDEX

A A

Printed and bound by Antony Rowe Ltd, Eastbourne

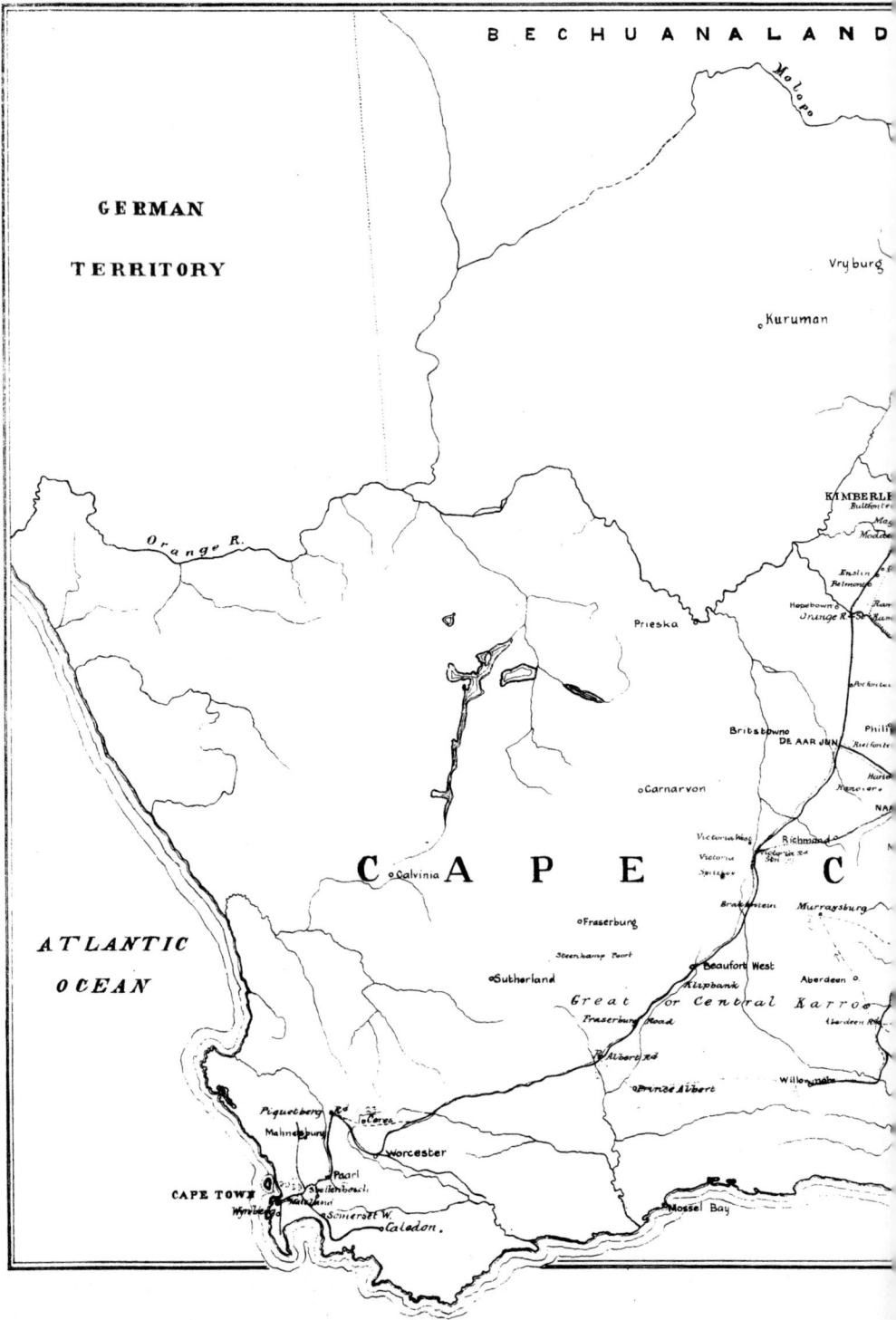

T R A N S V A A L

Zeerust

Roossenekal

Middelburg

MAFEKING
o Lichtenburg

Krugersdorp

PRETORIA
Diamond Hill
Belfast

Komati Poort

JOHANNESBURG

LOURENCO MARQUES

Delagoa Bay

Potchefstroom

Heidelberg
Vereeniging

S W A Z I
L A N D

Piet Retief

Klerksdorp

Bremersdorp

Ermelo

Bloemhof

Hoopstad

KROONSTAD

New Amsterdam

Volksrust

Charlestown

Utrecht

Paul Pietersburg

Christiana

Vrede

Reitz

Newcastle

Vryheid

Z U L U L A N D

O R A N G E   R I V E R

Bethlehem

Harrismith

Glencoe
Dundee

St Lucia Bay

C O L O N Y

Senekal

Winburg
Brandfort

Ladysmith

Spion Kop
Colenso

Greytown

BLOEMFONTEIN

Ladybrand

Maseru

Estcourt

B A S U T O

N A T A L

Howick

Saddler

L A N D

PIETERMARITZBURG

DURBAN

I N D I A N   O C E A N

Philippolis

G R I Q U A
L A N D

Harding
Kokstad

Aliwal North

Burghersdorp

ROSMEAD JUNC.
Starkstream

Stormberg

O L O N Y

Cradock

Gt Fish R.

King Williamstown

EAST LONDON

Grahamstown

Port Alfred

PORT ELIZABETH

SKETCH   MAP
OF PART OF **SOUTH AFRICA**
Showing Marches
of
INNISKILLING DRAGOONS
During BOER WAR.

Marches 1899-1900
1901
1902

Scale of English Miles.
20 10   0   20   40   60   80   100

The Numbers on Routes represent Dates.